The Best 125 Lowfat Fish and Seafood Dishes

Susann Geiskopf-Hadler
and
Mindy Toomay

Prima Publishing
P.O. Box 1260BK
Rocklin, CA 95677
(916) 786-0426

Composition by Janet Hansen, Alphatype
Production by Carol Dondrea, Bookman Productions
Copyediting by Sandra Su
Interior design by Judith Levinson
Cover design by The Dunlavey Studio
Illustrations by Renee Deprey
Cover illustration by Francis Livingston

Prima Publishing
Rocklin, CA

Library of Congress Cataloging-in-Publication Data

Geiskopf-Hadler, Susann, 1950–
    The best 125 lowfat fish and seafood dishes / Susann
Geiskopf-Hadler and Mindy Toomay.
        p.   cm.
    ISBN 1-55958-302-9 (pbk.)
        1. Cookery (Fish)   2. Cookery (Seafood)   3. Quick
and easy cookery.   I. Toomay, Mindy, 1951–
    II. Title.   III. Title: Best one hundred twenty-five lowfat
fish and seafood dishes.
TX747.G45   1993   92-39919
641.6'92—dc20   CIP

93 94 95 RRD 10 9 8 7 6 5 4 3 2 1

Printed in the United States of America

How to Order:
Single copies may be ordered from Prima Publishing, P.O. Box 1260BK, Rocklin, CA 95677; telephone (916) 786-0426. Quantity discounts are also available. On your letterhead, include information concerning the intended use of the books and the number of books you wish to purchase.

As always, we dedicate this book
to our first and best cooking teachers—our mothers—
and to M.F.K. Fisher (1908–1992), with gratitude
for her inspiring books about food and life.

Acknowledgments

Making a good book, like making a good meal, requires attention, creativity, patience, and energy. Throughout the process of producing *The Best 125 Lowfat Fish and Seafood Dishes*, these qualities have been offered in abundance by every member of the team.

Thanks first to Prima Publishing, particularly our editor, Jennifer Basye, for encouraging us to keep cooking creatively so this third volume in the Best 125 series could be released so soon. The good-natured efficiency of Carol Dondrea at Bookman Productions was essential in transforming our manuscript into a finished book in record time. Lindy Dunlavey of The Dunlavey Studio worked her usual magic with color and design on the cover, and Francis Livingston painted another enticing, impressionistic cover illustration.

As we reiterate throughout this book, freshness is the key to wonderful fish and seafood cooking. Thanks to the knowledgeable, friendly folks at our favorite local fish counters—Corti Brothers Market and the Sacramento Natural Foods Co-op—who care about quality as much as we do.

Both our husbands gave up their wives once again, with very little whining, to the all-consuming process of birthing a cookbook. Guy Hadler provided expertise at the grill and valuable dinner hour critiques. Cooking is therapeutic for Guy, and we deprived him of it for several months. He says he forgives us. Tad Toomay was often called away from his own creative work to be kitchen assistant or gracious host, and he played both roles admirably. His musical contributions to our book release celebrations have set the festive tone for sharing our accomplishments with family and friends.

To test our recipes on a variety of palates, we counted on numerous friends to taste and comment. We acknowledge all of them for being willing and happy guinea pigs during several months of intense experimentation.

No cookbook can be successful without the enthusiastic response of adventurous cookbook users. Most of you will remain unknown to us, but you are part of the team, nonetheless. We appreciate you all.

Contents

Almost Instant Recipes

This book amply demonstrates that fish and seafood are nutritious and delicious. But the benefits don't stop there. For many of today's busy cooks, the greatest appeal of fish and seafood is the speed with which they can be prepared. The following list includes recipes that we have labeled "Almost Instant." This designation, which appears under the recipe title for each applicable dish, means that it can be prepared in 30 minutes or less from start to finish. For the simplest of our dishes, preparation time is as little as 15 or 20 minutes.

Introduction

We offer this assurance to food lovers everywhere: The recipes in this book are so delicious, satisfying, and varied you will forget you're eating lowfat fare! We are conscientious about nutrition, but pleasure at the table is our prime concern.

These are exciting times for creative, health-conscious cooks. More and more people the world over are coming to believe that a true culinary masterpiece is based on fresh ingredients, simply prepared, with a minimum of fat and sodium. What began as California cuisine and spa food has been embraced by good cooks and sophisticated chefs everywhere. Healthy eating is becoming synonymous with fine dining, and we couldn't be more delighted.

Naturally low in fat and cholesterol, yet high in beneficial omega-3 fatty acids, fish and seafood deserve top billing in this approach to a healthy diet. With this in mind, we stock our pantries with a wide variety of ingredients that bring out the best in seafood. Light and healthy citrus juices, fresh and dried herbs and spices, fine vinegars and mustards, and wines and spirits are among our favorite lowfat flavor enhancers. We also utilize the tastes, textures, and colors of various vegetables and fruits. In addition, many of our recipes include rice, beans, or pasta for hearty appetites; healthy eating is not about sacrifice!

We have drawn inspiration from many international culinary traditions—Thai, Italian, and Greek, to name a few—and we haven't neglected such American classics as Manhattan Style Clam Chowder, Crab Newburg, and Crab and Bay Shrimp Louis. However, we specialize in innovation. Scallop Soup with

Saffron and Green Grapes, Prawn Scampi with Anise Liqueur, Halibut Baked in Coconut Lime Sauce, and Risotto with Shark, Sage, Tomatoes, and Mozzarella are just a few of our tantalizing nontraditionals.

Our extensive section on grilled dishes provides ample inspiration for summer dinner party fare. We've also emphasized such simple yet underutilized techniques as baking in parchment, broiling, and poaching.

We believe this collection of lowfat fish and seafood dishes offers something for everyone: basic start-up information and simple instructions for the novice as well as new and different flavor combinations to inspire the expert chef. And, as in our previous books, we include a special index to our many Almost Instant recipes (see page xii) for busy cooks who want dinner on the table in half an hour.

As always, we wish you good health, good eating, and joy in the kitchen.

If you have any feedback for us about this book, or if you would like to hear about our other offerings, please write to us in care of our publishers:

> Susann Geiskopf-Hadler and Mindy Toomay
> c/o Prima Publishing
> P.O. Box 1260BK
> Rocklin, CA 95677

Thanks for buying this book.

The Fish Market

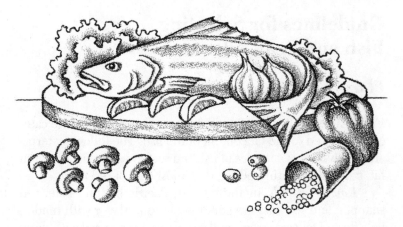

Choosing a Fish Market

If you intend to do much fish and seafood cooking, cultivate a rapport with a reputable local fishmonger. He or she will become a great ally in your search for the freshest fish for your table.

Most towns of any size have markets that specialize in fresh and frozen fish, and grocery stores catering to gourmet cooks usually offer a wide array of good quality fish and seafood. Look around for a fish department that displays fish unwrapped and on ice in a closed refrigerator case rather than sealed in plastic, where bacteria can flourish.

Feel free to ask questions about where fish was caught, how it was transported to market, and how long it's been there. A conscientious fishmonger will know all about the fish in the case and will steer you toward the very freshest product.

Guidelines for Selecting Fish and Seafood

Flavors and Textures

Fish can generally be divided into three flavor and texture categories related to the fat content of the fish. The following terms are relative; most varieties of fish and seafood are much lower in fat, particularly saturated fat, than most cuts of red meat.

Lower-fat fish, including cod, Pacific halibut, sole, red snapper, and sea bass are generally mild in flavor with tender, pale flesh. Delicately seasoned sauces are best paired with these lighter-flavored fishes. They dry out quickly and are good choices for moist-heat cooking methods such as steaming, poaching, and baking en papillote (in parchment paper).

Medium-fat fish, including Atlantic halibut, yellowfin tuna, and swordfish are a bit firmer in texture than those lower in fat and are suitable for any seasoning and cooking method.

Higher-fat fish, including salmon, albacore and bluefin tunas, and herring usually have a pronounced flavor with firmer, "meaty" flesh that is deeper in color than lower-fat varieties. They are good choices for grilling, baking, and other dry-heat methods, and they combine well with strong seasonings.

Selecting Fresh Fish and Seafood

Fish and shellfish are among the most perishable of all foods. Make the fish counter your last stop at the market and get your purchase into your home refrigerator immediately. If you live more than a short distance from the market, ask your fishmonger to pack the fish in ice and transport it home in a small ice chest.

- *Whole fish,* such as trout, salmon, and catfish, should have clear, not cloudy, eyes. Skin should be intact and shiny and scales should not appear dry. Gills should be moist and deep red in color. Check the stomach cavity—it should be well-cleaned and the ribs still firmly connected to the flesh. Whole fish should feel firm and the flesh should spring back when touched. The slippery, natural moisture clinging to the outside of the fish should be transparent, not milky. An "off" odor—ammonialike or "fishy"—indicates a fish is past its prime.

- *Steaks and fillets,* regardless of species, should have a moist, freshly cut appearance. There should be no discoloration or browning around the edges. They should feel firm and resilient, not mushy, to the touch. Fresh fish cuts will have no ammonia, iodine, or strong "fishy" odor.

- *Crab* is typically available freshly cooked, either in or out of the shell. Where our recipes call for crab meat, we prefer to pick meat from cooked, whole crabs just before using. Have your fishmonger clean and crack the whole crabs for you. If you purchase cooked crab meat already picked from the shells, it should be moist, translucent, and white, although leg and claw meat will have some red coloration.

- *Lobster tails* are the most commonly available form of this crustacean, either freshly cooked and iced in the fish market or frozen. Shells should be bright pink and intact, and meat should be moist and snowy white.

- *Shrimp* is usually frozen before shipping, then thawed at the retail market. Fresh (that is, never frozen) shrimp is available only in certain parts of the country where it can be purchased directly off the shrimp boat. In other regions, what appears as fresh in the markets is thawed raw shrimp. It should not be refrozen at home. Thawed raw shrimp is gray or greenish in color, but all species turn bright pink when cooked. Any hint of ammonia odor in raw shrimp is an indication of staleness. Cooked shrimp is also available at many fish markets. It should be plump, moist, and pink in color.

- *Prawns* and shrimp are interchangeable for all culinary intents and purposes. The term *prawns* typically refers to the larger varieties.

- *Clams and mussels* are seasonally available live in their shells. They should be displayed in the market on ice. The shells should not be cracked and should be tightly closed. The fishmonger may wrap the shellfish in plastic for purchase. This prevents their juices from contaminating other foods in the shopping bag, but it cuts off their oxygen supply. Be sure to get them home as soon as possible, and remove them from the plastic before placing in the refrigerator in a bowl loosely covered with a damp cloth or paper towel.

- *Live oysters* should be handled as described above for clams and mussels. However, our recipes call for shucked oysters, which are available in nearly every supermarket packed in a jar with their natural juices and displayed on ice at the fish counter. Packed this way, they should appear plump and their liquid should be transparent, not milky.

- *Scallops* usually are presented in the market out of their shells. Both tiny bay scallops and larger sea scallops should be white or ivory, not grayish, in color and should be an irregular round shape.

Selecting Frozen Fish and Seafood

Flash-frozen fish can have a better flavor and texture than "fresh" fish that may have spent several days out of the water before arriving at market. Fish labeled "flash-frozen" or "IQF"—individually quick frozen—is usually a good bet. Frozen fish should feel solid as a rock. If possible, choose frozen fish wrapped in clear packages so you can see the contents. There should be no sign of freezer burn, indicated by light-colored or cottony spots, or any ice crystals present inside the package. Yellow discoloration and/or a "fishy" odor can be signs of rancidity. Avoid ripped or broken packages. If the package carries a date, select the most recent one. Feel free to sort through the packages—those in the lower part of the freezer case may be coldest and therefore more thoroughly frozen for better quality.

Put frozen fish in your supermarket cart just before checking out, and get it home and into the freezer immediately or ask your fishmonger to pack it in ice and transport it home in a small ice chest. Date frozen fish packages before placing them in your home freezer, and use them within three to six months of purchase. Optimum freezer life varies from species to species. For specific information, call the U.S. Food and Drug Administration's Seafood Hotline at 1-800-332-4010.

Selecting Canned Fish and Seafood

When possible, we select water-packed canned fish to avoid the added fat. Sardines, tuna, and salmon are examples of fish that are readily available packed in water. When oil-packed fish is all you can find (as is the case with smoked oysters, for instance), pour off as much liquid as possible, then toss the contents with fresh-squeezed lemon juice and drain again. The juice will carry away some of the remaining oil.

Read the labels. Particularly with canned clams and crab, excessive additives may be present. We prefer the fish we consume to be as free of chemicals as possible, so we choose varieties that have the fewest extra ingredients listed on the label.

The tuna fishing industry has for years been accused of fishing practices that result in the destruction of large numbers of dolphins caught along with the tuna in huge drift nets. Due to consumer concern, however, major well-known brands of canned tuna in the United States are now confirmed to be dolphin-safe.

Seafood Serving Sizes

Needless to say, amounts of fish and seafood per person will vary according to appetite, and smaller amounts will be needed when combined in a dish with other substantial foods. The following rules of thumb apply when buying fish and seafood that is to be the dominant part of a meal:

- Steak and fillet cuts: 5 ounces per person.
- Crab and lobster in the shell: 1 pound per person.
- Crab meat and lobster meat: 4 ounces per person.
- Mussels or clams in the shell: 1 pound per person.
- Peeled, deveined shrimp or prawns: 4 ounces per person.
- Scallops: 4 ounces per person.

Home Storage and Handling

Refrigeration

Fish and seafood are among the most perishable of all foods, so proper refrigeration and handling are essential. Generally speaking, fish should be handled as little as possible, kept as cold as possible, and cooked as soon as possible after purchase.

If you purchase fish from a fishmonger who has just wrapped it for you, keep it in its original wrapper. Fresh fish purchased prepackaged in plastic wrap should be gently removed from its package, rinsed in cold water, patted dry, and rewrapped in butcher or wax paper. In all cases, keep fish and seafood in the lower part of the refrigerator, where the temperature is coldest.

Live clams, mussels, and oysters should be removed from plastic wrap as soon as possible and placed in a bowl in the refrigerator loosely covered with a damp cloth or paper towel. Live shellfish should be used within twenty-four hours of purchase.

Freezing and Thawing

Home freezers aren't cold enough to accomplish the flash-freezing used by commercial packers. Commercially frozen fish can be stored six to twelve months in home freezers, depending on the species, whereas fresh fish and seafood frozen at home should be eaten within three to six months, depending on species. Generally speaking, leaner fish varieties can be frozen for longer periods than oilier varieties. Call the U.S. Food and Drug Administration's Seafood Hotline at 1-800-332-4010 for instructions on freezing particular species.

Wrap meal-size portions in plastic or other airtight wrap, label with variety and date, and freeze immediately. Thawed fish should never be refrozen, so if you intend to freeze your purchase, ask the fishmonger if it was previously frozen.

What appears to be fresh raw shrimp or prawns in the fish case are almost always previously frozen, so they should not be refrozen at home. Since clams, mussels, and oysters in their shells are alive, they are also not suitable for freezing.

Fish and seafood should never be thawed at room temperature or in hot water. Use one of the following safe methods for thawing:

- Transfer the package from the freezer to the bottom of the refrigerator, on a plate to catch the juices. Most fish will thaw in twelve hours, depending on the thickness.
- Thaw in your microwave oven according to manufacturer's directions.
- For quick-thawing when a microwave oven isn't available, unwrap the fish and place it in a pan of cold water to cover until thawed—about one to two hours, depending on the thickness of the fish. If fish pieces are frozen together, separate them as they thaw to expose all surfaces to the water. Check thawing fish frequently. If fish is thawed before you are ready to proceed with the recipe, place it on a plate in the refrigerator, loosely covered with a moist cloth or paper towel.

Detecting Spoilage

Your sense of smell is your best spoilage detector. Fresh fish smells clean and of the sea. A "fishy" odor is caused by a chemical compound produced as fish and seafood deteriorate, so spoiling fish smells bad. Don't be overly sensitive, however. Particularly with plastic-wrapped supermarket fish cuts, a *slight* fish odor will be noticeable. Rinse the fish, pat dry, and cook thoroughly to kill any bacteria that may be present. The finished dish may not taste as fresh as possible, but it won't make you sick. For best results, buy fish freshly wrapped from a reputable fishmonger and cook it as soon as possible. Learn to trust your nose and, "When in doubt, throw it out!"

On the subject of fish smells, many people complain that cooking fish or seafood at home produces unpleasant odors that can last for days. Fish odor lingering in the house comes from uncooked juices on the packaging. Put fish wrappers in a plastic bag, seal, and discard immediately in your outdoor garbage can to avoid this problem.

Rinsing or Soaking Before Cooking

Although experts do not agree that rinsing or soaking fish or seafood before use is necessary, we choose to do so, to remove any particles of skin or fin that may cling to the flesh. Use a thin stream of cold water for rinsing to avoid splattering, as fish juices may carry bacteria that can contaminate other foods, utensils, and kitchen surfaces.

Seafood Safety

According to a 1991 report of the U.S. Food and Drug Administration, seafood is responsible for only 1 illness in every 2 million servings. Chicken, by contrast, is responsible for 1 illness in every 25,000 servings. These statistics should put to rest any concerns about the safety of eating fish and seafood. If it is truly fresh when purchased—and if it is stored, handled, and cooked properly—it can be considered a safe, lowfat source of excellent protein and other important nutrients. Please be sure to read this entire chapter to learn about techniques for selecting, storing, and handling fish and seafood to maximize safety.

The National Academy of Sciences reports that eight out of ten cases of seafood illness are due to eating raw oysters, clams, or mussels. Thoroughly cooking these molluscs is the only sure way to destroy disease-causing organisms. One potential contaminant is a one-celled organism called dinoflagellate, which renders some shellfish toxic. Commonly referred to as "red tide," these algae bloom during the summer months and clams, mussels, and oysters that live in the wild feed on it.

To eliminate the risk of eating red-tide-contaminated shellfish, a good rule of thumb is to avoid eating shellfish in the months without an *R* in their names: May, June, July, and August.

Chemical contaminants, such as mercury and lead, and industrial wastes like dioxins and PCBs are occasionally found in fish. Most of these problems occur in inland or coastal areas, where water pollution may be a concern. Deep-sea waters, where most commercial fishing occurs, remain clean. Eating a variety of species in modest portions will minimize any possible risk of chemical contamination.

As for commercially farmed fish, the U.S. Department of Commerce operates a voluntary inspection program with which most domestic aquaculture farms comply. These plants, which produce most of the trout and catfish available for purchase in our markets, are modern and sanitary.

Safety Tips

- It is extremely important to avoid cross-contamination of fish with other foods in your kitchen. After handling raw fish or seafood, wash your hands with soap and hot water before touching anything else. Use a nonporous cutting board for raw fish and seafood. Clean your knife, cutting board, and any other utensils that have contacted raw fish in hot, soapy water before using them with other foods.

- Fish and seafood deteriorate rapidly, even at cold temperatures, so plan your fish purchase close to when you anticipate cooking it to minimize the risk of spoilage. If you do not eat the fish on the day of purchase, store it in the lower part of your refrigerator, where the temperature is coldest, and eat it within two days. To hold for longer periods, fish may be frozen (see "Freezing and Thawing" above).

- Many people are concerned about swallowing fish bones. It's wise to chew slowly, removing any bones you detect in the process. However, if you don't notice a bone until you're in the process of swallowing it, don't panic. Simply eat an entire piece of bread to help the bone pass through your throat. Seafood steak cuts generally don't have small bones embedded in the flesh, and most bones are removed from fillets when they are cut by the fishmonger. You can manually inspect for bones and remove any remaining ones with a pair of kitchen tweezers or pliers before cooking.

Stocking the Pantry

A diet based primarily on fish and seafood, vegetables, and whole grains and beans is naturally low in fat but high in flavor and variety. In our recipes, these simple, nutritious foods are combined with herbs, spices, fruits and their juices, wines and spirits, and other carefully chosen seasonings. We think the results are delicious and innovative.

In this chapter, we provide a glimpse into our cupboards. Keeping the same ingredients on hand in your pantry will make lowfat seafood cookery easy and convenient.

Please consult our previous books, *The Best 125 Meatless Pasta Dishes* and *The Best 125 Meatless Main Dishes* (both

Prima, 1992) for more information about creative, healthy cooking.

Grains

Among the whole grains we most frequently recommend as seafood companion dishes are bulgur wheat and various types of rice. Brown rice contains substantially more nutrients than polished white rice, and we usually prefer it, though most of our Louisiana-inspired recipes call for white rice, which is traditional. In addition to long-grain and short-grain brown rice, we often use an aromatic rice from India called basmati, which is sometimes sold as "aromatic rice." It is available for purchase virtually everywhere.

Another specialty rice we frequently use is the round-grain Italian type usually sold as "riso arborio." Its unique shape yields a superbly creamy cooked rice. See the chapter on "Risotto and Rice Dishes," page 165, for more information on this type of rice. Italian specialty markets and gourmet food stores often carry the varieties of round-grain rice suitable for risotto.

In addition to starring in a chapter of its own, pasta is a frequently recommended companion dish. So many shapes are available, and pasta's compatibility with different seasonings makes it an excellent side dish. Don't miss the "Seafood Pasta" chapter on page 197, which offers more information on selecting pasta, along with our favorite main-course pasta recipes.

Dried Beans and Peas

Dried beans and peas (also known as legumes) are wonderfully nutritious, delicious, and economical and are key ingredients in a few of our recipes. With a little advance planning, it is easy to cook dried beans at home. Cook more than you need for a particular recipe and freeze the remainder for use at a later time (see page 36 for detailed cooking instructions). When time is short, you may substitute canned beans for fresh-cooked ones. Be aware, however, that salt, sugar, and various preservatives are often present in canned beans, sometimes in large quantities. Be sure to read the labels, and choose beans without these added ingredients when possible. If they contain unwanted additives, drain and rinse canned beans thoroughly before using them in a recipe.

Vegetables

Shop for fresh vegetables just before you'll use them, since nutrient values diminish rapidly after picking. Texture as well as color should be robust, so select produce that is firm, not limp, dry, or rubbery. In keeping with the U.S. Department of Agriculture's Food Guide Pyramid, which recommends three to five servings of vegetables per day (see page 20 for more information), we utilize them as an important ingredient in many of our fish and seafood recipes. In addition to flavor, color, and texture, they are excellent sources of vitamins, minerals, and dietary fiber.

Because mushrooms are succulent and rich in flavor, they play an important role in our seafood cuisine. The fresh button mushroom most familiar to Americans is versatile and delicious. Choose button mushrooms that are evenly white or light brown in color, with caps tightly closed against the stem. Also available fresh in well-stocked produce markets are shiitake—the rich, black mushroom used by Chinese chefs—oyster, and enoki mushrooms. Dried mushrooms also expand the variety of mushroom textures and flavors. Dried shiitakes can be found in every Asian market and at gourmet food shops.

Canned, fresh, and dried tomatoes are also often called into duty in our kitchens. Purchase low-sodium or sodium-free canned tomato products whenever possible. Dried tomatoes have an intensified tomato sweetness and add a unique texture and flavor to some of our recipes. They can be purchased at well-stocked markets, either in bulk or in cellophane packages. Some varieties are tender enough to be used as is; others are so dry they must be reconstituted in liquid before using (see page 37 for instructions). Dried tomatoes are also available marinated in olive oil. When our recipes call for minced dried tomatoes, however, we are referring to the oil-free type.

Fruits and Fruit Juices

Like vegetables, fresh fruits are packed with vitamins and minerals and are a good source of carbohydrates and dietary fiber. They are low in calories and sodium, and are practically fat-free. The sweetness of fruits and their juices pairs well with certain types of seafood, while the tart citrus flavors of lemon, lime, and grapefruit complement others.

Most fruits can be purchased just before use, but tropical fruits, such as papaya, mango, and kiwi, usually arrive at the market unripe and require a few days of further ripening at home. Place these fruits in a basket at room temperature and check daily for characteristic signs of ripeness. Papayas and mangoes are ripe when they yield to gentle pressure and are primarily orange or golden, rather than green, in color. Kiwis won't alter in appearance, but will become slightly soft to the touch when ripe.

We use citrus juices frequently in our recipes, and we recommend fresh-squeezed juices in all cases. All citrus fruits are readily available; it takes only a moment to squeeze a small amount of fresh juice, and the flavors and nutritional benefits are far superior to those of frozen or bottled varieties.

Dairy Products and Eggs

In our lowfat seafood cooking, we don't rely heavily on dairy products for obvious reasons. Whole milk derives almost half its calories from saturated fat, and most cheeses contain abundant fat and sodium. When we do use milk, yogurt, sour cream, or cheese, we prefer varieties that are lowfat, light, nonfat, or part-skim.

Goat and sheep milk cheeses, such as crumbly feta and soft chevre, have a unique piquant flavor that we enjoy in Mediterranean-inspired recipes. The French variety of feta is milder in flavor and lower in fat and sodium than its Greek counterpart. Specialty markets carry it, as do many supermarkets.

Sometimes we use butter, always in small amounts, when its flavor seems right for a particular dish. We prefer the unsalted variety for its purity and sweetness. We do not recommend substituting margarine for butter because of the health concerns associated with the hydrogenation process used to harden liquid oils into solid form.

Though eggs are an excellent source of protein, their fat-to-calorie ratio is high, and they contain quite a bit of cholesterol. For these reasons, people on a lowfat dietary regimen should limit the number of eggs they consume. For types of preparations which would typically use eggs—such as salmon cakes and crab cakes—we have called for egg whites only, since the yolk carries little protein and most of the fat. A general rule of thumb for eliminating egg yolks is to substitute twice as many egg whites for the number of whole eggs called for in a recipe. It won't work in every case—successful soufflés, for instance, require at least a couple of yolks—but usually you will be happy with the results.

Oils, Nuts, and Seeds

Olive oil and canola oil, both low in saturated fat and cholesterol-free, are our preferences for cooking when oil is called for. Extra virgin olive oil has a robust olive aroma and flavor. The flavor of canola oil is lighter, almost bland, so it won't overpower a delicately flavored dish. We also use both light and dark sesame oils occasionally, particularly in Asian-inspired dishes. The dark variety is pressed from toasted sesame seeds. Its smoky flavor is absolutely unique and quite delicious. Where it is called for in our recipes, there is no suitable substitute.

Nuts and seeds are high in fats, so we use them sparingly and we usually toast them to make the most of their rich flavor (see page 34 for toasting instructions). We call for fresh, raw, unsalted nuts and seeds, and nut butters made without additives like sugar or salt.

Seasonings

A cupboard well stocked with dried herbs and spices and other lowfat flavor enhancers is a treasure trove for creative cooks. They add very little fat or calories but provide abundant flavor. The herbs and spices most frequently used in our recipes include: (1) dried basil, dill, oregano, rosemary, sage, tarragon, thyme, bay leaves, and saffron; (2) whole nutmeg, coriander, and anise, to be ground just before using; (3) commercially ground cinnamon, cumin, chili powder, paprika, curry blends, and peppers; and (4) whole mustard, celery, cumin, and dill seeds. Herbs and spices do lose their potency, so buy them in small quantities. Natural food stores often sell them in bulk, enabling you to buy as much or as little as you like. Store in airtight containers, and discard and replace after about a year.

Some of our recipes call for the brighter flavors of fresh herbs. Herbs are easy to grow in even a small garden space, or you can now find a good selection at well-stocked produce markets. Though the results won't be quite the same, dried herbs can sometimes be substituted when fresh ones are called for in our recipes. Use half as much dried as you would fresh. Dried rosemary, oregano, tarragon, and dill are acceptable alternatives when fresh is not available. Parsley and cilantro should always be used fresh since the dried varieties tend to be flavorless.

Wines and Spirits

In moderation, fermented grape and grain beverages have a place in our diets. We find many culinary uses for vermouth, port, dry sherry, and brandy, as well as red and white wines and, occasionally, beer. The Japanese rice wine called sake, and mirin, its sweet wine counterpart, show up in a number of our Asian dishes. They are available at Asian specialty food shops and some well-stocked supermarkets.

Wines and spirits add interesting flavors without adding fat. In every case, the amounts used are small, so the quantity of alcohol in each serving is negligible. Because the flavors of these wines and spirits are essential to certain dishes, we suggest that those who object to their use simply bypass the recipes containing them.

Thickening Agents

There are many ways to thicken sauces without using butter or oil. In our recipes, we sometimes call for dissolving flour in cold water, then whisking the mixture into hot liquid until thickened. For a moderately thick sauce, a good rule of thumb is 1 tablespoon unbleached flour dissolved in 3 tablespoons cold water to thicken 1 cup of liquid. As the liquid cooks over medium heat, it should be stirred or whisked frequently. It will take about 10 to 15 minutes to thicken. This method is especially suitable for cream sauces and yields a velvety consistency.

For creating sauces for sautés and stir-fried dishes, our preferred thickener is arrowroot powder, the ground dried root of a starchy tropical tuber. It is dissolved in a little cold water, then stirred or whisked into hot liquid. It will thicken the liquid almost immediately and should not be cooked longer, as this will result in a gummy rather than smooth consistency. The standard formula is 1½ tablespoons arrowroot powder dissolved in 3 tablespoons cold water to thicken 1 cup of liquid.

Cornstarch is interchangeable with arrowroot powder in our recipes. We prefer arrowroot because it is a less highly processed food. Arrowroot powder is available (sometimes sold as arrowroot flour) in natural food stores and some well-stocked supermarkets.

Nutrition Alert

Nutritionally speaking, there are many good reasons to make fish and seafood a regular part of our diets. Most varieties are lower in fat and calories than other sources of concentrated protein, and fish and seafood are the best sources of the nutrients called omega-3 fatty acids, which recently have been discovered to be valuable in reducing the risk of heart disease. (For more information, see "Fats," below.)

People who are concerned about nutrition balance their food intake based on factors beyond the outmoded "five basic food groups" concept. In 1992, the U.S. Department of Agriculture released the Food Guide Pyramid, presenting the food groups with a new and different emphasis. At the base of the pyramid are the foods from which we should get most of our calories. At the tip are the foods that should supply us with the fewest calories. (To order a brochure that depicts the Food Guide Pyramid and discusses the concept in detail, order Home and Garden Bulletin #252 from USDA, Human Nutrition Information Service, 6505 Belcrest Road, Hyattsville, MD 20782.)

The basic message of the pyramid is to cut down on fats and added sugars, as well as to eat a variety of foods from the different food groups. The chief eating goals, says the USDA, should be variety, moderation, and balance. It is the overall picture that counts—what you eat over a period of days is more important than what you eat in a single meal.

A diet primarily comprised of grains and cereal products (six to eleven servings per day), vegetables (three to five servings per day), and fruits (two to four servings per day), combined with lowfat protein sources (two to three servings per day) and lowfat dairy products (two to three servings per day) conforms to the Food Guide Pyramid, creating a well-balanced mix of proteins, carbohydrates, and fats. Fish and seafood are particularly favored in the protein category because, unlike red meat, they contain almost no saturated fat, the type of fat implicated in the development of heart disease.

The Surgeon General and the American Heart Association are proponents of what is described as a "semi-vegetarian" approach to eating, which is based primarily on grains, vegetables, and fruits. Those of us who occasionally eat fish and seafood with what is otherwise a vegetarian diet fit this description. The Food Guide Pyramid and other expert recommendations support semi-vegetarianism as an important aspect of a healthy life-style. The major shift for many Americans is to view meat, if it is to be consumed at all, as a side dish or condiment.

Many studies are being conducted to determine optimum levels of various food components in the human diet. Our intent here is to provide an introduction to basic nutrition. For further investigation, check with your local librarian or bookseller for thorough reference works.

The recipes in this book have been analyzed for calories, protein, carbohydrates, cholesterol, sodium, and various types of fat—including beneficial omega-3 fatty acids. In addition, we indicate the percentage of calories derived from fat for each recipe. We discuss below the importance of each of these components.

Calories

It is important to be aware of your total caloric intake in a day but most important to note where the calories are coming from. Calories derive from three primary sources: protein, carbohydrates, and fats. Fats contain a greater concentration of calories than do carbohydrates or protein, and they are much harder for the body to metabolize. The U.S. Food and Drug Administration therefore suggests that the average American diet should be adjusted so that fewer calories come from fatty foods and more from carbohydrates. They specifically recommend that no more than 30 percent of the calories in our overall diets be derived from fat.

Fish and seafood are very low in fat and calories—most types of freshwater and saltwater fish have less than 150 calories in three ounces, and single-digit fat levels. When combined with carbohydrate-rich foods—such as rice, pasta, or starchy vegetables, as we suggest in this book—and little added fat, fish and seafood fit the guidelines perfectly.

The nutritional analysis presented with each of our recipes includes percentage of calories from fat. Occasionally, the calories are so low for a dish that, despite the small number of fat grams it contains, the percentage is over 30 percent. In these cases, remember that our recommended companion dishes will round out the calories and carbohydrates in the meal, bringing the percentage down to well within the recommended range of 30 percent or less.

Fats

Our bodies need some fat, as it is an essential component in energy production, but it is estimated that most of us consume six to eight times more fat than we need. High-fat diets are implicated not only in heart disease, but also in the development of some cancers, most notably of the colon and breast. It is likely to contribute to a healthier—perhaps even longer—life to learn the basics about dietary fat.

There are nine calories in a gram of fat. A gram of protein or carbohydrate contains only four calories. Obviously, therefore, the less fat one consumes, the lower one's intake of calories and the lower one's ratio of calories from fat. Calories derived from dietary fats are more troublesome than calories from any other source, as the body is most efficient at converting fat calories into body fat.

Consider that the average tablespoon of oil contains fourteen grams of fat and 120 calories, while almost no fat is contained in a half cup of steamed brown rice (206 calories) or a cup of cooked broccoli (44 calories). This illustrates the volume of food that can be eaten without increasing one's fat-to-calories ratio.

Another way of monitoring one's fat intake is by counting fat grams consumed. In the nutritional analysis provided with each of our recipes, fat is listed in total grams per serving to facilitate this. An easy way to calculate how much fat you should consume is to divide your body weight in half. This number is an estimate of the maximum fat in grams that a moderately active person should ingest over the course of a day to maintain that weight.

Our nutritional analyses also break down total fat per recipe into monounsaturated, polyunsaturated, and saturated fat values. The term *saturation* refers to the number of hydrogen atoms present in the fat, with saturated fats containing the most.

The primary reason to pay attention to the saturation level of fats is because diets high in saturated fats increase levels of blood cholesterol in some people—a risk factor in heart disease. Not only do monounsaturated and polyunsaturated fats not harm our hearts, they actually appear to help reduce cholesterol levels in the blood when eaten in moderation as part of an overall lowfat diet.

Therefore, it is wise to choose foods higher in polyunsaturated or monounsaturated fats than in saturated fats. To assist in making this determination, remember that most saturated fats are from animal origin and are hard at room temperature (such as butter and cheese) and most unsaturated fats are of vegetable origin and are liquid at room temperature (such as olive and canola oils).

Omega-3 Fatty Acids

Omega-3 fatty acids, found primarily in fish oils, are super-polyunsaturated. The most important health benefit attributed to the omega-3s is that they make the blood less likely to coagulate, or clot, thereby reducing the risk of heart attack and stroke. In addition, they appear to play an important role in fetal and infant development.

Research suggests that the body needs omega-3s in high concentrations, but manufactures them in very small amounts. Though a certain type of omega-3 is present in some plant oils, such as linseed, canola, and walnut, the largest concentrations and the most beneficial types are found only in seafood.

Study of the omega-3 fatty acids is ongoing. Some scientists suggest that they may be helpful in the treatment of such debilitating conditions as high blood pressure and arthritis. While we await definitive results, eating seafood and the omega-3s they contain once or twice a week may be beneficial.

Protein

Since our bodies store only small amounts of protein, it needs to be replenished on a daily basis. However, though protein is needed for growth and tissue repair, it is not needed in great abundance. The National Academy of Science's Food and Nutrition Board recommends forty-five grams of protein per day for the average 120-pound woman and fifty-five grams for the average 154-pound man. Some nutritionists think this is more protein than needed on average. Recent nutritional studies suggest, in fact, that the detrimental effects of excessive protein consumption should be of greater concern to most Americans than the threat of protein deficiency.

While this debate continues, it makes sense to choose protein sources that are low in fat and, thus, calories. Fish and seafood are an excellent choice.

Carbohydrates

There is a common misconception that carbohydrates such as pasta, grains, and potatoes are high in calories and low in nutritive value. However, starchy complex carbohydrates do not present a calorie problem; the problem lies with the fats that are typically added to them.

Nutritional experts now suggest that more of our daily calories come from carbohydrates than from fats or protein, since the body provides energy more economically from carbohydrates. Carbohydrates are quickly converted into glucose, the body's main fuel.

In addition, complex carbohydrates are low in fat and are a good source of fiber. Insoluble fiber is the nondigestible part of plant food. It passes through the digestive system intact, keeping the intestines clear. The soluble fiber from legumes and grains also may decrease blood cholesterol levels, which is an added bonus to our heart health.

Although fish and seafood are generally low in carbohydrates, most of our recipes combine them with higher-carbohydrate grains and vegetables. Therefore, the overall balance of protein, fat, and carbohydrates fits the optimum-nutrition profile.

Cholesterol

Many volumes have been written on this subject in recent years, and much is being discovered about the role of cholesterol in overall health and nutrition. Cholesterol is essential for cell wall construction, the transmission of nerve impulses, and the synthesis of important hormones. It plays a vital role in the healthy functioning of the body and poses no problem when present in the correct amount. However, in excess, cholesterol is a major risk factor in heart disease. The U.S. Senate Select Committee on Nutrition and Human Needs recommends that the average person consume no more than 300 milligrams of cholesterol per day. Have your cholesterol level checked by your doctor and follow his or her specific guidelines.

Recent studies have shown that the total amount of fat a person eats—especially saturated fats—may be more responsible for the cholesterol level in the body than the actual cholesterol count found in food.

With the exception of some shellfish, seafood and fish are low in cholesterol. In addition, unsaturated fats like those found in vegetable oils and most fish actually are considered beneficial, because they help lower the harmful type of blood cholesterol (called LDL) when included in a diet low in overall fat.

Sodium

The American Heart Association recommends that sodium intake be limited to 3,000 milligrams per day (a teaspoon of salt contains 2,200 milligrams of sodium). However, the actual physiological requirement is only 220 milligrams a day.

Sodium, like other food components that we ingest, plays an important role in the functioning of the body. It is essential for good health, since each cell of the body must be bathed continually in a saline solution. High sodium intake disrupts this balance and is associated with high blood pressure and such life-threatening conditions as heart and kidney disease and strokes.

Many foods naturally contain some sodium, so you do not need to add much when cooking to achieve good flavor. Particularly if you have salt-related health concerns, dishes that taste a little bland unsalted can be seasoned with herbs or other salt-free alternatives. When our recipes do call for salt, you may add less than the recommended amount, or none at all, if your doctor has drastically reduced your sodium intake.

Monitoring your intake of the above food components is important; however, unless you're under a doctor's instructions, you needn't be overly rigid. It is preferable to balance your intake over the course of a day, or even several days, rather than attempt to make each meal fit the pattern recommended by nutritional experts. This rule of thumb allows you to enjoy a recipe that may be higher in fat or salt, for instance, than you would normally choose, knowing that at your next meal you can eliminate that component altogether to achieve a healthy daily balance.

The information given here is not set in stone; the science of nutrition is constantly evolving. The analyses for our recipes is provided for people on normal diets who want to plan healthier meals. If your physician has prescribed a special diet, check with a registered dietitian to see how these recipes fit into your guidelines.

We encourage you to spend some time learning about how foods break down and are used by the body as fuel. A basic understanding of the process and application of a few simple rules can contribute to a longer and—more important—a healthier life.

An Introduction
to the Recipes

You will notice that our recipes list ingredients in an unconventional format: The name of the food is in the first column, and the quantity required is in a separate column to the right. This allows the quickest perusal of the ingredients, so you can determine whether you're in the mood for a certain dish and whether you have the required foods on hand. We find this format particularly easy to follow and hope you will agree.

In an introduction to each chapter, we have provided pertinent tips and techniques for successful preparation. Please read those introductions for a comprehensive overview. The information below ensures a smooth and enjoyable cooking experience when working from written recipes.

Tips for Successful Cooking from Recipes

- Use only the freshest, best quality ingredients. Your finished dish will be only as good as the individual components that go into it, so don't compromise on quality.

- Read a recipe all the way through before beginning to cook. This will allow you to take care of any preliminary steps, such as bringing ingredients to room temperature, and it will give you a solid grasp of the entire process.

- Set your ingredients and equipment out on the work surface before you begin. This will save you walking from one end of the kitchen to the other to rummage in a cupboard for the long-lost paprika, for instance, while neglecting whatever's cooking on the stove.

- For certain ingredients, quantities are by nature somewhat approximate. When we call for a large carrot, for instance, the one you use may be more or less large than the one we used. This is nothing to worry about. When it is essential to the success of a dish to use a very specific amount, we will provide cup or pound measurements. Otherwise, use your own judgment to decide which carrot in the bin is "large." Garlic amounts in our recipes refer to medium-size cloves. If you are using elephant garlic or the tiny cloves at the center of a garlic bulb, adjust accordingly the number of cloves you use.

- Seasonings are a matter of personal taste. We have provided recipes for dishes that taste good to us, seasoned as we like them. Certain people will prefer more or less of certain seasonings such as salt or garlic.

- When serving hot food, use warmed serving dishes and warmed individual plates so the food stays at optimum temperature as long as possible. This is easily accomplished by placing the dishes near the heat source as you cook; or warm your oven several minutes before dinnertime, turn off the heat, and place the dishes there until needed.

Seafood Cooking Tips

Tips and techniques specific to certain fish and seafood cooking methods are covered in detail in the introduction to each chapter in this book. Here we mention some general guidelines to assist you in successful seafood cooking.

- Because fish has so little connective tissue, it cooks very rapidly. Therefore, have the rest of the meal well under way before you put the fish on to cook.
- Generally, fish is cooked for a few minutes on one side, then turned to ensure even cooking. Thin fillets, however, may not need to be turned, even when broiling or grilling. Refer to specific recipe instructions for more information.
- The single most common mistake made with fish and seafood is overcooking. Some species of fish become dry and dull in flavor when overcooked; others become tough or rubbery. Our best advice is to pay close attention and test frequently until you begin to develop a knack for sensing when fish is perfectly cooked.
- Raw fish is moist and translucent—you can almost see into the flesh. Fish is properly cooked when it is mostly opaque, but still barely translucent at the very center. You will need to cut into the thickest part of the fish to perform this visual test.

- With many varieties of thin fillets, fish is done when it "flakes" easily. Gently insert a fork into the thickest part and twist—fish is done if layers separate easily.

- Keep in mind that fish will continue to cook for a few moments after it is removed from the heat, so learn to allow for this when assessing doneness.

- If cooking fish is new to you, be conservative in your timing. It is preferable to undercook than to overcook, since you can always return the fish to the heat for a little longer, if necessary.

- Clams, mussels, and oysters in their shells will pop open when cooked. Remember to discard any that *aren't* tightly closed when you put them in the pot or that *are* closed when you take them out! They cook very rapidly and become tough when cooked too long, so watch the pot closely. Shucked oysters also cook very rapidly, and curl at the edges when done.

- Shrimp, scallops, lobster, and crab turn from translucent to opaque when done—cut to test. Shrimp turns from gray or greenish to bright pink within a minute or two and should be removed from the heat immediately. Don't overcook delicate seafood as it will become dry and tasteless.

Some Secrets of Lowfat Cooking

The first step to decreasing fat in your diet is to change old habits of thinking. There is a tendency for many people to believe that food without added fat can't taste good when, in fact, excellent flavor depends on expert seasoning. Delicious dishes are easy to achieve using well-chosen fat-free or lowfat ingredients. Stocking the pantry with garlic, ginger root, miso, lemons and other citrus fruits, wines and spirits, and a wide variety of fresh and dried herbs and spices will prepare you for a full-flavored, lowfat cooking adventure. See "Stocking the Pantry" on page 12 for more detailed information.

Read the chapter entitled "Nutrition Alert" on page 20 to learn how the body uses fat and how many grams of fat you should consume to maintain your ideal weight. Understanding the metabolism process will help you make informed decisions and can be a great boon to your motivation to cook—and eat—in a healthy manner.

Lowfat Cooking Tools and Tips

We prefer heavy-bottomed cast-iron or stainless steel cookware because it distributes heat evenly and is much less prone to sticking and scorching than thinner surfaces. When properly tempered, cast iron requires very little oil, even for frying griddle cakes. To temper a cast-iron pan, preheat the oven to 300 degrees F. Wash the new pan with mild soap and hot water. Rinse and dry thoroughly. Heat the pan in the oven for a few minutes, then rub it with a very thin and even layer of olive or canola oil. Return it to the hot oven for 20 minutes, then rub again with a very thin and even layer of oil. Put it back in the oven for 20 minutes, then turn off the heat and allow the pan to cool in the oven. After every use, wash a tempered pan in hot water, without soap and without hard scrubbing, and dry immediately over a hot burner. If the oil coating turns gummy or wears off, or if rust develops, wash the pan thoroughly and repeat the tempering process. When cared for in this way, cast-iron pans will serve you well for a lifetime.

Don't think you need to buy expensive cooking sprays in order to cut down on oil. If you are cutting fats down to a bare minimum, a fraction of a teaspoon is enough to coat the bottom of a pan, for either baking or stovetop cooking. A small pastry brush or flexible rubber spatula works well for distributing it evenly over the surface. When sautéing with a minimum of oil, stir food frequently so it doesn't stick.

Many of our recipes utilize moist-heat cooking methods, such as steaming, poaching, and baking en papillote (in parchment paper), which do not require oil and prevent fish from drying out during cooking. Getting acquainted with these lowfat methods will revolutionize the way you cook.

Techniques for the Basics

Here we explain some basic techniques used in various recipes in this book. They are simple and quick procedures. Once you have mastered them, you will find them quite useful.

Toasting Seeds and Nuts

Place nuts or seeds in a single layer in a cast-iron skillet over medium-high heat on the stove top. Shake the pan frequently and soon the nuts or seeds will be golden brown and will emit a wonderful roasted aroma. Remove immediately from the pan and set aside until needed.

Blanching Vegetables

Some recipes call for blanching (also called parboiling) vegetables to cook them just a little before adding to a recipe. The purpose of blanching is to brighten the color and soften the texture.

Wash the vegetables. Boil several cups of water in a large lidded pot. When the water boils, drop in the vegetables. Blanching time will vary, usually from about two to five minutes depending on the size and density of the particular vegetable. Test a piece from time to time to check for doneness; it should still be quite firm, but not as crunchy as its raw counterpart. When done, cool immediately in cold water, and drain.

To blanch fresh tomatoes, drop them into boiling water. Within a minute or two, their skins will begin to split and pull away from the flesh. Remove the tomatoes with a slotted spoon to a bowl of cold water. When cool enough to handle, remove the skins and cut out the stems.

A recipe will sometimes call for seeding the tomatoes after blanching. When cooled, cut the peeled tomatoes in half crosswise and gently squeeze to remove the juicy seed pockets.

Roasting Vegetables

Certain vegetables develop a delightful smoky flavor when roasted. Peppers, tomatoes, and small eggplants lend themselves most readily to this type of preparation. Place the vegetable, whole or cut, under a very hot broiler or on a hot grill and turn every few minutes until the entire surface is charred black. When blackened, remove to a paper bag, fold to close, and set aside. The steam in the bag will finish the cooking and the vegetable will become quite soft. When cooled, remove from the bag and peel off the charred skin. Remove stems and/or seeds and proceed with the recipe.

Baking Garlic

Preheat the oven or toaster oven to 350 degrees F. Rub off as much papery skin as possible from the garlic bulb, but do not break it up into individual cloves. Slice about ½ inch off the pointed end of the bulb, rub the cut surface evenly with ⅛ teaspoon olive oil, and place in a covered clay or glass dish (alternatively, you may wrap the bulb in foil). Bake for 45 minutes to 1 hour. Garlic is done when the bulb is very soft when gently squeezed. Take the roasted garlic out of the oven and allow to cool.

Remove the garlic from the skin by squeezing the cloves from the bottom. The garlic will slide out the cut end as a soft paste. Patiently remove all bits of skin that may cling to the garlic paste and proceed with the recipe. Whole baked garlic bulbs may also be served as a delicious lowfat spread for bread or crackers.

Cooking Beans

Before cooking beans, rinse them thoroughly to remove surface dirt and sort them carefully. Often small dirt clods, pebbles, or other foreign objects will find their way through the factory sorters and into the market bean bin. Also discard beans and peas that are shriveled or discolored.

Most beans are soaked for several hours to soften them before cooking. Cover with plenty of fresh water and leave at room temperature overnight, loosely covered with a tea towel or lid. A quicker method is to cover the beans with boiling water and leave them to soak, loosely covered, for a few hours. Drain off the starchy soaking liquid. Cover the beans with fresh water and boil until tender. You may wish to add garlic, bay leaves, and/or chili flakes to the cooking water, but wait to salt the pot until the beans are tender and ready for their final seasoning, because cooking in salt can give beans a tough or rubbery texture. As a general rule of thumb, 1 cup of dried beans will yield 2 to 2½ cups of cooked beans.

For most uses, the beans should be boiled until they yield easily to the bite, but are not mushy. If they are to be cooked further after boiling, as in a casserole, take them from the pot when barely al dente.

Beans freeze well. Cook in larger quantities than called for in a recipe and freeze the rest in small, measured portions.

Reconstituting Dried Fruits and Vegetables

To get optimum flavor from fruits and vegetables that have been dried, and to soften them to a chewable consistency, reconstitute before using.

The technique for fruits is to immerse them in warm water, fruit juice, brandy, or wine and allow them to sit at room temperature until softened. The amount of time will vary from fruit to fruit. Do not let fruit sit any longer than necessary in the liquid, as the flavor and color will leach out.

Each variety of dried tomato—from paper dry to leathery to plump—calls for a slightly different technique. Paper dry or leathery ones should be covered with boiling water and allowed to plump 15 to 30 minutes. The desired result is an easily chewable, not mushy, texture. Depending on their chewiness, the plumper variety may not need reconstituting. Drain well, reserving the liquid, if desired, for use in a soup or sauce, and chop or mince the tomatoes as called for in the recipe.

All varieties of dried mushrooms are reconstituted before use by soaking them for 30 minutes or so in warm water. Usually, the recipe will suggest straining and saving the soaking water to use where liquid is needed in the dish. Certain dried mushrooms, like shiitakes, must be washed under a thin stream of running water after soaking to remove particles of grit that are lodged in the membranes under the cap.

Often-Used Homemade Ingredients

When our recipes call for such ingredients as salsa or chutney, you may purchase commercial varieties. For optimum quality, however, make your own. It's easier than you think to keep homemade convenience foods on hand.

Bread Crumbs and Cubes

If you have a partial loaf of bread that has dried in the bin, simply whirl it in a food processor to either coarse or fine crumb consistency. It is sometimes useful to have seasoned bread crumbs on hand. Mix dried herbs and granulated garlic into the crumbs before storing.

You can also prepare dried bread crumbs from fresh bread. Preheat the oven to 350 degrees F. Use your hands to crumble bread onto a dry cooking sheet. Place in the oven for 15 minutes, then turn off the heat and leave the crumbs in the oven to dry for about half an hour longer. When recipes call for bread cubes, simply cut fresh bread into the desired size and proceed with baking as described above. Dried bread crumbs and cubes will keep for long periods in a dry place in an airtight container.

Cajun Blackening Spice Mix

Yield: 1 cup

Dried thyme	2 tablespoons
Dried oregano	2 tablespoons
Granulated garlic	2 tablespoons
Onion powder	2 tablespoons
Chili powder	2 tablespoons
Cayenne	1 tablespoon
Ground cumin	1 tablespoon
Black pepper	1 tablespoon
White pepper	1 tablespoon
Ground cinnamon	1 teaspoon

Place all spices in a small food processor work bowl and pulse to crumble and combine ingredients. Store in a covered jar.

Each 1 tablespoon provides:

18	Calories	0 g	Omega-3
1 g	Protein	0.5 g	Fat
4 g	Carbohydrate		19% of calories from fat
12 mg	Sodium		0 g saturated fat
0 mg	Cholesterol		0.1 g polyunsaturated fat
			0 g monounsaturated fat

Salsa Fresca

Yield: 5 cups

Fresh tomatoes	**2½**	**pounds**
Whole mild green chilies	**1**	**7-ounce can**
Fresh-squeezed lemon juice	**¼**	**cup**
Onion	**1**	**medium, finely diced**
Fresh cilantro, minced	**⅓**	**cup**
Garlic	**3**	**cloves, minced**
Salt	**⅛**	**teaspoon**
Pepper		**A few grinds**

Blanch and peel the tomatoes (see page 34). Coarsely chop them, drain off as much juice as possible, and set aside in a bowl. Drain the liquid from the canned green chilies. Finely chop them and add to the tomatoes. Add the lemon juice to the tomato mixture, along with the onion, cilantro, garlic, salt, and pepper. Though its flavor improves over time, this salsa can be enjoyed immediately. Store the portion you don't use right away in a tightly closed container in the refrigerator for several days, or freeze for longer periods. If you are accustomed to canning foods, this recipe may be made in larger quantities and put up for the pantry.

Each 1 cup provides:

71	Calories	0 g	Omega-3
3 g	Protein	1 g	Fat
16 g	Carbohydrate		9% of calories from fat
82 mg	Sodium		0.1 g saturated fat
0 mg	Cholesterol		0.3 g polyunsaturated fat
			0.1 g monounsaturated fat

Basil Pesto

Yield: 1 cup

Fresh basil leaves	**2**	**cups, firmly packed**
Olive oil	**⅓**	**cup**
Pine nuts	**¼**	**cup**
Garlic	**6**	**cloves, chopped**
Parmesan cheese, finely grated	**¾**	**cup**

Wash the basil, discard the stems, and spin dry. In a food processor or blender, puree basil with ¼ cup of the olive oil, the pine nuts, garlic, and Parmesan until thick and homogenous. With the machine running, add the remaining olive oil in a thin stream to form a smooth paste.

Note: If you are harvesting basil from the garden at season's end, a few simple tips will facilitate cleaning the leaves. Use your clippers to snip off the main stems near the base of the plant, rather than pulling the plants up by the roots. Put a spray attachment on your hose and wash down the harvested branches of basil before bringing them into the kitchen.

Each ¼ cup provides:

305	Calories	0 g	Omega-3
9 g	Protein	28 g	Fat
6 g	Carbohydrate		81% of calories from fat°
362 mg	Sodium		9 g saturated fat
15 mg	Cholesterol		3 g polyunsaturated fat
			18 g monounsaturated fat

°Standing alone, this recipe appears high in fat. When combined with lower-fat ingredients in our recipes, however, the fat ratio will be balanced.

Mango Chutney

Yield: 4 half-pints

Orange	1	medium
Apples	3	medium
Mangoes	2	medium
Lemon	1	
Onion	1	medium
Honey	1	cup
Cider vinegar	1	cup
Water	1	cup
Fresh ginger, finely chopped	2	tablespoons
Dried red chili flakes	1	teaspoon
Peppercorns	1	teaspoon
Allspice	1	teaspoon
Mustard seed	1	teaspoon
Whole cloves	1	teaspoon
Celery seed	1	teaspoon
Raisins	¾	cup

Chop the fruits and onion into small pieces. Combine with honey, vinegar, and water in a large saucepan or stockpot. Tie the ginger and dried spices in a square of cheesecloth. Cook it all for about 20 minutes, then add the raisins and continue to cook

until thick. Remove spice bag. Spoon into half-pint jars, seal tightly, and store in the refrigerator for several weeks, or follow standard canning procedures and put up for the pantry.

Each tablespoon provides:

32	Calories	0 g	Omega-3
0.2 g	Protein	0.1 g	Fat
9 g	Carbohydrate		2% of calories from fat
1 mg	Sodium		0 g saturated fat
0 mg	Cholesterol		0 g polyunsaturated fat
			0 g monounsaturated fat

Companion Dishes

Each of our recipes includes recommendations for companion dishes, designed to balance the flavors and to keep the fat content of an entire meal at or under 30 percent calories from fat. These suggestions can help those interested in maximizing flavor while minimizing fat achieve this goal—but they are only suggestions. You may find them particularly useful when preparing a dish that relies on seasonings or cooking methods unfamiliar to you. However, feel free to use your own tried-and-true side dishes instead.

This chapter contains the recipes for the companion dishes referred to throughout this book.

Steamed Basmati Rice

Yield: 4 servings

Water	**2 cups**
Green onions	**2, minced**
Basmati rice, uncooked	**1 cup**

Bring water and onions to a boil. Add rice, return to a boil, cover, and reduce heat to low. Steam 20 minutes. Without disturbing the lid, allow to sit 5 minutes. Fluff with a fork and serve.

Each serving provides:

172	Calories	0 g	Omega-3
3 g	Protein	1.3 g	Fat
36 g	Carbohydrate		7% of calories from fat
71 mg	Sodium		0.3 g saturated fat
0 mg	Cholesterol		0.5 g polyunsaturated fat
			0.5 g monounsaturated fat

Steamed Brown Rice

Yield: 4 servings

Water	**2**	**cups**
Short-grain brown rice,		
uncooked	**1**	**cup**
Salt	**⅛**	**teaspoon**
Pepper		**A few grinds**

Bring the water to a boil in a 2-quart saucepan over high heat.
Add the rice, salt, and pepper and bring back to a boil over high
heat, cover, and reduce heat to low. Simmer gently 45 minutes,
then turn off heat and let stand an additional 5 minutes before
removing the lid. Serve hot.

Each serving provides:

172	Calories	0 g	Omega-3
4 g	Protein	1.3 g	Fat
36 g	Carbohydrate		7% of calories from fat
71 mg	Sodium		0.3 g saturated fat
0 mg	Cholesterol		0.5 g polyunsaturated fat
			0.5 g monounsaturated fat

Spanish Rice

Yield: 8 servings

Olive oil	1	tablespoon
Garlic	3	cloves, minced
Chili powder	2	teaspoons
Dried thyme	¼	teaspoon
Long-grain brown rice, uncooked	2	cups
Water	4	cups
Low-sodium tomato paste	¼	cup
Salt	¼	teaspoon
Cayenne		A pinch
Peas, fresh or frozen	1	cup

In a heavy-bottomed pot with a tight-fitting lid, heat the olive oil over medium-low heat. Sauté the garlic with the chili powder and thyme for a minute or two, then stir in the rice. Stir and cook 5 minutes, then add the water, tomato paste, salt, and cayenne. Stir to incorporate the tomato paste. Bring to a simmer over high heat, cover, reduce heat to very low, and cook 45 minutes. Remove the lid, pour the peas on top of the rice, and replace the lid. Let stand 10 minutes. Stir the peas into the rice and serve very hot.

Each serving provides:

212	Calories	0 g	Omega-3
5 g	Protein	3 g	Fat
41 g	Carbohydrate		14% of calories from fat
83 mg	Sodium		0.5 g saturated fat
0 mg	Cholesterol		0.5 g polyunsaturated fat
			2 g monounsaturated fat

Wild Rice Pilaf

Yield: 6 servings

Raw unsalted slivered almonds	¼	**cup**
Low-sodium vegetable broth cube	1	**large**
Hot water	2½	**cups**
Unsalted butter	1	**tablespoon**
White onion, diced	¼	**cup**
Green bell pepper, diced	⅓	**cup**
Long-grain brown rice, uncooked	1	**cup**
Wild rice, uncooked	¼	**cup**

Toast the almonds (page 34) and set aside. Dissolve the vegetable broth cube in the hot water. Melt the butter in a two-quart saucepan over medium heat. Sauté the onion and bell pepper 5 minutes, then add the rices, stirring to coat with the butter and vegetables. Add the hot broth and bring to a boil over high heat. Cover, reduce heat to very low, and cook 45 minutes. Allow to sit, covered, for 10 minutes before serving. Top with the toasted almonds and serve immediately.

Each serving provides:

190	Calories	0 g	Omega-3
5 g	Protein	6 g	Fat
31 g	Carbohydrate		26% of calories from fat
149 mg	Sodium		2 g saturated fat
6 mg	Cholesterol		1 g polyunsaturated fat
			3 g monounsaturated fat

Steamed Bulgur

Yield: 4 servings

Water	**2 cups**
Salt	**⅛ teaspoon**
Pepper	**A few grinds**
Green onions (optional)	**2, minced**
Bulgur wheat, uncooked	**1 cup**

Over high heat, bring the water to a boil with the salt and pepper. For a variation, add 2 minced green onions to the water along with the salt and pepper. Stir in bulgur, cover, reduce heat to low, and simmer 20 minutes. Let stand an additional 5 minutes before removing the lid. Serve hot.

Each serving provides:

146	Calories	0 g	Omega-3
6 g	Protein	1.5 g	Fat
31 g	Carbohydrate		8% of calories from fat
64 mg	Sodium		0.3 g saturated fat
0 mg	Cholesterol		0.4 g polyunsaturated fat
			0.4 g monounsaturated fat

Seasoned Black Beans

Yield: 4 servings

Cooked black beans	**2**	**cups, or 1 16-ounce can**
Granulated garlic	**¼**	**teaspoon**
Ground cumin	**⅛**	**teaspoon**
Chili powder	**¼**	**teaspoon**

Cook the beans according to instructions on page 36, or use canned beans. Heat the beans, along with ½ cup of their cooking liquid or all of the liquid from the can. Add the garlic, cumin, and chili powder, bring to a simmer over medium-low heat, and cook 10 to 12 minutes, stirring frequently, until beans are very hot. Serve immediately.

Each serving provides:

115	Calories	0 g	Omega-3
8 g	Protein	0.5 g	Fat
21 g	Carbohydrate		4% of calories from fat
82 mg	Sodium		0.2 g saturated fat
0 mg	Cholesterol		0.2 g polyunsaturated fat
			0.1 g monounsaturated fat

Steamed Couscous

Yield: 4 servings

Water	**1½**	**cups**
Granulated garlic	**½**	**teaspoon**
Olive oil	**1**	**tablespoon**
Dried couscous	**1**	**cup**
Salt and pepper (optional)		**To taste**

Bring water, garlic, and olive oil to a boil. Stir in the couscous, cover, and immediately turn off the heat. Let stand 5 minutes, then remove the lid and transfer to a serving bowl, fluffing with a fork to break up any large clumps. Serve hot.

Each serving provides:

204	Calories	0 g	Omega-3
6 g	Protein	4 g	Fat
36 g	Carbohydrate		17% of calories from fat
5 mg	Sodium		0.5 g saturated fat
0 mg	Cholesterol		0.4 g polyunsaturated fat
			2.5 g monounsaturated fat

Mediterranean Pasta

Yield: 6 servings

Dried pasta spirals	**12 ounces**
Fresh-squeezed lemon juice	**2 tablespoons**
Capers, drained and minced	**2 tablespoons**
Reduced-fat feta cheese, crumbled	**1 ounce (⅓ cup)**
Pepper	**Several grinds**

Bring several quarts of water to a boil and cook the pasta until al dente. Toss with the lemon juice, then with the capers, feta cheese, and pepper. Place in a warmed bowl and serve immediately.

Each serving provides:

226	Calories	0 g	Omega-3
9 g	Protein	3 g	Fat
41 g	Carbohydrate		11% of calories from fat
107 mg	Sodium		1 g saturated fat
54 mg	Cholesterol		1 g polyunsaturated fat
			1 g monounsaturated fat

Poppy Seed Noodles

Yield: 6 servings

Dried pasta spirals	8	ounces
Olive oil	2	tablespoons
Garlic	2	cloves, minced
Salt	¼	teaspoon
Poppy seeds	1	tablespoon

Bring several quarts of water to a boil and cook the pasta until al dente. Drain well and transfer to a warm serving bowl. Meanwhile, measure the olive oil into a tiny pan and add the garlic and salt. You do not really sauté the garlic, but simply heat it over medium heat in the oil. This takes only a moment. Pour this over the cooked pasta and toss well to coat. Sprinkle with the poppy seeds and toss again to distribute evenly. Serve immediately.

Each serving provides:

193	Calories	0 g	Omega-3
6 g	Protein	7 g	Fat
28 g	Carbohydrate		31% of calories from fat°
97 mg	Sodium		1 g saturated fat
36 mg	Cholesterol		1 g polyunsaturated fat
			4 g monounsaturated fat

°This companion dish is recommended for meals that are otherwise low in fat.

Grilled Red Potatoes

Yield: 6 servings

Baby red potatoes	**2**	**pounds**
Olive oil	**1**	**tablespoon**
Granulated garlic	**¼**	**teaspoon**

If using a coal grill, prepare the coals to be a medium-high temperature. A gas grill should be preheated 10 minutes before you grill the potatoes. Scrub the potatoes, but do not peel. Slice into ½-inch disks. Use your hands to rub the oil on the potato slices. Sprinkle with half of the granulated garlic. Place garlic side down on the grill. Cook for 5 minutes, sprinkle with the remaining garlic, then turn and continue to cook for 5 minutes. Turn and cook 5 additional minutes on each side. Serve immediately.

Each serving provides:

131	Calories	0 g	Omega-3
4 g	Protein	2.5 g	Fat
24 g	Carbohydrate		17% of calories from fat
5 mg	Sodium		0.3 g saturated fat
0 mg	Cholesterol		0.2 g polyunsaturated fat
			1.7 g monounsaturated fat

Parsley Potatoes

Yield: 4 servings

Baby red or white potatoes	1	**pound**
Olive oil	1	**tablespoon**
Fresh parsley, minced	¼	**cup**
Granulated garlic	⅛	**teaspoon**
Pepper		**A few grinds**
Salt		**A pinch**

Wash the potatoes and dice them. Drop into boiling water and cook about 10 minutes, until tender but not mushy. Drain well and toss in a bowl with olive oil, then parsley, garlic, pepper, and salt. Serve hot.

Each serving provides:

113	Calories	0 g	Omega-3
3 g	Protein	3.5 g	Fat
18 g	Carbohydrate		28% of calories from fat
58 mg	Sodium		0.5 g saturated fat
0 mg	Cholesterol		0.3 g polyunsaturated fat
			2.5 g monounsaturated fat

Garlic Mashed Potatoes

Yield: 6 servings

Russet potatoes	4	large
Garlic	6	cloves, peeled
Olive oil	1	tablespoon
Salt	¼	teaspoon
Cayenne	⅛	teaspoon

You may peel the potatoes if you prefer a perfectly smooth texture, but we usually leave the skins on for the nutrients they hold. Dice the potatoes, put in a large pot with enough water to submerge them and the peeled whole garlic cloves. Boil until very tender, about 15 minutes after a hard boil has been achieved. Drain, but reserve ¼ cup of the cooking water.

Whip the potatoes with a whisk or whir in a food processor with a tablespoon of the reserved potato water, oil, salt, and cayenne. Continue adding potato water a little at a time until you've achieved your desired consistency. Serve very hot.

Each serving provides:

189	Calories	0 g	Omega-3
6 g	Protein	3 g	Fat
36 g	Carbohydrate		12% of calories from fat
96 mg	Sodium		0.3 g saturated fat
0 mg	Cholesterol		0.2 g polyunsaturated fat
			2 g monounsaturated fat

The Best 125 Lowfat Fish and Seafood Dishes

Cornbread

Yield: 8 servings

Canola oil	1	teaspoon plus 2 tablespoons
Coarse yellow cornmeal	1	cup
Whole wheat pastry flour	½	cup
Baking powder	2	teaspoons
Salt	¼	teaspoon
Egg	1	large
Honey	3	tablespoons
Cultured lowfat buttermilk	1	cup

Preheat oven to 375 degrees F. Rub an 8-inch square pan with 1 teaspoon of the oil. In a large bowl, stir together the cornmeal, flour, baking powder, and salt. In a smaller bowl, beat the egg with honey and remaining 2 tablespoons oil until smooth, then add the buttermilk and blend thoroughly. Pour wet ingredients into cornmeal mixture and beat vigorously until smooth.

Pour mixture into the oiled pan and bake 25 to 30 minutes. When a toothpick inserted in the center comes out clean, the cornbread is done. Remove from the oven and let stand in the pan 15 minutes. Serve warm or at room temperature.

Each serving provides:

169	Calories	0 g	Omega-3
4 g	Protein	5 g	Fat
27 g	Carbohydrate		27% of calories from fat
112 mg	Sodium		1 g saturated fat
28 mg	Cholesterol		1 g polyunsaturated fat
			0.4 g monounsaturated fat

Roasted Garlic Bread

Yield: 6 servings

Baked garlic	**2 bulbs**
Parmesan cheese, finely grated	**2 tablespoons**
Dried oregano	**¼ teaspoon**
Salt	**⅛ teaspoon**
Pepper	**A few grinds**
Olive oil	**1 tablespoon**
Fresh sourdough bread	**Half a one-pound loaf**

Bake the garlic according to instructions on page 35. Meanwhile, stir the cheese, oregano, salt, and pepper into the olive oil until well combined. When the garlic is cool enough to handle, use your hands to squeeze the soft garlic out of the skin. Take your time and remove all of the garlic, picking out any tiny pieces of skin that may come off.

Beat the olive oil mixture with the garlic until smooth and well combined. Cut the half-loaf of bread in half lengthwise to expose the soft inner part. Spread evenly with the garlic mixture. Wrap in foil and bake for 10 minutes, then remove the foil and place under a hot broiler for a minute, if you wish, to create a crispy texture.

Each serving provides:

145	Calories	0 g	Omega-3
5 g	Protein	5 g	Fat
21 g	Carbohydrate		31% of calories from fat°
266 mg	Sodium		1 g saturated fat
2 mg	Cholesterol		0.5 g polyunsaturated fat
			3 g monounsaturated fat

°This companion dish is recommended for meals that are otherwise low in fat.

Tofu Garlic Spread

Yield: 6 2-tablespoon servings

Firm-style tofu	**5**	**ounces**
Plain nonfat yogurt	**½**	**cup**
Low-sodium soy sauce	**1**	**teaspoon**
Garlic	**3**	**cloves, minced**
Dark sesame oil	**½**	**teaspoon**

Slice the tofu and wrap in a tea towel to drain for several minutes. Pat it dry and combine it in a blender or food processor with the yogurt, soy sauce, garlic, and oil. Puree until smooth. Serve immediately, or cover and refrigerate for several hours to allow the flavors to combine. You may make this ahead and refrigerate up to 4 days. Great on crackers or bread, and delicious with vegetables.

Each serving provides:

29	Calories	0 g	Omega-3
3 g	Protein	1 g	Fat
3 g	Carbohydrate		29% of calories from fat
56 mg	Sodium		0.1 g saturated fat
0.4 mg	Cholesterol		0.2 g polyunsaturated fat
			0.2 g monounsaturated fat

Tartar Sauce

Yield: 9 2-tablespoon servings

Reduced-calorie mayonnaise	¼ **cup**
Plain nonfat yogurt	¼ **cup**
Capers, drained and minced	1 **teaspoon**
Gherkins, diced	2 **teaspoons**
Garlic	1 **clove, minced**
Fresh dill, minced	1 **tablespoon**
Fresh tarragon leaves, minced	1 **teaspoon**

Whisk together the mayonnaise and yogurt. Stir in the capers, gherkins, garlic, dill, and tarragon. If possible, make ahead and set aside in the refrigerator so the flavors can blend. This sauce will keep in the refrigerator up to a few weeks in a tightly closed container.

Each serving provides:

27	Calories	0 g	Omega-3
0.4 g	Protein	2 g	Fat
1 g	Carbohydrate		76% of calories from fat°
70 mg	Sodium		0.4 g saturated fat
2 mg	Cholesterol		1 g polyunsaturated fat
			0.2 g monounsaturated fat

°Standing alone, this recipe appears high in fat. When served as part of an overall lowfat meal, the fat ratio will be balanced.

Mustard Tarragon Sauce

Yield: 16 ½-tablespoon servings

Dijon mustard	¼ cup
Honey	1 tablespoon
Tarragon wine vinegar	1 tablespoon
Olive oil	2 tablespoons
Fresh tarragon leaves, minced	1 tablespoon
Capers, minced	1 teaspoon

In a bowl, stir together the mustard, honey, and vinegar. Whisk in the oil, then stir in the tarragon and capers. Serve immediately, or refrigerate until needed. This sauce will keep in the refrigerator for up to a few weeks.

Each serving provides:

21	Calories	0 g	Omega-3
0.1 g	Protein	2 g	Fat
1 g	Carbohydrate		75% of calories from fat°
47 mg	Sodium		0.2 g saturated fat
0 mg	Cholesterol		0.4 g polyunsaturated fat
			1 g monounsaturated fat

°Standing alone, this recipe appears high in fat. When served as part of an overall lowfat meal, the fat ratio will be balanced.

Yogurt Thyme Sauce

Yield: 10 1-tablespoon servings

Plain nonfat yogurt	½ **cup**
Dijon mustard	2 **tablespoons**
Fresh-squeezed lemon juice	1 **tablespoon**
Green onion	1, **minced**
Dried thyme	½ **teaspoon**

Whisk together the yogurt, mustard, lemon juice, and onions. Grind the thyme with a mortar and pestle, or crumble between the palms of your hand, then stir into the yogurt mixture. Warm slightly in a tiny saucepan or microwave oven just before serving. This sauce can be made ahead of time, and will store for up to a week in the refrigerator.

Each serving provides:

9	Calories	0 g	Omega-3
1 g	Protein	0.1 g	Fat
1 g	Carbohydrate		10% of calories from fat
49 mg	Sodium		0 g saturated fat
0.3 mg	Cholesterol		0.1 g polyunsaturated fat
			0 g monounsaturated fat

Steamed Vegetables

The following chart provides recommended steaming times for a wide variety of vegetables. Place the vegetables on a steaming tray over a couple of inches of water in a lidded pot at the beginning of meal preparation, then turn on the burner to high heat and set your timer at just the right moment. Time the steaming of the vegetables so that they will be done at the same time your main course is ready.

For people raised on canned spinach and frozen corn who have decided they hate vegetables, steamed fresh ones will be a revelation. Most vegetables taste best when cooked to the "al dente" stage (when they are tender enough to chew easily but still have a little crunch). Overcooking brings out the bitterness in some vegetables and renders others mushy and tasteless. Worst of all, too much cooking depletes the excellent nutrient value offered by fresh vegetables.

For good health's sake, avoid mayonnaise, butter, and creamy sauces. Instead, try tossing fresh vegetables with lemon juice or vinegar, a small amount of ground sesame seeds, or a little of your favorite fresh or dried herb. Serve hot or at room temperature.

The cooking times below are estimates for average-size vegetables. Adjust accordingly.

Vegetable Steaming Times

Artichokes, whole	35 minutes
Asparagus	8 minutes
Beans, green	9 minutes
Beets, whole	25 minutes
Broccoli	10 minutes
Brussels sprouts, whole	15 minutes
Cabbage, wedges	9 minutes
Carrots, medium slices	12 minutes

Cauliflower, flowerets	15 minutes
Corn, fresh kernels or ears	8 minutes
Onions, pearl	20 minutes
Peas, edible pod or shelled	8 minutes
Potatoes, cubes	15 minutes
Rutabagas, cubes	18 minutes
Spinach and other greens	5 minutes
Summer squash	8 minutes
Yams or sweet potatoes, 1-inch slices	30 minutes

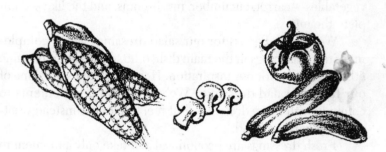

Side-Dish Salads

Almost every meal that appears on our tables includes a salad. Raw vegetables are low in fat and calories, and provide good quantities of vitamins, minerals, and insoluble fiber. They satisfy our desire for textural variety, providing a crunchy counterpoint to other foods. Leafy salads have a refreshing effect on the palate and aid digestion. In short, salads are delicious health foods and should be enjoyed daily, so long as you don't drown the vegetables in fat-laden salad dressings!

A vast variety of salad ingredients is available in every supermarket. Butter, red leaf, and romaine are only a few of the possible lettuce options (standard head lettuce—often called iceberg—just doesn't compare in nutritional value or flavor). Rocket, radicchio, chicory, dandelion, and mustard are other greens that add delicious variety to salads. Your favorite vegetables—carrot, cucumber, mushrooms, and the like—complete the mix.

We choose flavors for our salad dressings which complement the seasonings in the main dish, often drawing on the same ethnic tradition for our inspiration. Here are recipes for some of our favorite salad dressings. We've suggested ingredients to combine with these dressings, but feel free to use instead whatever you have on hand.

Fresh dressings are economical and take only a moment to prepare from ingredients you probably have on hand in your kitchen. They will keep well in the refrigerator, but the flavors will be most distinct if small portions are brought to room temperature before tossing with salad ingredients. We recommend keeping a variety of homemade dressings on hand.

Basil Balsamic Salad

Dressing yield: ¾ cup

The dressing

Low-sodium tomato sauce	½	cup
Fresh-squeezed lemon juice	2	tablespoons
Balsamic vinegar	2	tablespoons
Dried basil	2	teaspoons
Garlic	2	cloves, minced
Salt	¼	teaspoon
Pepper		Several grinds

Whisk together all ingredients until smooth. Toss 2 tablespoons per serving with salad ingredients. This dressing will keep up to two weeks in a covered jar in the refrigerator, but bring it back to room temperature before serving.

The salad

Lettuce and other greens
Mushrooms
Cucumber
Fresh and/or dried tomato

Each 1 tablespoon of dressing provides:

17	Calories	0 g	Omega-3
0.5 g	Protein	0.03 g	Fat
4 g	Carbohydrate		1% of calories from fat
96 mg	Sodium		0.01 g saturated fat
0 mg	Cholesterol		0.01 g polyunsaturated fat
			0 g monounsaturated fat

Buttermilk Cucumber Salad

Dressing yield: 2 cups

The dressing

Cucumber	1	medium
Cultured lowfat buttermilk	1	cup
Light sour cream	1	tablespoon
White wine vinegar	1	tablespoon
Garlic	1	clove, minced
Fresh dill, minced (or 1 teaspoon dried)	2	teaspoons
Salt		A pinch
Pepper		A few grinds

Peel, seed, and mince the cucumber and place it in a medium bowl. Whisk together the remaining ingredients and stir into the cucumber. Toss 1 tablespoon per serving with salad ingredients. Dressing not used immediately can be kept for up to one week in the refrigerator, but bring small portions to room temperature before using.

The salad
Lettuce and other greens
Cooked garbanzo beans (chickpeas)
Carrot
Fresh tomato

Each 1 tablespoon of dressing provides:

5	Calories	0 g	Omega-3
0.3 g	Protein	0.1 g	Fat
1 g	Carbohydrate		23% of calories from fat
15 mg	Sodium		0.1 g saturated fat
0.5 mg	Cholesterol		0 g polyunsaturated fat
			0 g monounsaturated fat

Southwest Salad

Dressing yield: 1 cup

The dressing

Raw unsalted pumpkin seeds	2	tablespoons
Fresh-squeezed orange juice	⅓	cup
Light sesame oil	2	tablespoons
Fresh-squeezed lime juice	2	tablespoons
Cider vinegar	2	tablespoons
Garlic	2	cloves, minced
Fresh cilantro, minced	2	tablespoons
Salt	¼	teaspoon
Cayenne	⅛	teaspoon

Toast the pumpkin seeds (see page 34). Combine all ingredients in a food processor or blender and process until well combined. Toss 1 tablespoon per serving with salad ingredients. Dressing not used immediately can be kept for up to two weeks in the refrigerator, but bring small portions to room temperature before using.

The salad
Lettuce and other greens
Fresh tomatoes
Corn kernels
Diced jicama
Avocado
Cooked pinto beans

Each 1 tablespoon of dressing provides:

28	Calories	0 g	Omega-3
0.5 g	Protein	3 g	Fat
1 g	Carbohydrate		78% of calories from fat°
34 mg	Sodium		0.4 g saturated fat
0 mg	Cholesterol		1 g polyunsaturated fat
			1 g monounsaturated fat

°Standing alone, this recipe appears high in fat. When combined with the recommended salad ingredients and served as part of an overall lowfat meal, the fat ratio will be balanced.

Middle East Salad

Dressing yield: 1 cup

The dressing

Tahini (sesame butter)	¼	cup
Plain nonfat yogurt	⅓	cup
Water	¼	cup
Fresh-squeezed lemon juice	3	tablespoons
Low-sodium soy sauce	2	teaspoons
Curry powder	1	teaspoon
Garlic	2	cloves, minced
Fresh parsley, minced	2	tablespoons
Green onions	2,	minced
Cayenne	⅛	teaspoon

Combine all ingredients in a food processor or blender and process until well combined. Toss 1 tablespoon per serving with salad ingredients. Dressing not used immediately can be kept for up to one week in the refrigerator, but bring small portions to room temperature before using. You may thin out with a small amount of water or more lemon juice, as needed.

The salad
   Lettuce and other greens
   Cooked garbanzo beans (chickpeas)
   Cucumber
   Fresh tomato
   Sesame seeds

Each 1 tablespoon of dressing provides:

20	Calories	0 g	Omega-3
1 g	Protein	1.5 g	Fat
1 g	Carbohydrate		58% of calories from fat*
31 mg	Sodium		0.2 g saturated fat
0.1 mg	Cholesterol		0.6 g polyunsaturated fat
			0.5 g monounsaturated fat

---

*Standing alone, this recipe appears high in fat. When combined with the recommended salad ingredients and served as part of an overall lowfat meal, the fat ratio will be balanced.

Asian Salad

Dressing yield: 1¼ cups

The dressing

Rice wine vinegar	¼	**cup**
Fresh-squeezed pink grapefruit juice	¼	**cup**
Dark sesame oil	2	**tablespoons**
Mirin	1	**tablespoon**
Low-sodium soy sauce	1	**teaspoon**
Honey	1	**teaspoon**
Granulated garlic	¼	**teaspoon**

Combine all ingredients together in the blender or food processor and puree to a smooth sauce consistency. Toss 1 tablespoon per serving with salad ingredients. Dressing not used immediately can be kept for up to a month in the refrigerator, but bring small portions to room temperature before using.

The salad
Lettuce and other greens
Mung bean sprouts
Mushrooms
Radicchio

Each 1 tablespoon of dressing provides:

15	Calories	0 g	Omega-3
0.03 g	Protein	1.4 g	Fat
1 g	Carbohydrate		77% of calories from fat*
11 mg	Sodium		0.2 g saturated fat
0 mg	Cholesterol		0.6 g polyunsaturated fat
			0.5 g monounsaturated fat

---

*Standing alone, this recipe appears high in fat. When combined with the recommended salad ingredients and served as part of an overall lowfat meal, the fat ratio will be balanced.

Honey Mustard Salad

Dressing yield: 1 cup

The dressing

Olive oil	2	tablespoons
White wine vinegar	2	tablespoons
Water	2	tablespoons
Honey	1	tablespoon
Dijon mustard	1	tablespoon
Plain nonfat yogurt	¼	cup
Capers, drained and minced	2	teaspoons
Dried tarragon	1	teaspoon
Granulated garlic	½	teaspoon
Pepper		Several grinds

Whisk together the oil, vinegar, water, honey, and mustard, then whisk in yogurt. Stir in the capers, tarragon, granulated garlic, and pepper. Toss 1 tablespoon per serving with salad ingredients. Dressing not used immediately can be kept for up to a month in the refrigerator, but bring small portions to room temperature before using.

The salad
   Lettuce and other greens
   Fresh tomato
   Cucumber
   Green onions

Each 1 tablespoon of dressing provides:

23	Calories	0 g	Omega-3
0.3 g	Protein	2 g	Fat
1.6 g	Carbohydrate		67% of calories from fat*
21 mg	Sodium		0.4 g saturated fat
0.06 mg	Cholesterol		0.2 g polyunsaturated fat
			1.3 g monounsaturated fat

*Standing alone, this recipe appears high in fat. When combined with the recommended salad ingredients and served as part of an overall lowfat meal, the fat ratio will be balanced.

Appetizers and First Courses

Our favorite seafood appetizers and first courses that appear in this chapter range from the classic to the avant-garde. Any of the recipes in the "Appetizers" section could be served as part of a spectacular buffet of finger foods. Dishes that would be perfect as the starter course of a special dinner party menu have been grouped under the "First Courses" subheading. The Salmon Cakes, Crab Cakes, or Salmon Quesadillas could even become the main course for supper, combined with our recommended companion dishes.

Most of these delicacies are served chilled or at room temperature, with the exception of the Salmon Cakes and Salmon Quesadillas, which we prefer hot.

If including an appetizer on the menu sounds like too much trouble, remember that many of these recipes take only a few minutes to prepare, not counting chilling time, so they can be made quickly and simply and well in advance. Most spreads and dips actually improve with age and are best made several hours—or even a day—ahead of serving time. Store them tightly covered in the refrigerator and allow to come to room temperature for about thirty minutes before serving. Restir dips and transfer to a pretty bowl or platter, garnish, and set out where you want your guests to congregate. Serving a wonderful appetizer gives them something to nibble on when they arrive. This takes the pressure off the cook's timetable, contributing to a relaxed mood.

If you're accustomed to serving traditional chips and dips or cheese and crackers before a meal, this refreshing selection of appetizers will expand your horizons.

Tools . . .

- Invest in a cast-iron skillet for cooking our salmon and crab cakes and quesadillas, as well as for many other uses. Once properly tempered, very little oil is needed for frying. (For detailed instructions for tempering cast-iron pans, see page 33.)
- A selection of pretty serving bowls and platters is essential for dips and composed appetizers.
- Specially made individual cocktail cups are available, which allow the bowls that hold the food to be nestled in larger bowls of crushed ice, so each serving can remain cold. Small cocktail forks are particularly nice, though not essential, for this type of dish.

. . . and Tips

- Always marinate in a nonmetal container as acids can react with the metal, causing off-flavors and discoloration. Marinating raw fish in acidic liquid for several hours will cure it, so that no further cooking is required, as in the classic south-of-the-border preparation called Ceviche. The fish will be extremely tender and well-saturated with the flavors of the marinade. Be sure to use absolutely fresh fish from a trusted source for such "raw-cured" preparations.

- Appetizers provide a great opportunity to be creative about presentation. There are many wonderful garnishes that do not contain fat or sodium. Our favorites include flower petals or whole blossoms, fresh herb sprigs, and citrus peel curls.

Australian Clam Dip

This wonderfully fresh-tasting dip is traditionally served with potato chips. Use a baked, rather than fried, variety that is lightly salted and the nutritional picture won't be too troublesome. The healthiest alternative, however, is to serve it with raw vegetables for dipping.

Yield: 8 servings

Minced clams	2	6-ounce cans
Light cream cheese	4	ounces
Fresh-squeezed lemon juice	3	tablespoons
Worcestershire sauce	2	teaspoons
Garlic	2	cloves, minced
Cayenne		A pinch

Drain all but 2 tablespoons of liquid from one can of clams. Drain all the liquid from the other can into a food processor. Add reserved clam juice, cream cheese, lemon juice, Worcestershire sauce, garlic, and cayenne and blend until thick and well combined. Stir in the clams, chill for at least an hour, and serve.

Recommended companion dishes: raw broccoli spears and/or cucumber slices, or lightly salted baked potato chips

---

Each serving provides:

183	Calories	0.1 g	Omega-3
20 g	Protein	5 g	Fat
4 g	Carbohydrate		25% of calories from fat
152 mg	Sodium		2 g saturated fat
40 mg	Cholesterol		1 g polyunsaturated fat
			2 g monounsaturated fat

Smoked Herring, Tarragon, and Caper Spread

The smoked herring has a distinctive pungent flavor that is perfectly complemented by cocktail rye bread. It is especially well matched with Eastern European cuisine, such as the Braised Shark with Sauerkraut and Carrots (page 274).

Yield: 12 servings

Smoked skinless herring	1	**ounce**
Lowfat cream cheese	4	**ounces**
Plain nonfat yogurt	3	**tablespoons**
Fresh-squeezed lemon juice	1	**tablespoon**
Fresh tarragon leaves, minced	1	**teaspoon**
Green onions	2,	**minced**
Capers, drained and minced	2	**teaspoons**
Prepared horseradish	1	**teaspoon**

Coarsely chop the herring and place it in a food processor. Add the cream cheese, yogurt, and lemon juice. Pulse to combine. Add the tarragon, green onions, capers, and horseradish. Puree

until smooth. Transfer to a serving bowl, cover, and refrigerate at least 1 hour—or up to a day—before serving to allow the flavors to blend.

Recommended companion dish: cocktail rye bread

Each serving provides:

25	Calories	0 g	Omega-3
1 g	Protein	2.5 g	Fat
1 g	Carbohydrate		44% of calories from fat°
96 mg	Sodium		1 g saturated fat
6 mg	Cholesterol		0.2 g polyunsaturated fat
			1 g monounsaturated fat

°Standing alone, this recipe appears high in fat. When served as part of an overall lowfat meal, the fat ratio will be balanced.

Spread with Chevre, Dill Seed, and Dried Tomato

Spread on crusty sourdough slices, this makes a very special appetizer. The delicate flavor of chevre and the pungency of the dill seed season the crab nicely.

Yield: 12 servings

Dried tomatoes, minced	1	**tablespoon**
Soft chevre	3	**ounces**
Plain nonfat yogurt	2	**tablespoons**
Fresh-squeezed lemon juice	1	**teaspoon**
Brandy	1	**teaspoon**
Garlic	1	**clove**
Dill seed	½	**teaspoon, crushed**
Pepper		**Several grinds**
Crab meat*	8	**ounces (about 1½ cups)**

*If purchasing cooked whole crab, ask for 2 pounds of crab. Have your fishmonger crack and clean it. Pick all the meat from the shell, being careful to discard all the bits of shell and cartilage.

Reconstitute the tomatoes if they are too dry to mince (see page 37). Stir together the chevre, yogurt, dried tomatoes, lemon juice, brandy, garlic, dill seed, and pepper until well combined. Gently fold in the crab meat. Chill an hour or two before serving.

***Recommended companion dish:* sliced sourdough baguette**

Each serving provides:

34	Calories	0.06 g	Omega-3
4 g	Protein	2 g	Fat
1 g	Carbohydrate		38% of calories from fat*
81 mg	Sodium		1 g saturated fat
18 mg	Cholesterol		0.2 g polyunsaturated fat
			0.5 g monounsaturated fat

---

*Standing alone, this recipe appears high in fat. When served as part of an overall lowfat meal, the fat ratio will be balanced.

Smoked Oyster Spread with Fresh Basil

The flavor of this rich spread is deliciously mysterious. Even smoked oyster detractors will enjoy it, never guessing its main ingredient. You will find the pickled peppercorns in the spice section of your supermarket. They provide a wonderful mellow heat without the harshness of an equivalent amount of dried peppercorns.

Yield: 8 servings

Smoked oysters	1	3¾-ounce tin
Fresh-squeezed lemon juice	1	tablespoon
Lowfat cream cheese	4	ounces
Fresh basil leaves, chopped	½	cup
Plain nonfat yogurt	¼	cup
Fennel seed, finely crushed	1	teaspoon
Pickled green peppercorns, drained	1	teaspoon
Garlic	2	cloves, minced
Salt		A pinch
Red bell pepper, finely minced	¼	cup

Drain the oil from the oysters, toss with the lemon juice, and drain again immediately to remove as much oil as possible. Combine everything except the red bell pepper in a food processor. Puree until smooth. Transfer to a serving dish. Stir in the minced bell pepper until well distributed. Cover and refrigerate for at least an hour—or up to a day— before serving to allow the flavors to blend.

***Recommended companion dish:* sliced sourdough baguette or cocktail rye bread**

Each serving provides:

46	Calories	0.1 g	Omega-3
3 g	Protein	3 g	Fat
2 g	Carbohydrate		35% of calories from fat°
142 mg	Sodium		1.5 g saturated fat
14 mg	Cholesterol		0.4 g polyunsaturated fat
			1 g monounsaturated fat

°Standing alone, this recipe appears high in fat. When served as part of an overall lowfat meal, the fat ratio will be balanced.

Smoked Oyster and
Fresh Dill Lovash

Lovash is Armenian cracker bread. It is most commonly sold with three large crisp rounds in a package. Some specialty stores in ethnic neighborhoods will sell it "soft" rolled, in which case you don't need to dampen it as described below. Either way works well in this recipe. You can serve the rolls as part of an appetizer spread at a party or pack them in with a picnic.

Yield: 24 servings

Lovash rounds	2	**large**
Smoked oysters	1	**3¾-ounce tin**
Fresh-squeezed lemon juice	2	**tablespoons**
Light cream cheese	12	**ounces**
Green onions	2,	**minced**
Fresh dill, minced	2	**tablespoons**
Prepared horseradish	1	**teaspoon**

Lightly spray the crisp lovash rounds on each side with water and place them between moistened tea towels. Allow to soften for 2 hours, until pliable but not sticky. Drain the oil from the smoked oysters, toss oysters with 1 tablespoon of lemon juice, and drain them again immediately to remove as much oil as possible. Place the oysters, cream cheese, green onions, dill, remaining 1 tablespoon of lemon juice, and horseradish in a food processor. Pulse until well combined, but not totally smooth. Lay the moistened crackers on the counter and spread the oyster mixture evenly over them with a rubber spatula. Roll one side to the middle, jellyroll fashion, then roll the other side to meet it in the middle. Slice between the rolls and wrap each of the resulting 4 rolls in waxed paper. Refrigerate for several hours. Before serving, remove the paper and slice into half-inch rounds. Arrange on a platter and serve.

Each serving provides:

53	Calories	0.02 g	Omega-3
2 g	Protein	2 g	Fat
4 g	Carbohydrate		26% of calories from fat
126 mg	Sodium		1 g saturated fat
7 mg	Cholesterol		0.2 g polyunsaturated fat
			0.8 g monounsaturated fat

Hearts of Palm with Crab and Fresh Dill

ALMOST INSTANT

This appetizer is very easy to make, and can be made up to a day in advance. The presentation is festive, and the flavor is delicious. We recommend using meat from a cooked whole crab, reserving the remainder for another use.

Yield: 16 servings

Hearts of palm, water-packed	1	14-ounce can, drained
Reduced-calorie mayonnaise	1	tablespoon
Plain nonfat yogurt	1	tablespoon
Fresh dill, minced	1	teaspoon
Fresh-squeezed lemon juice	1	teaspoon
Granulated garlic	⅛	teaspoon
Crab meat	2	ounces
Fresh dill sprigs	30	¼-inch pieces

Cut the hearts of palm into ½-inch lengths and set cut end up on a serving dish. Mix together the mayonnaise, yogurt, dill, lemon juice, and garlic. Use a spoon to place a dollop of sauce on top of

each palm round. Distribute the crab evenly on top, along with a small sprig of dill. Serve immediately, or cover and chill for up to one day.

Each serving provides:

18	Calories	0 g	Omega-3
1 g	Protein	1 g	Fat
2 g	Carbohydrate		32% of calories from fat*
31 mg	Sodium		0.1 g saturated fat
2 mg	Cholesterol		0.3 g polyunsaturated fat
			0.1 g monounsaturated fat

---

*Standing alone, this recipe appears high in fat. When served as part of an overall lowfat meal, the fat ratio will be balanced.

Lobster Lime Cocktail

This is a delightful way to begin a meal. The servings are small, but they're big on flavor.

Yield: 6 servings

Lobster meat*	¾	pound
Dry white wine	⅓	cup
Fresh-squeezed lime juice	¼	cup
Olive oil	1	tablespoon
Lime zest	1	teaspoon
Butter lettuce	6	large leaves

Rinse the lobster meat, pat dry, and cut into bite-size pieces. Set aside. Put the wine, lime juice, oil, and lime zest in a wok or skillet and cook over medium heat for 2 minutes. Increase the temperature to medium-high, add the lobster, and stir-fry for 2 minutes, until lobster is hot and opaque all the way through.

*If purchasing fresh or frozen whole lobster tails in the shell, ask for 1¼ pounds. If frozen, thaw according to directions on page 8. Rinse the lobster and cut the shells front and back with kitchen scissors. Gently remove the meat and pat it dry.

Transfer lobster and pan juices to a small bowl and chill for at least 1 hour. To serve, place a lettuce leaf in the bottom of each of six chilled cocktail cups or small dessert bowls and mound the lobster on top. Garnish each with a lime wedge, if you wish.

Recommended companion dish: **Roasted Garlic Bread (page 58)**

Each serving provides:

95	Calories	0.2 g	Omega-3
24 g	Protein	3 g	Fat
2 g	Carbohydrate		30% of calories from fat
101 mg	Sodium		0.5 g saturated fat
40 mg	Cholesterol		0.5 g polyunsaturated fat
			2 g monounsaturated fat

Classic Crab Cocktail

ALMOST INSTANT

Here is a cocktail sauce just like our mothers used to make, tangy but not so hot that the crab's delicacy is smothered. The addition of the celery hearts is our only variation on this old standard. The sauce can be prepared several hours—or even a day—ahead of time. In fact, ahead-of-time preparation is preferable, as the flavor will improve.

Yield: 4 servings

Low-sodium tomato puree	¾	cup
Fresh-squeezed lemon juice	2	tablespoons
Prepared horseradish	1½	tablespoons
Worcestershire sauce	2	teaspoons
White onion, grated	3	tablespoons
Granulated garlic	¼	teaspoon
Tabasco sauce		A few drops
Salt		A pinch
Crab meat°	12	ounces (about 2 cups)
Celery, heart portion, thinly sliced	¾	cup
Butter lettuce	4	large leaves
Lemon wedges	4	

°If purchasing cooked whole crab, ask for 3 pounds of crab. Have your fish-monger crack and clean it. Pick all the meat from the shell, being careful to discard all the bits of shell and cartilage.

Whisk together the tomato puree, lemon juice, horseradish, Worcestershire sauce, onion, garlic, Tabasco sauce, and salt. Chill at least 15 minutes or as long as several hours. Toss the crab and celery together, then toss with the sauce. Line four chilled cocktail cups or small dessert bowls with lettuce leaves and mound on the crab mixture. Serve very cold with a wedge of lemon at each place.

Recommended companion dish: **sliced sourdough bread**

Each serving provides:

110	Calories	0.3 g	Omega-3
16 g	Protein	1 g	Fat
10 g	Carbohydrate		8% of calories from fat
422 mg	Sodium		0.2 g saturated fat
50 mg	Cholesterol		0.4 g polyunsaturated fat
			0.2 g monounsaturated fat

Prawns with Tomato Mustard Sauce

ALMOST INSTANT

This is a spicier version of the classic cocktail sauce, so a little goes a long way. Serve it as the first course of a strongly seasoned meal.

Yield: 6 servings

Bay leaves	3	
Peeled and deveined raw prawns*	1	**pound**
Plain nonfat yogurt	½	**cup**
Low-sodium tomato paste	2	**tablespoons**
Fresh-squeezed lemon juice	2	**tablespoons**
Worcestershire sauce	1	**tablespoon**
Prepared horseradish	1	**teaspoon**
Dry mustard	1	**teaspoon**
Butter lettuce	6	**large leaves**

Fill a medium pot with several quarts of water, add the bay leaves, and bring to a boil. Rinse the prawns and add to the boiling water. Cook for about 1 minute, until they turn pink and float to the top. Prawns cook very quickly; do not wait for water to return to a boil before timing begins. Transfer to a colander to drain. Place the prawns in the refrigerator to chill. Whisk together the yogurt, tomato paste, lemon juice, Worcestershire sauce, horseradish, and mustard. Chill for at least 15 minutes or as long as several hours before serving.

*If you purchase unpeeled raw shrimp or prawns, break away the shells and cut a shallow slit along the back so you can remove the dark vein.

To serve, place a lettuce leaf in the bottom of each of six chilled cocktail cups or small dessert bowls. Distribute the sauce evenly among the cups, then place equal portions of prawns on top. Pass lemon wedges, if desired.

Recommended companion dish: **bread sticks**

Each serving provides:

103	Calories	0.5 g	Omega-3
16 g	Protein	2 g	Fat
4 g	Carbohydrate		14% of calories from fat
164 mg	Sodium		0.3 g saturated fat
117 mg	Cholesterol		0.5 g polyunsaturated fat
			0.2 g monounsaturated fat

Scallop and Sea Bass Ceviche

This classic Spanish preparation calls for the very freshest fish, which will be cured in citrus juices rather than being cooked. We feel the scallops are essential here, but red snapper, halibut, or another mild-flavored fish could be substituted for the bass. This recipe is a slightly spicy version—add additional minced jalapeño if you like it hotter.

Yield: 6 servings

Scallops (bay or sea)	½	pound
Sea bass fillet	¾	pound
Fresh-squeezed lime juice	¾	cup
Fresh-squeezed lemon juice	¾	cup
Salt	¼	teaspoon plus ⅛ teaspoon
Pepper		Several grinds
Fresh tomatoes	2	large (1 pound), diced
Zucchini	1	medium, finely diced
Red onion	½	medium, minced
Fresh cilantro, finely minced	2	tablespoons
Fresh jalapeño pepper, minced	1½	teaspoons

Rinse the scallops and drain them well. If they are large, cut into ½-inch pieces. Rinse the sea bass and pat it dry. Remove any skin and bones—with tweezers if necessary—and cut into ½-inch chunks. Place the scallops and bass in a nonmetallic bowl. Combine the lime juice, ½ cup of the lemon juice, salt, and pepper and pour over the fish (fish must be completely submerged—add more lime and/or lemon juice, if necessary). Refrigerate, stirring occasionally, for 7 hours or longer to allow it to cure completely.

Meanwhile, combine the tomatoes, zucchini, onion, remaining ¼ cup lemon juice, cilantro, and jalapeño in a nonmetallic bowl. Refrigerate, stirring occasionally, until you are ready for it—several hours is best. Drain the fish when curing time is up, reserving ¼ cup of the juice. Stir the reserved juice into the tomato mixture and toss with the fish. Serve cold, in chilled cocktail cups or small dessert bowls.

Recommended companion dish: sourdough French bread

Each serving provides:

108	Calories	0.4 g	Omega-3
15 g	Protein	1 g	Fat
10 g	Carbohydrate		11% of calories from fat
232 mg	Sodium		0.3 g saturated fat
30 mg	Cholesterol		0.5 g polyunsaturated fat
			0.2 g monounsaturated fat

Salmon Cakes with Corn and Sweet Pepper Relish

The secret to creating salmon cakes with the proper consistency is saltine crackers! Bread crumbs may be substituted, but the consistency and flavor are not the same. This is a dazzling first course at a very special dinner party or a wonderful light dinner entrée for six when combined with the companion dishes recommended below. Be sure to use a well-tempered cast-iron pan so you will need little oil for frying.

Yield: 12 servings

The relish

Mirin	1	tablespoon
Garlic	2	cloves, minced
Red bell pepper	1	small, diced
Green onions	2,	minced
Corn kernels, fresh or frozen	1	cup
Fresh-squeezed lime juice	2	tablespoons
Honey	1	tablespoon
Dried red chili flakes	¼	teaspoon
Fresh cilantro, minced	¼	cup

The salmon cakes

Salmon fillets	1½	pounds
Egg whites	2	large
Yellow onion, minced	¼	cup
Dijon mustard	1	tablespoon
Fresh parsley, minced	2	tablespoons
Fresh tarragon leaves, minced	1	tablespoon
Pepper		Several grinds
Saltine cracker crumbs	1½	cups
Olive oil	1	tablespoon

Begin by making the relish. Heat the mirin in a medium skillet over medium heat. Stir in the garlic, bell pepper, and onion until well combined, then stir in the corn. Sauté 3 minutes, then add the lime juice, honey, and chili flakes. Increase heat to medium-high and cook 5 minutes to reduce the liquid. Stir in the cilantro and transfer mixture to a serving bowl. Set aside while you prepare the salmon cakes. You may prepare the relish ahead of time and hold over in the refrigerator, but bring it to room temperature before serving.

Rinse the salmon and place in a shallow pan large enough to hold it in a single layer. Add enough water to just cover the fish. Remove the fish and bring the water to a boil. Lay the salmon back in the pan in a single layer. Cover the pan tightly and bring back to a boil. Simmer 3 to 5 minutes, depending on the thickness of the fillet. Fish is done when it is mostly opaque but still slightly translucent at the very center. Remove from the pan, drain, and cool.

Whisk the egg whites briefly in a mixing bowl; add the onions, mustard, parsley, tarragon, and pepper. Stir in 1 cup of the cracker crumbs. Flake the salmon and gently stir it in. Shape into twelve patties and set aside on a cutting board. Preheat the oven to 200 degrees F. and place a serving platter in to warm. Put the remaining ½ cup of cracker crumbs in a shallow bowl and lightly coat each patty on both sides.

Rub ½ teaspoon of the oil on the bottom of a large cast-iron skillet and heat over medium heat. When it is hot enough to sizzle a drop of water, spoon in enough batter to create 2-inch cakes, as many as will fit in the pan at one time without touching each other. Cook for 3 to 5 minutes on each side, until they are golden brown. Add more oil, ½ teaspoon at a time, if needed. You should need no more than a total of 1 tablespoon (3 teaspoons) oil. As they are done, place them on the platter in the oven to keep warm as you cook the remaining patties. Serve hot with the Corn and Sweet Pepper Relish.

***Recommended companion dishes:* Honey Mustard Salad (page 76), steamed broccoli (see page 64), and Cornbread (page 57)**

	Each serving provides:		
209	Calories	0.4 g	Omega-3
16 g	Protein	5 g	Fat
23 g	Carbohydrate		24% of calories from fat
242 mg	Sodium		1 g saturated fat
45 mg	Cholesterol		1 g polyunsaturated fat
			2 g monounsaturated fat

Fluffy Crab Cakes with Mango and Blueberry Salsa

These morsels will come as a delicious surprise to anyone accustomed to traditional crab cakes. The airy texture of the cakes and their unconventional pairing with fruit will delight your friends. They can serve as the hearty first course in a southwestern feast for six, or you can center a spring brunch or summer supper for four around them—see recommended companion dishes below to complete the meal. Be sure to used a well-tempered cast-iron pan so you will need little oil for frying.

Yield: 6 servings

The salsa

Mango, peeled and minced	½	**cup (1 medium fruit)**
Blueberries, chopped	¼	**cup**
Green onions	2,	**minced**
Fresh-squeezed lemon juice	1	**tablespoon**
Salt		**A pinch**

The cakes

Cultured lowfat buttermilk	⅓	cup plus 2 tablespoons
Reduced-calorie mayonnaise	2	tablespoons
White onion, grated	2	tablespoons
Pickled jalapeño, seeded and minced	1	tablespoon
Ground cumin	½	teaspoon
Celery seed	½	teaspoon, crushed
Dry mustard	½	teaspoon
Fine cornmeal	⅓	cup
Unbleached flour	¼	cup
Baking powder	½	teaspoon
Crab meat°	12	ounces (about 2 cups)
Egg whites	2	large
Corn or canola oil	1½	teaspoons

Stir together the salsa ingredients and set aside at room temperature. In a bowl, whisk together the buttermilk and mayonnaise, then stir in the onion, jalapeño, cumin, celery seed, and dry mustard. In a separate bowl, stir together the cornmeal, flour, and baking powder. Stir together the buttermilk and cornmeal mixtures, combining well. Gently fold in the crab meat. Beat the egg whites by hand or with an electric mixer until soft peaks form. Gently fold into the crab mixture.

Rub ½ teaspoon of the oil on the bottom of a large cast-iron skillet and heat over medium heat. When it is hot enough to sizzle a drop of water, spoon in enough batter to create 3-inch cakes, as many as will fit in the pan at one time without touch-

°If purchasing cooked whole crab, ask for 3 pounds of crab. Have your fishmonger crack and clean it. Pick all the meat from the shell, being careful to discard all the bits of shell and cartilage.

ing each other. Cook about 4 minutes on one side, then turn and cook an additional 3 to 4 minutes. The cakes should be fluffy and golden brown. Add more oil, ½ teaspoon at a time, if needed. You should need no more than a total of 1½ teaspoons oil. As they are cooked, transfer the crab cakes to a pretty serving platter. Serve at room temperature with the salsa on the side. If you wish, you can create individual servings, including a spoonful of salsa on each plate.

Recommended companion dishes: **steamed corn on the cob (see page 64) and Buttermilk Cucumber Salad (page 68)**

Each serving provides:

141	Calories	0.2 g	Omega-3
13 g	Protein	4 g	Fat
14 g	Carbohydrate		25% of calories from fat
305 mg	Sodium		0.7 g saturated fat
36 mg	Cholesterol		1.6 g polyunsaturated fat
			0.7 g monounsaturated fat

Salmon Quesadillas with Cilantro and Salsa Fresca

ALMOST INSTANT

The combination of ingredients may sound unusual, but the resulting flavor is a wonderful marriage. This is a great first course, or it could be served as a main course for four, along with the recommended companion dishes mentioned below.

Yield: 8 servings

Salsa Fresca (see page 40)	1	cup
Salmon fillet	½	pound
Canola oil	½	teaspoon
Flour tortillas	4	large
Part-skim mozzarella cheese, grated	4	ounces (about 1½ cups)
Canned diced green chilies	1	4-ounce can
Fresh cilantro, minced	½	cup

Prepare the Salsa Fresca on page 40, or use a commercial variety. Preheat the broiler for 5 minutes. Rinse the salmon, pat it dry, and broil 4 inches from the flame for 4 minutes, then turn and cook about 3 minutes longer, depending on its thickness, until fish is mostly opaque but still barely translucent at the very center. Remove from the pan and allow to cool slightly, then remove any skin and bones, and break into bite-size pieces.

Rub ⅛ teaspoon of the oil on the bottom of a large cast-iron skillet. Heat for a moment over medium-high heat. Lay two flour tortillas in the skillet so the rounded edges meet the curve of the pan and the tortillas meet in the middle of the pan and are propped up against each other. Place a quarter of the cheese, salmon, chilies, and cilantro on each one. Fold the tops down and cook until golden brown, about 3 minutes. Remove the quesadillas momentarily and add ⅛ teaspoon oil to the pan. Replace the quesadillas and brown the other side. Keep them warm in the oven while you cook the remaining two, adding ⅛ teaspoon oil at the beginning and the remaining ⅛ teaspoon when you turn them. Serve hot with the salsa.

Recommended companion dishes: **Southwest Salad (page 70) and Seasoned Black Beans (page 50)**

Each serving provides:

153	Calories	0.2 g	Omega-3
11 g	Protein	5 g	Fat
15 g	Carbohydrate		30% of calories from fat
335 mg	Sodium		2 g saturated fat
23 mg	Cholesterol		1 g polyunsaturated fat
			2 g monounsaturated fat

Main Course Salads

In creating this collection of lowfat fish and seafood salads, we've moved far beyond the basic concept of iceberg lettuce and shrimp or tuna with a mayonnaise-based dressing. We set out to explore new territory by combining cold cooked fish with grains, beans, pasta, fruits, and vegetables—and a world of seasonings. We think you'll enjoy the results.

Our selection of favorite seafood salads ranges from light and leafy to dense and hearty, so there is something for every appetite. Though not all of our salads are "Almost Instant," most lend themselves to advance preparation and will provide leftovers for enjoyment over the course of a day or two when properly stored in a tightly covered container in the refrigerator.

These substantial salads are interesting and delicious enough for guests, so don't hesitate to plan a luncheon or summer dinner party around one of them.

Tools . . .

- Colander for washing vegetables and draining beans and pasta.
- Salad spinner (this inexpensive device dries greens quickly and efficiently through centrifugal force).
- Heavy-handled wire whisk for smooth combining of dressing ingredients.
- Large tossing bowl and pretty serving dishes.
- Large wooden spoons for tossing ingredients together and for serving.
- Chilled salad plates are preferred for leafy salads.

. . . and Tips

- Our seafood pasta salads specify cooking the pasta until "al dente." This Italian phrase means "to the tooth" and suggests that the tooth should meet a little resistance when biting into the pasta. Undercooked pasta has a tough center and an unpleasant starchy taste. Cooked too long, noodles break apart easily and turn to mush in the mouth. Use plenty of water (about 8 quarts per pound of pasta), keep the heat on high so pasta cooks at a good rolling boil, and stir the pot occasionally so it doesn't stick to the bottom.

- When you bring a head of lettuce home from the market, wash the leaves, shake off excess moisture, wrap in a dry cloth or paper towel, and store in a plastic bag in the refrigerator crisper. This is a great time-saver at mealtime.

- Store salads in the refrigerator, but allow to come to room temperature for thirty minutes before serving to heighten the flavors and improve the consistency of the dressing.

- Most salads can be served in individual portions on a bed of lettuce on pretty salad plates. If you wish to serve a salad family style, line a large platter or bowl with lettuce leaves and mound the salad on top.

Smoked Oyster, Artichoke, and Pasta Salad with Oregano Mustard Dressing

ALMOST INSTANT

Even our friends who claim to not like smoked oysters have enjoyed this rich and flavorful salad. It makes a popular potluck dish. The dressing can be prepared up to 2 days ahead of time—it will actually improve with age. The roasted red bell pepper that is sold in jars is fine here. Silken tofu—in firm and soft versions—is available in a vacuum pack at most large supermarkets.

Yield: 6 servings

The dressing

Dried oregano	1	teaspoon
Mustard seed	1	teaspoon
Chili powder	½	teaspoon
Silken firm tofu	4	ounces
Plain nonfat yogurt	¼	cup
Reduced-calorie mayonnaise	2	tablespoons
Fresh-squeezed lemon juice	2	tablespoons
Nonfat milk	2	tablespoons
Garlic	2	cloves, minced
Salt		A pinch
Cayenne		A pinch

The salad

Smoked oysters	2	3¾-ounce tins
Fresh-squeezed lemon juice	1	tablespoon
Artichoke hearts, water-packed	1	8½-ounce can, well-drained
Roasted red bell pepper	1	cup
Dried pasta spirals	10	ounces
Red onion, minced	2	tablespoons
Red wine vinegar	1	tablespoon
Fresh parsley, minced	2	tablespoons

In a heavy-bottomed dry pan over medium heat, combine the oregano, mustard seed, and chili powder. Stir for about 2 minutes, until a nutty aroma is emitted and the seeds are beginning to pop. Remove from the pan and set aside. In a blender or food processor, combine the remaining dressing ingredients with the toasted spices and puree. Set aside in the refrigerator so the flavors can blend.

In a stockpot, bring several quarts of water to a boil for the pasta. Drain the oil from the oysters, toss with the lemon juice, and drain again—thoroughly. The object is to remove as much oil as possible. If the oysters are large, cut them in half. You want about ½-inch pieces. Cut the artichoke hearts into ½-inch pieces, and the red bell pepper into thin strips. Cook the pasta in the boiling water until al dente. Cool under cold running water and drain briefly.

In a serving bowl, toss the pasta with the oysters, artichokes, bell pepper, and onion until well combined. Add the dressing and toss again to coat everything evenly. Drizzle on the vinegar, and sprinkle with parsley. Toss again and serve.

***Recommended companion dishes:* raw vegetables and crusty rolls**

Each serving provides:

277	Calories	0.2 g	Omega-3
13 g	Protein	5 g	Fat
46 g	Carbohydrate		17% of calories from fat
163 mg	Sodium		1 g saturated fat
59 mg	Cholesterol		1 g polyunsaturated fat
			1 g monounsaturated fat

Salmon, Orzo, and Cucumber Salad with Lemon Gorgonzola Dressing

Beautiful and scrumptious, this light dinner or lunch entrée lets the fresh flavors of cucumber and salmon shine through. Orzo is a rice-shaped pasta that is sold wherever a good selection of pasta is available. If you are serving it for dinner, perhaps include a hot soup on the menu.

Yield: 4 servings

The dressing

Cultured lowfat buttermilk	⅓	cup
Gorgonzola cheese, crumbled	2	ounces (½ cup)
Garlic	1	clove, minced
Lemon peel, finely minced	½	teaspoon
Pepper	⅛	teaspoon

The salad

Cucumbers	2	medium
Salmon steak	¾	pound
Dried orzo	¾	cup
Butter lettuce	8	large leaves
Lemon wedges	1	per serving

In a blender or food processor, combine the dressing ingredients and puree until smooth. Set aside in the refrigerator.

Peel the cucumbers, leaving a few very thin lengthwise strips of peel for color interest. Use a spoon to scoop out the seed portion and discard. Slice the cucumbers crosswise at a slant into thin strips. Place the cucumber slices in a colander in the sink or over a bowl. Sprinkle evenly with ¼ teaspoon salt, toss to distribute, and allow to drain for about 30 minutes.

Meanwhile, preheat the broiler for 5 minutes. Rinse the salmon and pat dry. Broil the fish 4 inches from the flame 4 minutes. Turn fish over and broil an additional 3 to 4 minutes, depending on the thickness of the fish. Fish is done when mostly opaque but still barely translucent at the very center. Remove from the broiler and set aside. When fish is cool enough to handle, remove any skin and bones and break up into bite-size pieces.

Bring 4 cups of water to a boil in a saucepan or stockpot, add the orzo, and cook until al dente. Cool under cold running water, drain very well, and set aside. Rinse the cucumbers thoroughly, squeezing gently with your hands to remove as much liquid as possible. Place them in a clean tea towel and squeeze gently to dry thoroughly. Toss the cucumbers, salmon, and orzo with the dressing until well combined.

Arrange the lettuce leaves on chilled individual serving dishes, and distribute the salad evenly among the four plates. Garnish each plate with a wedge of lemon.

Recommended companion dishes: plenty of crisp bread sticks and Chardonnay

---

Each serving provides:

262	Calories	0.5 g	Omega-3
25 g	Protein	8 g	Fat
23 g	Carbohydrate		28% of calories from fat
283 mg	Sodium		4 g saturated fat
74 mg	Cholesterol		1 g polyunsaturated fat
			3 g monounsaturated fat

Dill Marinated Rock Shrimp and Pasta Salad

This recipe calls for raw rock shrimp, which appear in the markets from early autumn through January. Raw medium shrimp may be substituted. You must use fresh dill to spark the flavor in this salad.

Yield: 8 servings

The marinade

Olive oil	¼	cup
White wine vinegar	2	tablespoons
Fresh-squeezed lemon juice	2	tablespoons
Capers, drained and minced	2	tablespoons
Fresh dill, minced	¼	cup
Garlic	2	cloves, minced
Pepper		Several grinds

The salad

Yellow onion	1	medium, sliced
Celery	1	rib, sliced
Bay leaves	2	
Peeled and deveined raw rock shrimp	1	pound
Dried pasta shells	1	pound
Cucumber	1	medium
Red onion, diced	½	cup
Yellow bell pepper	½	medium, diced

Whisk together the marinade ingredients and set aside at room temperature.

Combine 2 quarts hot water, onion, celery, and bay leaves in a stockpot; bring to a boil. Rinse the shrimp and immerse them in the boiling water. Cook 1 to 2 minutes, until they turn pink and float to the top (do not wait for the water to return to a boil; shrimp cook very fast). Drain well and discard the onion, celery, and bay leaves (you may save the cooking liquid to use in stock for risotto or soup). Add the shrimp to the marinade, toss to coat, cover, and refrigerate for 4 hours.

About 30 minutes before assembling the salad, bring several quarts of water to a boil in a stockpot and cook the pasta until al dente. Cool under cold running water, drain very well, and place in a large bowl.

Meanwhile, peel, seed, and slice the cucumber. Place in a colander and sprinkle with ¼ teaspoon salt. Let stand for 30 minutes, rinse, drain, and pat dry. Add to the pasta along with the red onion, bell pepper, shrimp, and marinade. Toss well. Refrigerate to allow the flavors to combine for about 1 hour or as long as overnight.

Recommended companion dishes: **sweet French bread and Fontina cheese**

Each serving provides:

362	Calories	0.3 g	Omega-3
20 g	Protein	10 g	Fat
45 g	Carbohydrate		26% of calories from fat
134 mg	Sodium		2 g saturated fat
140 mg	Cholesterol		2 g polyunsaturated fat
			6 g monounsaturated fat

Swordfish and Potato Salad with Paprika, Capers, and Horseradish

ALMOST INSTANT

This tangy and satisfying salad is a delicious seafood variation on the standard potato salad.

Yield: 4 servings

The dressing

Plain nonfat yogurt	½	cup
Capers, drained and minced	1½	tablespoons
Cider vinegar	1	tablespoon
Paprika	1	tablespoon
Prepared horseradish	2	teaspoons
Garlic	1	clove, minced
Granulated sugar	½	teaspoon
Salt	⅛	teaspoon
Pepper		A few grinds
Black olives, chopped	¼	cup

The salad

Red potatoes	¾	pound
Swordfish steak	¾	pound
Cucumber	1	medium, peeled, seeded, diced
Red bell pepper	½	medium, finely minced
Fresh parsley, minced	2	tablespoons
Lemon wedges	1	per serving

Whisk together all dressing ingredients except the olives. Stir in the olives and set aside at room temperature.

Bring a few quarts of water to a boil. Scrub the potatoes; do not peel them. Cut into large dice and drop into the boiling water. Return to a boil and cook 5 to 7 minutes, until potatoes are just barely tender. Immerse immediately in cold water to stop the cooking, and drain well.

Meanwhile, preheat the broiler 5 minutes. Rinse the swordfish, pat it dry, and broil it 4 inches from the flame 4 minutes, then turn and broil 3 to 4 minutes longer, depending on the thickness of the fish. Fish is done when mostly opaque but still barely translucent at the very center. Remove from the broiler and set aside. When cool enough to handle, remove any skin and bones and break up into bite-size pieces.

In a serving bowl, gently toss the potatoes and swordfish with the cucumber and bell pepper. Add the dressing and toss again until everything is well distributed. Sprinkle with the parsley and serve, passing the lemon wedges.

Recommended companion dishes: rye bread with Gruyère cheese

Each serving provides:

201	Calories	0.5 g	Omega-3
19 g	Protein	5 g	Fat
22 g	Carbohydrate		20% of calories from fat
342 mg	Sodium		1 g saturated fat
29 mg	Cholesterol		1 g polyunsaturated fat
			2 g monounsaturated fat

Tuna Rice Salad with Snow Peas and Spicy Sesame Sauce

This hearty and delicious salad is definitely a main course. The roasted sesame oil and wasabe give the dressing its rich Asian character, the perfect complement to the tuna, rice, and pea pods.

Yield: 6 servings

The salad

Short-grain brown rice, uncooked	⅔	cup
Tuna steak	¾	pound
Snow peas	½	pound
Red cabbage, finely shredded	¾	cup
Butter lettuce	6	large leaves
Lemon wedges	1	per serving

The dressing

Wasabe powder	2	teaspoons
Low-sodium soy sauce	1	tablespoon
Plain nonfat yogurt	½	cup
Reduced-calorie mayonnaise	2	tablespoons
Rice wine vinegar	1	tablespoon
Dark sesame oil	1	teaspoon
Granulated garlic	¼	teaspoon
Cayenne		A pinch
Green onions	3,	minced

Bring 1⅓ cups water to a boil in a saucepan over high heat. Stir in the rice, bring back to a boil, cover, reduce heat to very low, and simmer 45 minutes.

Place the wasabe powder in a small dish and stir in the soy sauce until smooth. Whisk this mixture with the yogurt, mayonnaise, vinegar, oil, garlic, and cayenne until well combined. Stir in the green onions and set aside in the refrigerator.

Preheat the broiler 5 minutes. Rinse the tuna, pat it dry, and broil it 4 inches from the flame 4 minutes, then turn and broil an additional 3 to 7 minutes, depending on the thickness of the fish. Fish is done when mostly opaque but still slightly translucent at the very center. Remove from the broiler and set aside. When cool enough to handle, remove any skin and bones and break into bite-size pieces.

String the snow peas and sliver them lengthwise. In a bowl, toss the rice with the snow peas and cabbage, then with the dressing. Add the tuna and gently toss again so that everything is well combined. Line 6 individual salad plates or bowls with the lettuce leaves. Mound the salad on top and serve with a lemon wedge.

Recommended companion dishes: sesame crackers and Tofu Garlic Spread (page 60)

Each serving provides:

164	Calories	0.1 g	Omega-3
17 g	Protein	3.5 g	Fat
16 g	Carbohydrate		19% of calories from fat
182 mg	Sodium		0.7 g saturated fat
28 mg	Cholesterol		1.4 g polyunsaturated fat
			0.7 g monounsaturated fat

Scallops, Beans, and Arugula with Cinnamon and Fresh Basil

ALMOST INSTANT

This intriguing blend of sweet and tart flavors is truly delectable. The addition of beans makes it a satisfying main course for lunch or the perfect light summer supper when combined with bread and, perhaps, a good cheese. You may make the dressing a few hours ahead of serving time, if you wish.

Yield: 6 servings

The salad

Cooked cannellini beans	1	cup
Bay scallops	1	pound
Cherry tomatoes	¾	pound, quartered
Yellow bell pepper, finely diced	¼	cup
Red onion, minced	2	tablespoons
Arugula leaves	1½	cups, washed and dried

The dressing

Fresh-squeezed orange juice	3	tablespoons
Balsamic vinegar	1	tablespoon
Olive oil	2	teaspoons
Garlic	2	cloves, minced
Ground cinnamon	¼	teaspoon
Salt	⅛	teaspoon
Pepper		A few grinds
Fresh basil leaves, minced	3	tablespoons

Cook cannellini beans according to directions on page 36, or rinse canned beans and drain them well. Set aside.

Whisk together the orange juice, vinegar, oil, garlic, cinnamon, salt, and pepper until well combined. Stir in the basil, cover, and set aside at room temperature.

Rinse the scallops. Place them in a skillet over medium heat and shake the pan occasionally as they sizzle and steam. Scallops are done when they are opaque all the way through— this will take only about 2 to 3 minutes, depending on their size. Set them aside to cool for a few minutes. In a serving bowl, combine the beans with the tomatoes, bell pepper, onion, and cooled scallops. Toss with the dressing, then add the arugula and toss again until well combined. Serve at room temperature.

***Recommended companion dishes:* crusty rolls and goat cheese**

Each serving provides:

145	Calories	0.2 g	Omega-3
16 g	Protein	2 g	Fat
15 g	Carbohydrate		15% of calories from fat
183 mg	Sodium		0.3 g saturated fat
25 mg	Cholesterol		0.5 g polyunsaturated fat
			1 g monounsaturated fat

Spinach Salad with Tuna and Mandarin Oranges

ALMOST INSTANT

This is a great twist on the ordinary spinach salad. The orange juice and rice wine vinegar add a nice sweetness, while the dark sesame oil contributes a nutty quality. The colors are bright and crisp. If serving this as a dinner entrée, you may wish to add sushi or a soup to the menu.

Yield: 6 servings

The dressing

Fresh-squeezed orange juice	¼	cup
Rice wine vinegar	2	tablespoons
Canola oil	1	tablespoon
Dark sesame oil	½	teaspoon
Low-sodium soy sauce	½	teaspoon
Fresh ginger, grated	½	teaspoon
Granulated sugar	½	teaspoon
Pepper		Several grinds

The salad

Raw sesame seeds	1	tablespoon
Fresh spinach	1	bunch (about ¾ pound)
Sliced water chestnuts	1	8-ounce can
Mandarin orange segments	1	11-ounce can
Albacore tuna, water-packed	1	6⅛-ounce can
Red onion, chopped	½	cup

Toast the sesame seeds (see page 34) and set aside. Whisk together the dressing ingredients and set aside at room temperature.

Carefully wash the spinach and spin it dry. Place in a large bowl and tear it into bite-size pieces. Drain the water chestnuts and the mandarin oranges and pat dry with a tea towel. Coarsely chop the water chestnuts. Drain the tuna, pressing with a spoon to remove as much liquid as possible. Add the water chestnuts, mandarin orange segments, tuna, and onion to the spinach. Toss well. Pour the dressing over the salad and toss again. Sprinkle the sesame seeds over the salad. Toss once more to combine, and serve.

Recommended companion dishes: sesame crackers with Tofu Garlic Spread (page 60)

Each serving provides:

133	Calories	0.2 g	Omega-3
11 g	Protein	5 g	Fat
14 g	Carbohydrate		29% of calories from fat
202 mg	Sodium		1 g saturated fat
13 mg	Cholesterol		2 g polyunsaturated fat
			1 g monounsaturated fat

Crab and Bay Shrimp Louis

ALMOST INSTANT

*Indulge in this lower-fat version of the classic Louis whenever fresh
steamed crabs are available. Our dressing has a satisfying spicy bite
and a creamy consistency. The colors, textures, and tastes of the
vegetables and seafood combine to create a salad that epitomizes
freshness.*

Yield: 4 servings

The dressing

Plain nonfat yogurt	⅔	cup
Reduced-calorie mayonnaise	⅓	cup
Chili sauce	⅓	cup
Prepared horseradish	1	teaspoon
Worcestershire sauce	2	teaspoons
Fresh-squeezed lemon juice	¼	cup
Tabasco sauce		Several drops
Pepper		Several grinds
Capers, minced	1	tablespoon
Green onions	2,	minced

The salad

Crab meat*	12	ounces (about 2 cups)
Cooked bay shrimp	8	ounces
Butter lettuce	2	large heads
Cherry tomatoes	¾	pound
Cucumber	1	medium
Green bell pepper	½	medium
Lemon wedges	1	per serving

Whisk together the yogurt, mayonnaise, chili sauce, horseradish, Worcestershire sauce, lemon juice, Tabasco sauce, and pepper until smooth. Stir in the capers and green onions. Set aside in the refrigerator.

Rinse the crab meat and shrimp separately, pat dry, and set aside in the refrigerator. Line 4 large individual salad plates with the outer leaves of the lettuce and gently tear remaining lettuce leaves into bite-size pieces, distributing them evenly among the plates. Cut the cherry tomatoes in half and arrange them around the outer rim of the lettuce. Peel and thinly slice the cucumber. Circle the plates with the slices. Cut the bell pepper into thin strips and place as spokes from the middle of the

*If purchasing cooked whole crab, ask for 3 pounds of crab. Have your fishmonger crack and clean it. Pick all the meat from the shell, being careful to discard all the bits of shell and cartilage. If using canned lump crab meat, rinse and drain well before using.

plate. Mound equal amounts of crab in the center of each plate and sprinkle the shrimp on top. Top with the dressing, and serve with a lemon wedge on each plate.

Recommended companion dish: Roasted Garlic Bread (page 58)

Each serving provides:

296	Calories	0.3 g	Omega-3
32 g	Protein	9 g	Fat
23 g	Carbohydrate		26% of calories from fat
913 mg	Sodium		2 g saturated fat
168 mg	Cholesterol		3 g polyunsaturated fat
			1 g monounsaturated fat

Shark and Corn Salad with Curry Pumpkin Seed Dressing

This pretty salad would make a fine warm-weather lunch or brunch entrée, served with a soft roll or cheese biscuit. For supper, you may wish to add a serving of hearty cooked vegetables, such as steamed artichokes. If delicately flavored Napa cabbage is not available, you may substitute regular green cabbage. In either case, it should be sliced into paper-thin shreds.

Yield: 4 servings

Fresh-squeezed orange juice	¼	cup
Fresh-squeezed lemon juice	¼	cup
Dry sherry	¼	cup
Garlic	3	cloves, minced
Shark steak	¾	pound
Plain nonfat yogurt	1	cup
Curry powder	1½	teaspoons
Granulated sugar	½	teaspoon
Salt	¼	teaspoon
Cayenne		A pinch
Raw unsalted pumpkin seeds	3	tablespoons
Cumin seed	1	teaspoon
Fennel seed	½	teaspoon
Fresh cilantro, minced	¼	cup
Corn kernels, fresh or frozen	12	ounces
Red bell pepper	½	medium
Napa cabbage, finely shredded	2	cups
Lemon wedges	1	per person

Combine orange and lemon juices, sherry, and 1 clove of the minced garlic in a shallow dish—a nonmetallic pie plate works well. Rinse the shark and pat dry. Place the shark in the marinade and refrigerate ½ hour, turning once midway through.

Meanwhile, whisk together the yogurt, curry powder, sugar, salt, cayenne, and remaining 2 cloves minced garlic. Combine the pumpkin, cumin, and fennel seeds and toast them (see page 34). In a food processor or blender, briefly grind the seeds to a coarse meal texture. Stir into the yogurt sauce, along with the cilantro. Set aside.

Bring a few cups of water to a boil over high heat. Stir in the corn kernels. When the water comes back to a boil, immediately drain the corn in a colander, rinsing with cold water to stop the cooking. Leave to drain for a few minutes to remove as much water as possible. Cut the bell pepper lengthwise into thin slivers, then slice the slivers crosswise into 1-inch pieces.

Preheat the broiler 5 minutes before marinating time is up. Remove the shark from the marinade and shake to remove excess moisture. Broil it 4 inches from the flame 5 minutes, then turn and broil 3 to 5 minutes longer, depending on the thickness of the fish. Fish is done when mostly opaque but still slightly translucent at the very center. Remove from the broiler and set aside. When fish is cool enough to handle, remove any skin and bones and break up into bite-size pieces. Toss the shark, corn, and bell pepper with the dressing until well combined.

The Best 125 Lowfat Fish and Seafood Dishes

Make a bed of shredded cabbage on each of four serving plates. Mound the corn mixture onto the cabbage beds and serve immediately with a lemon wedge on each plate.

Recommended companion dishes: **rolls or biscuits and steamed artichokes (see page 64)**

Each serving provides:

354	Calories	0.5 g	Omega-3
21 g	Protein	7 g	Fat
52 g	Carbohydrate		17% of calories from fat
188 mg	Sodium		1 g saturated fat
30 mg	Cholesterol		3 g polyunsaturated fat
			2 g monounsaturated fat

Crab, Papaya, Jicama, and Kiwi with Citrus Poppy Seed Dressing

Deliciously exotic, this salad promises a beautiful presentation and compliments to the chef. It makes a wonderful brunch served with poppy seed muffins and mimosas. Ripe kiwis yield slightly to pressure, like ripe avocados. Ripe papayas are an even yellow or orange color. If you can find only hard kiwis and green papayas, take them home and allow them to ripen at room temperature for a few days before making the salad. Select papayas and jicamas that are as unblemished as possible.

Yield: 6 servings

The dressing

Poppy seeds	1½	tablespoons
Plain nonfat yogurt	¼	cup
Fresh-squeezed orange juice	¼	cup
Fresh-squeezed lime juice	2	tablespoons
Orange zest	1	teaspoon
Granulated sugar	1	teaspoon
Ground ginger	½	teaspoon
Nutmeg, freshly grated	¼	teaspoon
Salt		A pinch
Cayenne		A pinch
Red onion, minced	2	tablespoons

The Best 125 Lowfat Fish and Seafood Dishes

The salad

Papaya	1	**large**
Jicama, peeled and diced	1	**cup**
Crab meat°	10	**ounces (about 1¾ cups)**
Kiwis	2	**large**

At least several hours or up to two days ahead of time, make the dressing. Toast the poppy seeds (see page 34). Whisk together the yogurt, orange and lime juices, orange zest, sugar, ginger, nutmeg, salt, cayenne, and toasted poppy seeds. Stir in the onion and refrigerate until ready to use.

Slice the papaya in half lengthwise. Scoop out and discard the seeds. Peel each half and dice into 1-inch cubes. Combine with the diced jicama in a medium bowl and toss gently with the dressing and crab meat. Peel the kiwis and discard the stem ends. Slice crosswise into ovals, exposing the pattern of black seeds. Arrange the kiwi slices around the edge of a medium serving plate. Mound the crab mixture into the center. Serve immediately or chill up to an hour.

Recommended companion dishes: muffins and mimosas

Each serving provides:

127	Calories	0.1 g	Omega-3
10 g	Protein	2 g	Fat
18 g	Carbohydrate		12% of calories from fat
193 mg	Sodium		0.2 g saturated fat
28 mg	Cholesterol		0.9 g polyunsaturated fat
			0.3 g monounsaturated fat

°If purchasing cooked whole crab, ask for 2½ pounds of crab. Have your fish-monger crack and clean it. Pick all the meat from the shell, being careful to discard all the bits of shell and cartilage. If using canned lump crab meat, rinse and drain well before using.

Soups, Stews,
and Chowders

No fish and seafood cookbook would be complete without a good selection of soups, stews, and chowders, since many of the best-loved soups are based on fresh seafood. Our reduced-fat versions of such American classics as Manhattan Clam Chowder, New England Oyster Stew, and Louisiana Gumbo deliver all the succulence of the originals without any sense of sacrifice. We've also drawn on the seasonings of Thailand, Italy, and Latin America to create full-flavored but lowfat soups and stews.

What distinguishes soups from stews and chowders is primarily their consistency. Chowders and stews most often include potatoes, which break up a little as they cook, thickening the broth with their starch. They make a satisfying meal in a bowl, requiring nothing more than a good bread and a beverage to complete the picture.

What we have called soups tend to have a thinner broth, but are often laden with vegetables, seafoods, and sometimes rice or noodles, so they should not be considered too insubstantial for dinner guests. Pay attention to our companion dish recommendations and you will satisfy even the heartiest appetite.

Though soups sometimes benefit from long simmering, we have chosen to include here only those with easy techniques and relatively short preparation times. Indeed, a few of our soups are Almost Instant.

Small amounts of seafood, combined with creamy ingredients, tomatoes, or clear broths, can be the basis of a truly special meal. Economical, nutritious, and quick to prepare, these seafood soups are sure to become standards in your repertoire.

Tools . . .

- Heavy-bottomed stockpot with a tight-fitting lid.
- Long-handled wooden spoons for stirring.
- Blender or food processor for pureeing.
- A soup tureen makes a pretty serving vessel.
- Ladles for serving.
- Individual serving bowls.
- Round-bowled soup spoons for diners are ideal.

. . . and Tips

- In the interest of quick preparation, many of our soups call for bottled clam juice or broth made with water and broth cubes. You can substitute homemade vegetable or fish stock, if you wish.

- The only way to ruin one of these soups is by overcooking the fish or seafood, rendering it tough and tasteless. Make sure the rest of the meal is ready when you add the fish to the soup.
- When pureeing is called for, do it in small batches to prevent hot liquid from splattering.
- Stir frequently to avoid sticking and scorching.
- Leftovers should be eaten the next day, or frozen if they are to be held for longer periods.

Mussels in Spicy Broth with Vegetables and Garbanzos

ALMOST INSTANT

This delicious clear broth stew is visually exciting, as well as nourishing. Be sure to buy or bake a really excellent crusty bread to soak up the broth.

Yield: 6 servings

Cooked garbanzo beans (chickpeas)	1½	**cups**
Dried tomatoes, minced	¼	**cup**
Baby red potatoes	¾	**pound**
Fresh green beans	½	**pound**
Whole baby corn	1	**15-ounce can**
Fresh spinach	1	**bunch (about ¾ pound)**
Clam juice	1	**8-ounce bottle**
Dry sherry	½	**cup**
Garlic	4	**cloves, minced**
Dried basil	2	**teaspoons**
Worcestershire sauce	1	**teaspoon**
Dried rosemary	1	**teaspoon, crushed**
Dill seed	½	**teaspoon, crushed**
Dried red chili flakes	½	**teaspoon**
Salt	⅛	**teaspoon**
Carrots	½	**pound, diced**
Live mussels in their shells	1½	**pounds**
Parmesan cheese, finely grated	⅓	**cup**

Cook the garbanzo beans according to directions on page 36, or rinse canned beans and drain them well. Set aside. Meanwhile, reconstitute the dried tomatoes if they are too dry to mince (see page 37).

Scrub the potatoes and quarter them—do not peel. Remove the stems from the beans and cut beans in half crosswise. Drain the corn and cut in half crosswise. Carefully wash the spinach and chop coarsely.

In a large stockpot, combine the clam juice, sherry, garlic, basil, Worcestershire sauce, rosemary, dill seed, chili flakes, and salt with 6 cups cold water. Bring to a simmer over high heat and add the potatoes and carrots. Bring back to a simmer, reduce heat to medium, and simmer, uncovered, for 10 minutes. Add the green beans, garbanzos, and dried tomatoes; bring back to a simmer over high heat, then reduce heat to medium and simmer, uncovered, about 5 minutes.

Meanwhile, scrub the mussels carefully and tug gently at the beard with your fingers or pliers to remove it. Any mussels that are not tightly closed after scrubbing should be discarded. Also discard any mussels with cracked or broken shells. Set the cleaned mussels aside in a colander. When potatoes and other vegetables are fork tender but not soft and falling apart, add the spinach and baby corn to the pot and stir. In a minute or two the spinach will be wilted. Pile the mussels into the pot and cover. Cook 2 to 3 minutes, until the mussels pop open. Check

carefully and discard any that have not opened. Transfer to a soup tureen or individual shallow serving bowls, making sure each bowl has a good balance of vegetables and mussels and plenty of broth. Serve very hot, passing the cheese.

Recommended companion dishes: crusty bread or rolls and Buttermilk Cucumber Salad (page 68)

Each serving provides:

438	Calories	0.2 g	Omega-3
22 g	Protein	7 g	Fat
69 g	Carbohydrate		15% of calories from fat
769 mg	Sodium		2 g saturated fat
21 mg	Cholesterol		2 g polyunsaturated fat
			2 g monounsaturated fat

Scallop Soup with Saffron and Green Grapes

This soup comes together amazingly fast. Choose it for a light supper before a play, along with the recommended companion dishes, or as an enjoyable luncheon. Be sure to warm the soup bowls.

Yield: 4 servings

Sea scallops	¼	pound
Seedless green grapes	¼	pound
Fish bouillon cube	1	large
Clam juice	1	8-ounce bottle
Dry sherry	2	tablespoons
Saffron threads	1	teaspoon

Rinse the scallops and slice them crosswise into ¼-inch disks. Remove the stem ends from the grapes and cut them in half. Set both aside. In a medium saucepan over high heat, bring 3 cups of water to a boil. Add the bouillon cube and stir to dissolve. Add the clam juice and sherry, return to a boil, and reduce heat to medium-high to maintain a rapid simmer. Stir in the saffron threads. Cook for about 2 minutes. Strain to remove the saffron so you have a clear broth. Return the broth to the pan and bring back to boiling, as you want it to be very hot. Distribute the raw

scallops among the warm soup bowls. Immediately ladle the boiling broth over the scallops. The high heat of the broth will cook the scallops in 2 minutes. Then distribute the grapes evenly among the bowls, and serve.

***Recommended companion dishes:* Buttermilk Cucumber Salad (page 68) and French bread with Brie cheese**

Each serving provides:

47	Calories	0.06 g	Omega-3
5 g	Protein	0.3 g	Fat
6 g	Carbohydrate		6% of calories from fat
176 mg	Sodium		0.1 g saturated fat
9 mg	Cholesterol		0.1 g polyunsaturated fat
			0.1 g monounsaturated fat

Shrimp and Rice Noodle Soup with Lemongrass

This nourishing, piquant soup combines all our favorite Southeast Asian seasonings. You can locate the unusual ingredients at an Asian market in your community.

Yield: 6 servings

Dried shiitake mushrooms	1	ounce
Dried rice cellophane noodles	½	pound
Snow peas	¼	pound, slivered
Clam juice	1	8-ounce bottle
Low-sodium soy sauce	1	tablespoon
Fresh jalapeño peppers, seeded and sliced	2	small
Fresh lemongrass, white portion, minced	1	tablespoon
White onion, thinly sliced	¼	cup
Mushrooms	½	pound, sliced
Firm-style tofu	3	ounces, cubed
Fresh basil leaves, minced	½	cup
Fresh cilantro, minced	¼	cup
Peeled and deveined raw shrimp*	1	pound
Mung bean sprouts	¼	pound
Unsweetened coconut milk	⅔	cup
Fresh-squeezed lime juice	3	tablespoons
Lemon wedges	1	per person

*If you purchase unpeeled raw shrimp or prawns, break away the shells and cut a shallow slit along the back so you can remove the dark vein.

Soak the dried mushrooms in 1½ cups hot water for 30 to 45 minutes. Gently lift them from the water and strain the soaking liquid through a paper coffee filter into a bowl. Set aside. Under a thin stream of running water, rinse the underside of the mushroom caps to remove any grit lodged in the membranes. Remove the stems and sliver the caps. Set aside. Rinse the dried rice noodles under cold water until very wet, then set aside to drain in a colander. String the snow peas and sliver them lengthwise. Set aside.

In a large stockpot over medium-high heat, bring the mushroom soaking liquid, clam juice, soy sauce, jalapeños, lemongrass, and onions to a boil with 2 cups of water. Reduce heat to medium to achieve a strong simmer. Stir in the two types of mushrooms, snow peas, tofu, basil, and cilantro, and bring back to a simmer. Add the shrimp and noodles and push with a wooden spoon to immerse them. Stir occasionally as everything simmers for 3 minutes. Remove pot from the heat and stir in the bean sprouts, coconut milk, and lime juice. Serve very hot in warmed, deep bowls, each one garnished with a lemon wedge and several sprigs of cilantro.

Each serving provides:

323	Calories	0.4 g	Omega-3
20 g	Protein	8 g	Fat
44 g	Carbohydrate		22% of calories from fat
320 mg	Sodium		4 g saturated fat
117 mg	Cholesterol		1 g polyunsaturated fat
			0.5 g monounsaturated fat

Tuscan Halibut Stew
with Cannellini Beans and Basil

This pretty and delicious stew combines some of the classic flavors of Northern Italy. If you can't locate cannellini beans in an Italian market, substitute another white bean.

Yield: 6 servings

Cooked cannellini beans	2½	cups
Dried tomatoes, minced	⅓	cup
Halibut steak or fillet	¾	pound
Olive oil	2	tablespoons
Red onion	1	medium, coarsely chopped
Garlic	4	cloves, minced
Dried rosemary	1	teaspoon
Zucchini	1	large, coarsely chopped
Carrot	1	large, coarsely chopped
Worcestershire sauce	1	tablespoon
Dry sherry	½	cup
Salt	¼	teaspoon
Cayenne	⅛	teaspoon
Broccoli, chopped	3	cups
Fresh basil leaves	2	cups, loosely packed
Parmesan cheese, finely grated	2	tablespoons

Cook cannellini beans according to directions on page 36, or rinse canned beans and drain them well. Set aside. Meanwhile, reconstitute the dried tomatoes if they are too dry to mince (see page 37).

Rinse the halibut and pat dry. Trim off any skin and remove any bones, using tweezers or pliers if necessary. Coarsely chop the halibut and set aside in the refrigerator.

Heat the oil in a stockpot over medium heat and sauté the onion, garlic, and rosemary 3 minutes, until onion is beginning to soften. Add the zucchini, carrot, and Worcestershire sauce, and stir and sauté 3 minutes longer. Add 2 cups of reserved bean liquid, 2 cups of water, sherry, salt, cayenne, and cooked beans (if you don't have 2 cups bean cooking liquid, add additional water to make 4 cups total liquid). Bring to a simmer and cook 5 minutes. Add the halibut, broccoli, basil, and dried tomato. Bring back to a simmer and cook 4 to 7 minutes, until fish chunks are opaque all the way through. Transfer the stew to a tureen if you have one, or serve from the pot. Serve very hot, sprinkled with the Parmesan.

Recommended companion dishes: Roasted Garlic Bread (page 58) and Basil Balsamic Salad (page 67)

Each serving provides:

286	Calories	0.2 g	Omega-3
25 g	Protein	7 g	Fat
32 g	Carbohydrate		22% of calories from fat
212 mg	Sodium		1 g saturated fat
20 mg	Cholesterol		1 g polyunsaturated fat
			4 g monounsaturated fat

Crab Bisque

While Susann and Guy were traveling in England, they wandered into a back alley French bistro for dinner one night. Much to their surprise, they were served the best crab bisque they had ever tasted! The waiter revealed the ingredients, and after many revisions, this lower-fat version is ready for you to enjoy.

Yield: 6 servings

Cooked whole crab	1	2-pound crab
Unsalted butter	2	tablespoons
Canola oil	1	tablespoon
Yellow onion	1	small, diced
Unbleached flour	3	tablespoons
Paprika	2	teaspoons
Salt	½	teaspoon
Low-sodium chopped tomatoes	1	cup
Condensed nonfat milk	1	12-ounce can
Dry sherry	1	teaspoon

Have the fishmonger crack and clean the fresh crab. Pick all crab meat from the shell, being careful to remove all the bits of shell and cartilage. Set the crab meat aside in the refrigerator. Rinse the shells, place them in a large stockpot, and cover with 6 cups water. Bring to a boil over high heat, reduce heat to low, and simmer 45 minutes. Strain the shell broth, retaining 3 cups. Set aside.

Heat the butter and canola oil in the stockpot over medium heat. Sauté the onion about 5 minutes, until soft, then stir in the flour, paprika, and salt. Stir and cook for 1 minute. Gradually add the reserved shell broth, whisking until smooth. Remove from the heat and stir in the tomatoes and crab meat. Transfer to a food processor or blender and puree until smooth (this may need to be done in several batches). Return the soup to the pot and stir in the condensed milk and dry sherry. Heat over low heat until steaming. Serve piping hot.

Recommended companion dishes: **steamed artichoke (see page 64), Basil Balsamic Salad (page 67), and French bread**

Each serving provides:

164	Calories	0.2 g	Omega-3
15 g	Protein	6 g	Fat
13 g	Carbohydrate		30% of calories from fat
442 mg	Sodium		2 g saturated fat
42 mg	Cholesterol		1 g polyunsaturated fat
			2 g monounsaturated fat

Quick and Light Oyster Stew

ALMOST INSTANT

The secret ingredient to this delicious soup is nutmeg! We prefer it freshly grated because the flavor is more intense, but you may substitute commercially ground nutmeg, if necessary.

Yield: 4 servings

Unsalted butter	1	**tablespoon**
Worcestershire sauce	2	**teaspoons**
Shucked oysters, with juice	2	**10-ounce jars**
Salt	½	**teaspoon**
Russet potatoes	2	**medium (about 1 pound)**
Lowfat milk	4	**cups**
Pepper		**Several grinds**
Nutmeg, freshly grated		**Several grinds**

Combine 2 cups of water with the butter, Worcestershire sauce, juice from the oysters, and salt in a stockpot and bring to a boil over high heat. Meanwhile, peel and cube the potatoes. Add the potatoes to the stockpot, reduce heat to medium-high, and cook for 20 minutes, stirring occasionally, until they are tender.

If the oysters are large, cut them in halves or thirds. When potatoes are fork tender, reduce the heat to medium and add the oysters. Cook until their edges curl, about 4 minutes. Meanwhile, scald the milk by placing it in a large saucepan and heating until bubbles begin to form around the edges. Be careful that it does not scorch. Pour this into the stockpot, add the pepper, heat through, and serve. Grind fresh nutmeg onto each serving.

***Recommended companion dishes:* Roasted Garlic Bread (page 58) and Honey Mustard Salad (page 76)**

Each serving provides:			
311	Calories	1 g	Omega-3
22 g	Protein	9 g	Fat
36 g	Carbohydrate		25% of calories from fat
546 mg	Sodium		4 g saturated fat
78 mg	Cholesterol		1 g polyunsaturated fat
			2 g monounsaturated fat

Rock Shrimp and Corn Chowder

This is the perfect dish to serve in the early autumn when rock shrimp first come into season and you can still get fresh corn. However, frozen corn can be used, so enjoy this chowder all winter as well. You may substitute peeled and deveined raw shrimp for the rock shrimp.

Yield: 6 servings

Salt	¼	teaspoon
Russet potatoes	2	medium
Olive oil	1	tablespoon
Yellow onion, diced	½	cup
Red bell pepper, diced	1	cup
Dried thyme	½	teaspoon
Low-sodium vegetable broth cube	1	large
Honey	1	teaspoon
Chili powder	½	teaspoon
Unbleached flour	1	tablespoon
Peeled and deveined raw rock shrimp	8	ounces, coarsely chopped
Lowfat milk	1½	cups
Corn kernels, fresh or frozen	1½	cups

Heat 6 cups of water to a boil in a stockpot. Add the salt and potatoes, return to a boil, then simmer over medium-high heat 10 minutes, until potatoes are fork tender. Meanwhile, put the olive oil in a skillet and sauté the onion, bell pepper, and thyme over low heat 5 minutes. Add to the potatoes, along with the vegetable broth cube, honey, and chili powder. Place ½ cup of the broth into a small jar that has a tight-fitting lid. Add the flour and shake vigorously to dissolve. Add to the simmering soup in a thin stream, whisking constantly. Cook over medium-high heat until thickened, about 20 minutes, stirring frequently. Remove from the heat and add half the shrimp. Transfer to a blender or food processor and puree until smooth (this will need to be done in several batches). Return to the stockpot, add the milk, and bring back to a simmer over medium-high heat. Add the remaining shrimp and corn and cook for 3 minutes. Serve very hot.

Recommended companion dishes: **Southwest Salad (page 70) and Cornbread (page 57)**

Each serving provides:

295	Calories	0.2 g	Omega-3
15 g	Protein	5 g	Fat
47 g	Carbohydrate		17% of calories from fat
195 mg	Sodium		1 g saturated fat
60 mg	Cholesterol		1 g polyunsaturated fat
			2 g monounsaturated fat

Curried Salmon and Artichoke Chowder with Chutney

ALMOST INSTANT

The sweetness of salmon is accentuated by the chutney, but the heat of the curry keeps the flavors in balance. Pretty and delicious, this soup is a good choice for company.

Yield: 6 servings

Salmon steaks or fillets	1	pound
Fresh-squeezed lemon juice	1	tablespoon
Artichoke bottoms, water-packed	1	13¾-ounce can
Light sesame oil	1	tablespoon
Garlic	4	cloves, minced
Curry powder	1	tablespoon
Russet potato	1	large, diced small
Carrot	1	medium, diced small
Mushrooms	½	pound, sliced
Salt	¼	teaspoon
Cayenne		A pinch
Plain nonfat yogurt	½	cup
Dry sherry	¼	cup
Fresh parsley, minced	¼	cup
Mango Chutney (see page 42)	3	tablespoons

Rinse the salmon and pat dry. Place in a skillet that has a tight-fitting lid. Add enough water to barely cover the fish. Remove the fish from the pan and set aside in the refrigerator. To create the poaching liquid, add lemon juice to the water in the skillet and bring to a boil over high heat. Add the fish, reduce heat to medium, cover, and cook 5 to 8 minutes, depending on the thickness of the fish. Fish is done when it is mostly opaque but still barely translucent at the very center. Remove it from the liquid and set aside. Measure the poaching liquid and add enough water to make 5 cups. Set the resulting broth aside in a bowl. When fish is cool enough to handle, remove any skin and bones and break up into bite-size pieces. Set aside.

Meanwhile, drain the artichokes, chop them coarsely, and set aside. In a stockpot, heat the oil over medium heat. Add the garlic and curry powder and stir, then add the potato and carrot. Stir and sauté about 3 minutes to brown a bit, then add the broth, artichokes, mushrooms, salt, and cayenne. Increase heat to high and bring to a simmer. Reduce heat to medium and simmer about 15 minutes, until potato and carrot are very tender.

Turn off the heat under the soup. Place the yogurt in a bowl and whisk in a few tablespoons of the hot soup to warm the yogurt. With a potato masher, lightly mash the ingredients in the pot—you want to break up some of the potatoes and carrots until a thick consistency is achieved. Stir in the yogurt, sherry, parsley, and chutney and cook 2 minutes over medium heat, adding the salmon for the last minute only. Serve very hot, passing additional yogurt as an optional topping.

Recommended companion dishes: **Middle East Salad (page 72) and whole-grain bread**

Each serving provides:

209	Calories	0.5 g	Omega-3
19 g	Protein	6 g	Fat
21 g	Carbohydrate		24% of calories from fat
191 mg	Sodium		2 g saturated fat
56 mg	Cholesterol		2 g polyunsaturated fat
			2 g monounsaturated fat

Corn and Green Chili Chowder with Clams

ALMOST INSTANT

This quick and simple Tex-Mex soup makes a wonderful early autumn supper, when corn and tomatoes are still at their best.

Yield: 4 servings

Olive oil	1	tablespoon
Garlic	3	cloves, minced
Red onion	½	large, minced
Ground cumin	½	teaspoon
Chili powder	½	teaspoon
Dried oregano	2	teaspoons
Corn kernels, fresh or frozen	1½	cups
Canned diced green chilies	1	4-ounce can
Cayenne		A scant pinch
Low-sodium vegetable broth cube	½	large
Nonfat milk	¼	cup
Chopped clams	1	6½-ounce can
Fresh cilantro, minced	¼	cup
Black olives, finely chopped	2	tablespoons
Parmesan cheese, finely grated	2	tablespoons
Fresh tomato	1	medium, seeded and diced
Green onions	2,	minced

Heat the oil in a stockpot over medium heat and sauté the garlic and onion for about 3 minutes, until onion is beginning to soften. Stir in the cumin, chili powder, and oregano, then add the corn, green chilies, cayenne, 3 cups of water, and the vegetable broth cube. Bring to a boil over high heat, reduce heat to medium-low, and simmer 15 minutes. Transfer half the soup to a blender jar and puree, then return to the pot, along with the milk, clams with their juice, cilantro, olives, Parmesan, and tomato. Return to a simmer and cook 2 minutes, until just heated through. Serve very hot, passing the green onions for garnish.

Recommended companion dishes: sliced fresh tomatoes and Roasted Garlic Bread (page 58)

Each serving provides:

377	Calories	0.1 g	Omega-3
21 g	Protein	9 g	Fat
55 g	Carbohydrate		22% of calories from fat
320 mg	Sodium		2 g saturated fat
34 mg	Cholesterol		2 g polyunsaturated fat
			4 g monounsaturated fat

Manhattan Style Clam Chowder

This classic red chowder is hearty and warming—a perfect choice for a winter day.

Yield: 4 servings

Chopped clams, with juice	2	6½-ounce cans
Dry white wine	½	cup
Russet potatoes	1	pound, diced
Yellow onion	1	large, diced
Garlic	4	cloves, minced
Carrot	1	large, diced
Dried tarragon	½	teaspoon
Dried basil	1	teaspoon
Dried oregano	½	teaspoon
Cayenne		A pinch
Salt	½	teaspoon
Pepper		Several grinds
Bay leaves	2	
Clam juice	1	8-ounce bottle
Low-sodium chopped tomatoes	1	28-ounce can
Low-sodium tomato paste	1	6-ounce can

Drain the liquid from the clams into a stockpot. Add the wine, potatoes, onion, garlic, carrot, tarragon, basil, oregano, and cayenne. Bring to a simmer over medium-high heat. Cook 10 minutes, then stir in the salt, pepper, bay leaves, bottled clam juice, tomatoes, and tomato paste. Bring back to a simmer, reduce heat to medium, and cook 30 minutes, stirring occasionally. Turn off the heat and stir in the clams. Serve immediately.

Recommended companion dishes: **Honey Mustard Salad (page 76) and Roasted Garlic Bread (page 58)**

Each serving provides:

309	Calories	0.1 g	Omega-3
17 g	Protein	2 g	Fat
58 g	Carbohydrate		6% of calories from fat
571 mg	Sodium		1 g saturated fat
60 mg	Cholesterol		0.5 g polyunsaturated fat
			0.5 g monounsaturated fat

Tomato Rice Soup with Scallops and Tarragon

This beautiful, warming soup is a perfect blending of flavors. We predict you will cook it often for favorite friends and family. If you have leftover rice, it comes together quite quickly.

Yield: 4 servings

Long-grain brown rice, uncooked	½	**cup**
Olive oil	1	**tablespoon**
Garlic	4	**cloves, minced**
Yellow onion	1	**large, diced**
Bell pepper	1	**small, diced**
Salt	⅛	**teaspoon**
Pepper		**Several grinds**
Dry sherry	½	**cup**
Low-sodium tomato puree	1	**14½-ounce can**
Bay scallops	¾	**pound**
Fresh tarragon, minced	¼	**cup, loosely packed**
Capers, drained and minced	2	**tablespoons**
Cultured lowfat buttermilk	¾	**cup**

In a saucepan over high heat, bring 1 cup of water to a boil. Stir in the rice, bring back to a boil, cover, reduce heat to very low, and cook 45 minutes.

Heat the oil in a stockpot over medium heat and sauté the garlic, onion, bell pepper, salt, and pepper for 10 minutes. Add the sherry and bring to a simmer. Stir in tomato puree and

1½ cups of water, bring to a boil over high heat, reduce heat to low, and simmer 20 minutes.

Meanwhile, rinse the scallops and drain well. Place them in a skillet over medium heat, along with the tarragon and capers. When sizzling begins, cover the pan and cook for 3 minutes, shaking occasionally. Scallops should turn from translucent to opaque. Set aside.

Place the buttermilk in a bowl and whisk in a few tablespoons of hot soup to warm it a little. When soup simmering time is up, stir in the buttermilk, rice, and cooked scallops, scraping the skillet with a rubber spatula to get all the bits of tarragon and capers into the soup. Serve immediately.

Recommended companion dishes: **French bread with cheese and Buttermilk Cucumber Salad (page 68)**

Each serving provides:

534	Calories	0.1 g	Omega-3
21 g	Protein	6 g	Fat
68 g	Carbohydrate		10% of calories from fat
309 mg	Sodium		1 g saturated fat
26 mg	Cholesterol		1 g polyunsaturated fat
			3 g monounsaturated fat

Scallop, Snapper, and Okra Gumbo

The word gumbo *is derived from an African word for okra—you can't have one without the other. This lowfat version of the Louisiana classic uses browned flour instead of the traditional oil-based roux.*

Filé powder is a blend of ground sassafras and thyme that lends a characteristic flavor to the soup base. You may substitute 1 teaspoon dried thyme, with less authentic results.

Yield: 6 servings

Unbleached flour	¼	cup
Olive oil	2	tablespoons
Yellow onions	2,	coarsely chopped
Bell peppers	2	medium, diced
Celery	1	rib, sliced
Garlic	6	cloves, minced
Dried red chili flakes	½	teaspoon
Low-sodium whole tomatoes	1	28-ounce can
Low-sodium vegetable broth cube	1	large
Okra, fresh or frozen	¾	pound, sliced
Filé powder	2	teaspoons
Dried oregano	1	teaspoon
Bay leaves	2	
Tabasco sauce		Several drops
Long-grain white rice, uncooked	¾	cup
Salt	¼	teaspoon
Sea scallops	¾	pound
Red snapper fillets	¾	pound

Place the flour in a heavy-bottomed saucepan over medium-low heat. Stir constantly as the flour browns for about 5 minutes. It is done when evenly tan in color. If it begins to blacken during this process, remove the pan from the heat, turn the burner down a bit, and resume the process. Remove the browned flour from the pan and set aside.

Heat the oil in a stockpot over medium heat. Sauté the onion, bell peppers, celery, garlic, and chili flakes for 10 minutes, stirring frequently. Meanwhile, chop the canned tomatoes coarsely, draining off their juice, and set aside. Stir the browned flour into the onion mixture, then add the tomatoes, 6 cups of hot water, vegetable broth cube, okra, file gumbo, oregano, bay leaves, and Tabasco sauce. Bring to a simmer over medium-high heat, then reduce heat to medium and simmer 10 minutes, stirring occasionally. Stir in the rice and salt, return to a simmer over medium-high heat, reduce heat to medium, and simmer 15 minutes, stirring frequently to prevent scorching and sticking.

Meanwhile, rinse the scallops and cut in half. Rinse the snapper and pat dry. Trim off any skin and remove any bones, using tweezers or pliers, if necessary. Stir the scallops and snapper into the pot, bring back to a simmer, cover, and simmer 5 to 7 minutes, until fish is opaque all the way through. Serve very hot, passing the Tabasco sauce for those who like it spicier.

Recommended companion dishes: Cornbread (page 57) and Southwest Salad (page 70)

Each serving provides:

345	Calories	0.3 g	Omega-3
28 g	Protein	6 g	Fat
45 g	Carbohydrate		16% of calories from fat
395 mg	Sodium		1 g saturated fat
40 mg	Cholesterol		1 g polyunsaturated fat
			4 g monounsaturated fat

Cioppino with Fresh Fennel and Brandy

There are as many versions of cioppino as there are great Italian cooks. This one includes two unusual ingredients: fresh fennel and brandy. Delicious! No cioppino feed would be complete without plenty of fruity red wine.

Yield: 4 servings

Low-sodium whole tomatoes	1	**28-ounce can**
Low-sodium stewed tomatoes	1	**14½-ounce can**
Green bell peppers	2	**medium, coarsely chopped**
Red onions	2	**medium, coarsely chopped**
Fresh fennel bulb	1	**medium, thinly sliced**
Garlic	6	**cloves, minced**
Dried basil	1	**tablespoon**
Bay leaves	2	
Fennel seed	½	**teaspoon**
Dried red chili flakes	½	**teaspoon**
Salt	⅛	**teaspoon**
Clam juice	1	**8-ounce bottle**
Live mussels in their shells	1	**pound**
Sea bass fillet	¾	**pound**
Olive oil	2	**tablespoons**

Peeled and deveined	
raw shrimp*	½ pound
Brandy	¼ cup

In a stockpot, combine both varieties of tomatoes with the bell peppers, onions, fresh fennel, 4 cloves of the garlic, basil, bay leaves, fennel seed, dried red chili flakes, salt, and clam juice. Bring to a simmer over medium-high heat, reduce heat to medium-low, cover, and simmer 30 minutes. Remove the lid and simmer 10 to 15 minutes longer, until sauce is reduced to a thick soup consistency.

Meanwhile, scrub the mussels carefully and tug gently at the beard with your fingers or pliers to remove it. Any mussels that are not tightly closed after scrubbing should be discarded. Also discard any mussels with cracked or broken shells. Set the cleaned mussels aside in a colander in the refrigerator. Trim off any skin and remove any bones from the sea bass, using tweezers or pliers, if necessary. Chop into 2-inch pieces. Heat the olive oil in a large skillet over medium-high heat and sauté the remaining 2 cloves of garlic for a minute or two. Add the sea bass and stir and sauté for 3 to 5 minutes, until fish is mostly opaque but still slightly translucent at the very center. Remove the fish and any pan juices to a plate and set aside. Add the shrimp to the skillet along with the brandy, and stir around for just 2 to 3 minutes, until all the shrimp turn bright pink. Remove shrimp and pan juices from the pan and set aside.

*If you purchase unpeeled raw shrimp or prawns, break away the shells and cut a shallow slit along the back so you can remove the dark vein.

When tomato sauce is ready, remove the bay leaves. Pile in the mussels in their shells. Cover and cook 3 to 5 minutes, until mussels have popped open. Check carefully and discard any that have not opened. Stir the cooked sea bass and shrimp into the stew and heat through. Serve the cioppino in shallow bowls, and have plenty of crusty rolls and napkins on hand!

***Recommended companion dishes:* crusty rolls and Basil Balsamic Salad (page 67)**

Each serving provides:

294	Calories	0.7 g	Omega-3
28 g	Protein	8 g	Fat
29 g	Carbohydrate		23% of calories from fat
375 mg	Sodium		1 g saturated fat
92 mg	Cholesterol		1 g polyunsaturated fat
			4 g monounsaturated fat

Risotto and Rice Dishes

Hearty and healthful, rice is a staple of our diets. Rice combines well with fish and seafood, as the recipes in this chapter demonstrate.

In addition to classics like paella and shrimp curry, we have included several innovative versions of the traditional northern Italian rice dish called risotto. Risotto uses a unique short, oval-shaped rice which releases its starch during the cooking process to create a creamy texture without the addition of fat-laden dairy products. This comfort-food quality makes risotto a frequent choice for us, and we think you'll agree these dishes are delicious enough to be prepared often. Cook them for friends and enlist their help in the stirring process.

Look for the special oval-grained risotto at a well-stocked supermarket or Italian specialty store. The most well-known variety is sold as Riso Arborio.

Though risotto does require close attention during cooking, it can be prepared in only about 40 minutes from start to finish. The seafood typically is cooked separately and added to the pot at the end of the cooking time.

We also offer in this chapter a few composed entrées for which a bed of rice is the perfect base. The rice is cooked separately, but is an integral part of the finished dish.

Tools . . .

- A selection of heavy-bottomed saucepans with lids.
- Large wooden spoon for stirring risotto.
- Pretty serving bowl, platter, or tureen.
- Large-bowled serving spoons.

. . . and Tips

- Stir risotto almost constantly as it absorbs each addition of liquid to prevent sticking or scorching. If risotto sticks even though you're stirring, reduce the heat slightly.
- The speed with which risotto cooks is affected by types of cookware, individual stove temperatures, and altitude. You may need to adjust the cooking time and the amount of liquid accordingly.
- Don't rinse risotto before cooking as you don't want to wash away any of the surface starches. Other types of

rice, such as basmati or brown rice, should always be rinsed to reduce stickiness and to clean off surface impurities.

- In the interest of quick preparation, our risotto recipes call for broth made with water and broth cubes. You may substitute homemade vegetable or fish stock, if you wish.
- If serving a dish on a bed of rice, start the rice in time so it is ready when you are.

Curried Risotto with Sea Bass, Garbanzos, Lime, and Cilantro

This nourishing, strongly seasoned rice dish is hearty and delicious. As a bonus, the combination of fish with both rice and beans delivers great protein and fiber.

Yield: 6 servings

Cooked garbanzo beans (chickpeas)	1	cup
Low-sodium vegetable broth cube	1	large
Olive oil	1	tablespoon
Garam masala or curry powder	1	tablespoon
Garlic	3	cloves, minced
Arborio rice, uncooked	1½	cups
Fresh tomato	1	medium
Salt	⅛	teaspoon
Pepper		Several grinds
Sea bass fillets	1	pound
Fresh-squeezed lime juice	2	tablespoons
Fresh cilantro, minced	¼	cup
Plain nonfat yogurt	3	tablespoons

Cook the beans according to the directions on page 36, or rinse and drain canned beans. Dissolve the vegetable broth cube in 5½ cups hot water and keep handy near the stove. In a large heavy-bottomed saucepan, heat ½ tablespoon of the olive oil over medium heat. Add the garam masala and 2 cloves minced garlic and sauté a minute or two. Add the rice and stir to coat with the oil and seasonings. Add 1 cup of the broth and stir gently until the liquid is absorbed. Add remaining broth ½ cup at a time, stirring almost constantly, and waiting until liquid is absorbed before each addition. When half the broth has been added, stir in the tomato, garbanzos, salt, and pepper and continue stirring and adding the remaining liquid ½ cup at a time.

Meanwhile, rinse the fish and pat dry. Trim off any skin and remove any bones, using tweezers or pliers, if necessary. Chop coarsely into 1-inch pieces. Heat ½ tablespoon olive oil in a heavy skillet over medium heat and add the sea bass chunks along with the lime juice and cilantro. Stir and sauté until fish is mostly opaque but still barely translucent at the very center. Remove from the pan and set aside, along with any pan juices.

When the last addition of broth has been absorbed and rice is tender, stir in the cooked fish and its juices. Heat through for 1 minute. Stir in the yogurt and and serve immediately in warmed shallow bowls.

Recommended companion dishes: Middle East Salad (page 72) and sesame crackers

---

Each serving provides:

350	Calories	0.5 g	Omega-3
21 g	Protein	7 g	Fat
50 g	Carbohydrate		18% of calories from fat
356 mg	Sodium		2 g saturated fat
33 mg	Cholesterol		1 g polyunsaturated fat
			3 g monounsaturated fat

Scallop and Mushroom Risotto with Tarragon

This dish melts in your mouth. The flavor is delicate and delicious.

Yield: 8 servings

Low-sodium vegetable broth cubes	1½	large
Olive oil	1	tablespoon
Garlic	3	cloves, minced
Mushrooms	½	pound, sliced
Red bell pepper	1	medium, diced
Yellow onion	1	medium, diced
Arborio rice, uncooked	2	cups
Dry white wine	1	cup
Bay scallops	1	pound
Dried tarragon	1	teaspoon
Fresh parsley, minced	⅓	cup
Parmesan cheese, finely grated	⅓	cup

Dissolve the vegetable broth cubes in 7 cups of hot water and keep handy near the stove. In a large heavy-bottomed stockpot, heat the oil over medium heat and add the garlic, mushrooms, red pepper, and onion. Sauté 7 minutes, then add the rice. Stir to coat with the oil and vegetables. Add the wine and stir gently until the liquid is absorbed. Add the broth ½ cup at a time, stirring almost constantly until liquid is absorbed before each addition.

The Best 125 Lowfat Fish and Seafood Dishes

Meanwhile, rinse the scallops and pat them dry. Add the tarragon, parsley, and scallops with the last ½ cup of broth, lower heat to medium-low, and cook until liquid is absorbed and the scallops are opaque. Serve immediately in warmed shallow bowls. Top with the Parmesan cheese.

Recommended companion dishes: steamed carrots (see page 64), Buttermilk Cucumber Salad (page 68), and Roasted Garlic Bread (page 58)

Each serving provides:

289	Calories	0.1 g	Omega-3
16 g	Protein	4 g	Fat
46 g	Carbohydrate		13% of calories from fat
336 mg	Sodium		1 g saturated fat
22 mg	Cholesterol		1 g polyunsaturated fat
			2 g monounsaturated fat

Risotto with Shark, Sage, Tomatoes, and Mozzarella

A wonderfully soul-satisfying dish, this earthy concoction is a good choice for a chilly evening. The distinctive flavor and texture of shark is a perfect match for the seasonings.

Yield: 6 servings

Low-sodium pear tomatoes, with juice	1	14½-ounce can
Garlic	4	cloves, minced
Dried rosemary	1	teaspoon, crushed
Rubbed sage	1	teaspoon
Salt	⅛	teaspoon
Pepper		Several grinds
Shark steaks	1	pound
Low-sodium vegetable broth cube	1	large
Olive oil	1	tablespoon
Dried oregano	½	teaspoon
Low-sodium tomato paste	1	tablespoon
Arborio rice, uncooked	1½	cups
Part-skim mozzarella cheese, grated	½	cup
Parmesan cheese, finely grated	2	tablespoons

In a skillet, combine the tomatoes, 2 cloves of the garlic, rosemary, sage, salt, and pepper. Bring to a simmer over medium heat. Lay the shark in this sauce, reduce the heat to low, cover, and simmer for about 5 minutes. Turn and simmer 4 to 8 minutes longer, depending on the thickness of the fish. Fish is done when mostly opaque but still barely translucent at the very center. Remove the fish to a plate to cool and turn off the heat under the tomato sauce. When fish is cool enough to handle, remove all skin and bones and break up into bite-size pieces. Stir any liquid that has collected on the plate into the sauce, along with the fish pieces. Set aside in a warm spot.

Dissolve the vegetable broth cube in 5½ cups hot water and keep handy near the stove. In a large heavy-bottomed saucepan, heat the olive oil over medium heat. Add the remaining 2 cloves of garlic, oregano, and tomato paste. Stir for a moment, then add the rice and stir to coat with oil and seasonings. Add 1 cup of the broth and stir gently until the liquid is absorbed. Add remaining broth ½ cup at a time, stirring almost constantly and waiting until liquid is absorbed before each addition. When the last addition of broth has been absorbed and the rice is tender, stir in the tomato fish mixture, mozzarella, and Parmesan. Heat for a minute longer and serve immediately in warmed shallow bowls. Serve very hot.

***Recommended companion dishes:* Basil Balsamic Salad (page 67) and bread sticks**

Each serving provides:

348	Calories	1 g	Omega-3
23 g	Protein	8 g	Fat
43 g	Carbohydrate		22% of calories from fat
343 mg	Sodium		2 g saturated fat
45 mg	Cholesterol		2 g polyunsaturated fat
			4 g monounsaturated fat

Clam Risotto with Dried Tomato and Peas

This robust risotto pairs canned clams with fresh steamed clams. The result is beautiful as well as delicious.

Yield: 4 servings

Dried tomatoes, minced	2	**tablespoons**
Canned minced clams	2	**6½-ounce cans**
Worcestershire sauce	2	**teaspoons**
Olive oil	1	**tablespoon**
Garlic	2	**cloves, minced**
Arborio rice, uncooked	1	**cup**
Dry white wine	½	**cup**
Fresh oregano leaves, minced	1	**tablespoon**
Shelled peas, fresh or frozen	2	**cups**
Fresh clams, in shell	1½	**pounds**
Lemon wedges	1	**per serving**

Reconstitute the tomatoes if they are too dry to mince (see page 37). Drain the canned clams, combining their liquid with 2½ cups hot water in a bowl. Stir in the Worcestershire sauce and keep this broth handy near the stove. Heat the oil in a large heavy-bottomed saucepan over medium heat and sauté the garlic for several seconds. Add the rice and stir to coat with the oil and garlic. Add the wine, stirring gently until liquid is absorbed. Add the broth ½ cup at a time, stirring almost constantly and waiting until liquid is absorbed before each addition. Add the oregano, tomatoes, canned clams, and peas with the last ½ cup of broth.

Meanwhile, scrub the fresh clams to remove grit from shells. Any clams that are not tightly closed after scrubbing should be discarded. Also discard any clams with broken shells. Set the cleaned clams aside in a colander. Put a few inches of water in a pot that has a tight-fitting lid and bring to a boil over medium-high heat. Add the fresh clams, cover, and steam 3 to 5 minutes. Check carefully and discard any clams that have not opened. Serve the risotto very hot, garnishing each dish equally with clams and a lemon wedge.

Recommended companion dishes: steamed broccoli (see page 64) and soft rolls

Each serving provides:

346	Calories	0.1 g	Omega-3
20 g	Protein	5 g	Fat
51 g	Carbohydrate		14% of calories from fat
113 mg	Sodium		1 g saturated fat
74 mg	Cholesterol		1 g polyunsaturated fat
			3 g monounsaturated fat

Risotto with Red Snapper, Spinach, Feta, and Nutmeg

Mediterranean influences are clearly evident in this great risotto. Because the spinach is steamed separately, it retains its bright, light flavor. You must use freshly grated nutmeg for optimum flavor—a simple nutmeg grater is an economical addition to your collection of essential culinary tools. The French feta is not as strong and salty as the traditional Greek version—it is worth seeking out.

Yield: 6 servings

Red snapper fillets	¾	pound
Granulated garlic	¼	teaspoon
Spinach	1	bunch (about ¾ pound)
Low-sodium vegetable broth cube	1	large
Olive oil	1	tablespoon
Garlic	4	cloves, minced
Dried oregano	½	teaspoon
Arborio rice, uncooked	1½	cups
French feta cheese, crumbled	2	ounces (½ cup)
Nutmeg, freshly grated	¼	teaspoon

Preheat the broiler 5 minutes. Rinse the red snapper and pat dry. Rub one side with half the granulated garlic. Broil the fish, garlic side up, 4 inches from the flame for 3 minutes, then turn, rub with the remaining granulated garlic, and broil an additional 2 to 4 minutes, depending on thickness of the fish. Fish is done when mostly opaque but still barely translucent at the very center. Set aside to cool. If liquid has collected in the broiler pan, pour into a measuring cup and set aside.

Carefully wash the spinach leaves, discarding large stems. Without drying them, place the leaves in a stockpot. Cover tightly and cook over medium heat 5 minutes, until spinach is wilted. Drain in a colander set over a bowl, pressing with a wooden spoon to release as much liquid as possible. Reserve the liquid. Set the spinach aside to cool.

Combine any spinach liquid with the fish juices saved from the broiler pan. Add enough hot water to measure 5½ cups total liquid and place in a bowl. Add the broth cube and stir to dissolve. Keep this broth handy near the stove.

When fish is cool enough to handle, remove any skin and bones and break up into bite-size pieces. When spinach is cool enough to handle, place on a cutting board and chop finely. Set fish and spinach aside.

In a large heavy-bottomed saucepan, heat the oil over medium heat. Add the garlic and oregano and sauté 3 minutes, then add the rice and stir to coat with the oil and seasonings. Add one cup of the broth and stir gently until the liquid is absorbed. Add the remaining broth ½ cup at a time, stirring almost constantly and waiting until liquid is absorbed before each addition. Add the spinach, feta cheese, and nutmeg with the last ½ cup of broth, lower heat to medium-low, and cook until liquid is absorbed and rice is tender. Transfer to a warmed serving bowl, stir in the fish, and serve hot.

Recommended companion dish: **Buttermilk Cucumber Salad (page 68)**

Each serving provides:

298	Calories	0.2 g	Omega-3
19 g	Protein	5 g	Fat
44 g	Carbohydrate		14% of calories from fat
350 mg	Sodium		1 g saturated fat
21 mg	Cholesterol		1 g polyunsaturated fat
			2 g monounsaturated fat

Risotto with Mahimahi, Sweet Red Peppers, and Basil

This is a simple but satisfying rendition of risotto. If you have a garden, late summer—when basil is at its peak—is the best time to try it.

Yield: 8 servings

Mahimahi steaks or fillets	1	**pound**
Granulated garlic	⅛	**teaspoon**
Low-sodium vegetable broth cube	1½	**large**
Olive oil	1	**tablespoon**
Garlic	4	**cloves, minced**
Yellow onion, diced	1	**medium**
Red bell peppers	2	**medium, diced**
Arborio rice, uncooked	2	**cups**
Dry white wine	1	**cup**
Fresh basil leaves, minced	¾	**cup**
Pepper	⅛	**teaspoon**
Lemon wedges	1	**per serving**

Preheat the broiler 5 minutes. Rinse the fish and pat it dry. Sprinkle one side with half the granulated garlic, then broil the fish garlic side up, 4 inches from the flame for 5 minutes. Turn, sprinkle on the remaining granulated garlic, and broil 3 to 4 minutes longer, depending on the thickness of the fish. Fish is done when mostly opaque but still barely translucent at the very center. Remove from the broiler and set aside. When cool enough to handle, remove any skin and bones and break up into bite-size pieces.

Meanwhile, dissolve the vegetable broth cubes in 7 cups hot water and keep handy near the stove. In a large heavy-bottomed stockpot, heat the oil over medium heat. Add the garlic, onion, and bell peppers and sauté 7 minutes. Add the rice and stir to coat with the oil and vegetables. Add the wine and stir gently until the liquid is absorbed. Add the broth ½ cup at a time, stirring almost constantly until liquid is absorbed before each addition. Add the basil, pepper, and mahimahi with the last ½ cup of broth. Serve immediately in shallow warmed bowls. Pass the lemon wedges.

Recommended companion dishes: steamed asparagus (see page 64) and Basil Balsamic Salad (page 67)

Each serving provides:

277	Calories	0.1 g	Omega-3
13 g	Protein	2 g	Fat
44 g	Carbohydrate		8% of calories from fat
209 mg	Sodium		0.4 g saturated fat
35 mg	Cholesterol		0.3 g polyunsaturated fat
			1 g monounsaturated fat

Szechwan Eggplant and Orange Roughy Risotto

This spicy creation has a lot of ingredients and several steps, but it is worth the effort. The rice wine, mirin, and chili oil are available at any Asian market and at many large supermarkets.

Yield: 6 servings

Dried shiitake mushrooms	½	**ounce**
Orange roughy fillets	1	**pound**
Fresh ginger, grated	2	**teaspoons**
Low-sodium soy sauce	2	**teaspoons**
Chili oil	1	**teaspoon**
Canola oil	1	**teaspoon**
Garlic	4	**cloves, minced**
Mustard seed	2	**teaspoons**
Eggplant	1	**medium (about 1 pound), diced**
Carrot	1	**large, diced small**
Sake	⅔	**cup**
Mirin	2	**tablespoons**
Cider vinegar	1	**tablespoon**
Ground cloves	⅛	**teaspoon**
Pepper		**Several grinds**
Dark sesame oil	2	**teaspoons**
Arborio rice, uncooked	1	**cup**
Green onions	4,	**minced**
Lemon wedges	1	**per person**

Soak the dried mushrooms in 1½ cups hot water for 30 to 45 minutes. Gently lift them from the water and strain the soaking liquid through a paper coffee filter into a large bowl. Set aside. Under a thin stream of running water, rinse the underside of the mushroom caps to remove any grit lodged in the membranes. Remove the stems and sliver the caps. Set aside.

Rinse the fish and pat dry. Bring 1 cup of water, the ginger, and 1 teaspoon of the soy sauce to a simmer in a skillet over medium heat. Lay the fish fillets in the liquid and bring back to a rapid bubble. Turn the fillets over, cover the pan, turn the heat down to low, and poach for 3 to 4 minutes. Fish is done when mostly opaque but still slightly translucent in the center. Remove the fish to a plate with a slotted spoon; set aside. Add the poaching liquid to the mushroom soaking liquid. When fish is cool enough to handle, use your hands to break it up into bite-size pieces.

In a large cast-iron skillet, heat the chili and canola oils over medium heat. Add 2 cloves of the garlic and the mustard seed and stir for a minute, then add the eggplant and carrot, stirring well to combine. Drizzle the remaining 1 teaspoon soy sauce evenly over the eggplant mixture. Stir and sauté about 12 minutes, until the carrot is fork tender. Turn off the heat and stir in ¼ cup water; it will sizzle and evaporate almost immediately, finishing the eggplant cooking. Put a lid on the pan to keep the mixture warm until you need it.

Meanwhile, add the sake, mirin, vinegar, cloves, and pepper to the mushroom/fish broth in the bowl. Measure this liquid and add enough water to make 3½ cups total. Heat the dark sesame oil in a large heavy-bottomed saucepan over medium heat. Add the remaining 2 cloves of garlic and stir for about a minute, then add the rice and stir to coat with the garlic and oil. Add ½ cup of the broth and stir gently until the liquid is absorbed. Add remaining broth ½ cup at a time, stirring almost constantly and waiting until liquid is absorbed before each addition. Add the mushrooms with the last ½ cup of broth.

When the last addition of broth has been absorbed and rice is tender, transfer it to a warmed serving bowl and gently stir in the eggplant mixture and the fish until well combined. Sprinkle the green onions evenly over the top and serve immediately with a wedge of lemon at each plate.

***Recommended companion dishes:* sesame crackers, steamed broccoli (see page 64), and fresh jicama slices**

Each serving provides:

425	Calories	0.01 g	Omega-3
15 g	Protein	5 g	Fat
35 g	Carbohydrate		17% of calories from fat
259 mg	Sodium		0.5 g saturated fat
15 mg	Cholesterol		2 g polyunsaturated fat
			2 g monounsaturated fat

Risotto with Spiced Shrimp, Beer, and Cheddar

The spice blend provides an intriguing dance of flavors. Unusual and delicious, this risotto is special enough for a dinner party.

Yield: 6 servings

The spice blend

Whole coriander	½	teaspoon
Fennel seed	½	teaspoon
Mustard seed	½	teaspoon
Cumin seed	½	teaspoon
Chili powder	¼	teaspoon
Dried thyme	¼	teaspoon
Dried red chili flakes	¼	teaspoon

The risotto

Olive oil	1	tablespoon
Garlic	3	cloves, minced
Red onion	1	medium, coarsely chopped
Yellow bell pepper	1	medium, coarsely chopped
Zucchini	2	medium, coarsely chopped
Salt		A pinch

Peeled and deveined		
raw shrimp*	¾	pound
Beer	⅓	cup
Low-sodium vegetable		
broth cube	1	large
Arborio rice, uncooked	1½	cups
Corn kernels, fresh or frozen	1	cup
Cheddar cheese, grated	2¼	ounces (¾ cup)

Combine the spices and grind to a coarse texture in a small food processor or with a mortar and pestle. Set aside.

In a large, heavy-bottomed skillet over medium heat, heat half the olive oil. Add half the spice blend and all the garlic and stir, then stir in the onion, bell pepper, zucchini, and salt. Sauté, stirring frequently, until vegetables are barely fork tender, about 7 to 9 minutes. Add the shrimp and beer all at once and stir constantly as the beer steams the shrimp. This will take about 3 minutes; shrimp are done when they have all turned bright pink. Remove the shrimp and vegetables immediately from the hot pan and set aside.

Dissolve the vegetable broth cube in 5½ cups hot water and keep handy near the stove. In a large heavy-bottomed saucepan, heat the remaining ½ tablespoon oil over medium heat. Add the remaining spice blend and stir, then add the rice and stir to coat with oil and seasonings. Add 1 cup of the broth and stir gently until the liquid is absorbed. Add the remaining broth ½ cup at a time, stirring almost constantly and waiting

*If you purchase unpeeled raw shrimp or prawns, break away the shells and cut a shallow slit along the back so you can remove the dark vein.

until liquid is absorbed before each addition. With the last ½ cup of broth, add the corn and cheese. Stir until liquid is absorbed and rice is tender. Stir in the shrimp and vegetables. Heat through for 1 minute, and serve in warmed shallow bowls.

Recommended companion dishes: Southwest Salad (page 70) and bread sticks

---

Each serving provides:

442	Calories	0.3 g	Omega-3
22 g	Protein	10 g	Fat
65 g	Carbohydrate		20% of calories from fat
368 mg	Sodium		4 g saturated fat
101 mg	Cholesterol		1 g polyunsaturated fat
			4 g monounsaturated fat

Orange Cilantro Scallops over Rice with Snow Peas

ALMOST INSTANT

The fresh orange juice brings out the sweetness of the scallops. The colors of this dish are particularly pretty.

Yield: 4 servings

Basmati rice, uncooked	1	cup
Snow peas	½	pound
Mushrooms	½	pound
Fresh-squeezed orange juice	¾	cup
Sea scallops	1	pound
Arrowroot powder or cornstarch	1	tablespoon
Fresh cilantro, minced	¼	cup
Poppy seeds	1	teaspoon

Bring 2 cups of water to a boil in a saucepan over high heat. Stir in the rice, return to a boil, cover, reduce heat to very low, and cook for 25 minutes.

Meanwhile, string the snow peas; leave them whole. Steam them 5 minutes, cool in a bowl of cold water, drain, and set aside in a warm spot. Wipe or brush any loose dirt particles from the mushrooms. Trim off their stem ends and slice the caps. Combine the orange juice with the mushrooms in a large skillet over medium-high heat. Bring to a simmer, reduce heat to medium, and cook 3 minutes.

Meanwhile, rinse the scallops and slice crosswise to create ¼-inch disks. Add the scallops to the orange juice and cook 3 to 4 minutes, until scallops are opaque all the way through. Remove the scallops and mushrooms with a slotted spoon, draining well, and set aside in a warm spot. Put 2 tablespoons water and the arrowroot powder in a small jar that has a tight-fitting lid and shake to dissolve. Combine this with the simmering juices in the skillet and stir constantly until thickened, about 2 minutes. Return the scallops and mushrooms to the pan, add the cilantro, and heat through about 1 minute. Fan the snow peas out around the edge of warmed serving plates and mound one-fourth of the rice in the center of each snow pea ring. Top the rice with the scallop mixture, then sprinkle with the poppy seeds. Serve immediately.

Recommended companion dishes: **Middle East Salad (page 72) and Roasted Garlic Bread (page 58)**

Each serving provides:

347	Calories	0.2 g	Omega-3
26 g	Protein	3 g	Fat
54 g	Carbohydrate		7% of calories from fat
189 mg	Sodium		0.2 g saturated fat
37 mg	Cholesterol		1 g polyunsaturated fat
			0.2 g monounsaturated fat

Crab Newburg

The traditional preparation of this dish calls for lots of butter, egg yolks, and heavy cream. We have lightened it up to take out much of the fat without sacrificing the flavor.

Yield: 4 servings

Basmati rice, uncooked	1	cup
Unsalted butter	2	tablespoons
Unbleached flour	3	tablespoons
Dry sherry	2	tablespoons
Lowfat milk	1½	cups
Egg yolk	1	medium
Crab meat*	8	ounces (about 1½ cups)
Dry white wine	2	tablespoons
Fresh-squeezed lemon juice	2	tablespoons
Salt	¼	teaspoon
Paprika	¼	teaspoon
Lemon wedges	1	per serving

Bring 2 cups of water to a boil in a saucepan over high heat. Stir in the rice, return to a boil, cover, reduce heat to very low, and cook for 25 minutes.

Melt the butter in a skillet over very low heat and blend in the flour. Quickly stir in the sherry, then gradually whisk in the milk and increase heat to medium. Cook, whisking frequently, about 10 minutes, until a thick sauce develops. In a small bowl,

*If purchasing cooked whole crab, ask for 2 pounds of crab. Have your fishmonger crack and clean it. Pick all the meat from the shell, being careful to discard all the bits of shell and cartilage. If using canned lump crab meat, rinse and drain well before using.

beat the egg yolk well, then stir a small amount of the hot sauce into it. Stir the egg yolk mixture into the sauce until incorporated. The sauce should be very thick. Stir in the crab, wine, lemon juice, salt, and paprika. Heat through for about 3 to 4 minutes. Divide the rice between warmed serving plates, then immediately spoon the Newburg sauce over the rice. Sprinkle an additional pinch of paprika over each serving and accompany with a lemon wedge.

***Recommended companion dishes:* steamed broccoli (see page 64), sourdough French bread, and Honey Mustard Salad (see page 76)**

Each serving provides:

376	Calories	0.2 g	Omega-3
18 g	Protein	9 g	Fat
51 g	Carbohydrate	23% of calories from fat	
351 mg	Sodium	5 g saturated fat	
107 mg	Cholesterol	1 g polyunsaturated fat	
		3 g monounsaturated fat	

Creole Catfish Dumplings and Rice

This recipe is one of Guy Hadler's specialties. We make our own blend of Cajun Blackening Spice Mix and share the recipe with you on page 39. You may substitute one of the commercially prepared varieties, if you wish, though they generally contain substantial amounts of salt.

Yield: 4 servings

Catfish fillets	¾	**pound**
Cajun Blackening Spice Mix		
(see page 39)	2	**tablespoons**
Egg whites	2	**large**
Unbleached flour	1	**cup**
Olive oil	1	**tablespoon**
Celery	2	**ribs, diced**
Green bell pepper	1	**medium, diced**
Yellow onion	1	**medium, diced**
Low-sodium chopped		
tomatoes	1	**14½-ounce can**
Low-sodium tomato sauce	1	**14½-ounce can**
Red wine	½	**cup**
Granulated garlic	1	**teaspoon**
Dried oregano	½	**teaspoon**
Dried thyme	½	**teaspoon**
Ground cumin	¼	**teaspoon**
Pepper		**Several grinds**
Basmati rice, uncooked	1	**cup**

Rinse the catfish and pat it dry. Trim off any skin and remove any bones, using tweezers or pliers, if necessary. Cut into 1-inch squares and coat on all sides with the Cajun spices. Lightly beat the egg whites in a bowl. Dip each piece of fish in the egg white, then coat on all sides with flour. Set aside.

Heat the oil in a large skillet over medium heat. Add the celery, bell pepper, and onion. Sauté 10 minutes, then add the tomatoes, tomato sauce, wine, garlic, oregano, thyme, cumin, and pepper. Gently place the catfish pieces into the tomato mixture, making sure they do not touch each other. Cover, reduce heat to medium-low, and cook 25 minutes.

Meanwhile, bring 2 cups of water to a boil in a saucepan over high heat. Stir in the rice, return to a boil, cover, reduce heat to very low, and cook 25 minutes. Place a serving of rice on each plate and spoon the dumplings and their sauce on top. Serve immediately.

Recommended companion dishes: Seasoned Black Beans (page 50), steamed corn on the cob (see page 64), and Cornbread (page 57)

Each serving provides:

548	Calories	0.3 g	Omega-3
27 g	Protein	8 g	Fat
87 g	Carbohydrate		13% of calories from fat
162 mg	Sodium		1 g saturated fat
42 mg	Cholesterol		1 g polyunsaturated fat
			4 g monounsaturated fat

Shrimp Curry with Pimiento Stuffed Olives

ALMOST INSTANT

In this recipe we use the individual curry spices to achieve the intense flavor found in traditional curry dishes. The sauce is quite thin so the rice can readily absorb it.

Yield: 4 servings

Basmati rice, uncooked	1	cup
Ground cumin	1	teaspoon
Ground turmeric	1	teaspoon
Ground coriander	½	teaspoon
Cayenne	¼	teaspoon
Salt	¼	teaspoon
Peeled and deveined raw shrimp°	¾	pound
Unsalted butter	1	tablespoon
Dry sherry	2	tablespoons
Red bell pepper	½	medium, chopped
Green onions	4,	minced
Garlic	2	cloves, minced
Fresh ginger, grated	1	teaspoon
Nonfat plain yogurt	2	cups
Pimiento stuffed olives, sliced	¼	cup
Lemon wedges	1	per serving

°If you purchase unpeeled raw shrimp or prawns, break away the shells and cut a shallow slit along the back so you can remove the dark vein.

Bring 2 cups of water to a boil in a saucepan over high heat. Stir in the rice, return to a boil, cover, reduce heat to very low, and cook 25 minutes.

Meanwhile, in a small bowl, stir together the cumin, turmeric, coriander, cayenne, and salt. Set aside. Rinse the shrimp and pat dry. Slice in half lengthwise. Set aside in the refrigerator. Melt the butter in a large skillet over medium heat. Add the sherry, bell pepper, green onions, and garlic. Cook 4 minutes, then stir in the spices and ginger. Cook for a minute, then add the yogurt and stir to incorporate. Heat through for 2 to 3 minutes, until hot, but do not allow it to boil. Gently fold in the shrimp. Cook 3 minutes longer, until all the shrimp are bright pink. Mound the hot rice on warmed serving plates and top with the shrimp curry. Sprinkle the olives over the top and serve immediately along with the lemon wedges.

***Recommended companion dishes:* Mango Chutney (see page 42), raisins, and roasted peanuts as condiments; steamed broccoli (see page 64); and Middle East Salad (page 72)**

Each serving provides:

378	Calories	0.4 g	Omega-3
28 g	Protein	5 g	Fat
52 g	Carbohydrate		13% of calories from fat
393 mg	Sodium		2 g saturated fat
140 mg	Cholesterol		1 g polyunsaturated fat
			1 g monounsaturated fat

Seafood Paella with Dried Tomato and Mango

Paella is the national dish of Spain. This version is a wonderful inter-play of mellow and spicy flavors showy enough for a very special occasion. A round, broad pan made especially for cooking paella yields the best results—you will need one at least 14 inches across and 2 inches deep to accommodate this recipe. You may substitute a skillet or dutch oven if you have one large enough. Ripe mangos are mostly orange or red, with no green, and they yield gently to pres-sure, like a ripe avocado. If necessary, ripen one at room temperature for a few days before making the paella.

Yield: 8 servings

Dried tomato, minced	¼	cup
Cod fillets	1	pound
Peeled and deveined raw shrimp°	1	pound
Squid tubes	½	pound
Live mussels in their shells	¾	pound
Saffron threads	1	teaspoon
Vegetable broth cube	1	large
Clam juice	2	8-ounce bottles
Olive oil	2	tablespoons
Yellow onions	2	large
Red bell peppers	2	large
Garlic	6	cloves, minced
Paprika	1½	teaspoons
Rubbed sage	1½	teaspoons

°If you purchase unpeeled raw shrimp or prawns, break away the shells and cut a shallow slit along the back so you can remove the dark vein.

Cayenne	⅛ teaspoon
Arborio rice	2½ cups
Mango, peeled and diced	
small	1 medium

Reconstitute the tomatoes if they are too dry to mince (see page 37). Rinse the cod and pat dry. Trim off any skin and remove any bones, using tweezers or pliers, if necessary. Cut into bite-size chunks. Rinse the shrimp and squid and pat dry. Set the cod, shrimp, and squid aside in the refrigerator on a plate loosely covered with a damp cloth or paper towel. Scrub the mussels carefully and tug gently at the beard with your fingers or pliers to remove it. Any mussels that are not tightly closed after scrubbing should be discarded. Also discard any mussels with cracked or broken shells. Put the mussels in a bowl in the refrigerator, loosely covered with a damp cloth or paper towel.

Combine the saffron threads with ¼ cup hot water and set aside. In a bowl, dissolve the vegetable broth cube in 3½ cups hot water and stir in the clam juice. Keep handy near the stove.

Preheat the oven to 375 degrees F. In the paella pan, heat the olive oil over medium heat. Add the onions, peppers, dried tomato, and garlic and sauté until beginning to soften, about 5 minutes. Stir in the saffron with its soaking liquid, paprika, sage, and cayenne. Stir the rice into the pan and sauté 5 minutes. Add the hot broth and stir to combine. Bring to a simmer over high heat, reduce heat to medium, and simmer 5 minutes without stirring the contents of the pan. Add the shrimp, cod, and squid, distributing evenly in the pan, pressing down to immerse among the rice grains. Do not stir or disturb the rice any more than necessary—you want all the rice to remain immersed.

Transfer to the oven and bake, uncovered, 15 minutes. Remove from the oven and add the mussels, pressing hinge side down into the rice. Distribute the mango evenly over the top. Bake, uncovered, 8 to 10 minutes, until the mussels have popped open and the rice is tender. Remove from the oven and cover with a clean tea towel. Allow to stand 5 to 10 minutes before transferring the hot pan to a trivet on the table.

Recommended companion dishes: **Basil Balsamic Salad (page 67), crusty bread or rolls, and fruity red wine**

Each serving provides:

399	Calories	0.5 g	Omega-3
23 g	Protein	6 g	Fat
62 g	Carbohydrate		13% of calories from fat
382 mg	Sodium		1 g saturated fat
158 mg	Cholesterol		1 g polyunsaturated fat
			3 g monounsaturated fat

The Best 125 Lowfat Fish and Seafood Dishes

Seafood Pasta

Pasta used to be thought of only as Italian food. Now, it has taken hold in mainstream America, appearing on the menus of all types of restaurants, often with nontraditional sauces. Anyone who eats out knows that fish and seafood are also popular restaurant offerings. Pair the two and you have a hot combination, indeed.

We have developed an extensive repertoire of seafood pasta dishes to satisfy this craving. The recipes range from classics such as Pasta with Clams, White Wine, and Mushrooms to innovations like Prawns and Pasta with Lemon Caviar Cream. We've also included our favorite quick-to-prepare stuffed pasta inventions.

All are delicious, low in fat, easy to make, and economical. Inexpensive dried pasta is just as delicious and lower in fat than the more expensive fresh pasta varieties, often made with eggs, now available in many supermarkets. In addition, a small amount of seafood goes a long way in a pasta dish.

There are so many good reasons to enjoy seafood pasta that we think you'll make these dishes often, for casual family dining and elegant dinner parties.

Tools . . .

- 10- to 12-quart stockpot with a tight-fitting lid.
- Large stainless steel or enameled colander for draining pasta.
- Long-handled wooden spoon for stirring the pot.
- Tongs, pasta claw, or long-handled wooden forks and/or spoons for serving.
- Large bowl for serving family-style pasta.
- Shallow individual serving bowls are a nice alternative to plates.

. . . and Tips

- Our seafood pastas specify cooking the pasta until "al dente." This Italian phrase means "to the tooth" and suggests that the tooth should meet a little resistance when biting into the pasta. Undercooked pasta has a tough center and an unpleasant starchy taste. Cooked too long, noodles break apart easily and turn to mush in the mouth. If using dried pasta, the package will give you the approximate cooking time. Set your timer for just a couple of minutes less than is recommended, so you can pull out a noodle and bite into it to test for doneness.

- Use plenty of water (about 8 quarts per pound of pasta), keep the heat on high so pasta cooks at a good rolling boil, and stir the pot occasionally so the pasta doesn't stick to the bottom.

- Drain cooked pasta immediately in a large colander, shaking to remove as much water as possible so it won't dilute the sauce. Toss immediately with the hot sauce. If you must hold the cooked pasta for a few minutes while you finish the sauce, toss with a bit of olive oil and return to the still hot, but dry, pasta cooking pot. Cover and set in a warm spot until needed.

- Use warmed serving bowls or plates so pasta stays hot as long as possible.

- If your finished pasta dish sits a bit too long before serving and turns sticky, toss in a little hot water, a tablespoon at a time, until desired consistency is achieved.

Pasta with Clams, White Wine, and Mushrooms

ALMOST INSTANT

This is likely to become an old standard for you, as it has for us. The ingredients are inexpensive, the preparation time is short, and the results are delicious.

Yield: 4 servings

Red bell pepper	½	medium, minced
Yellow onion	½	medium, diced
Garlic	2	cloves, minced
Mushrooms	½	pound, sliced
Salt	⅛	teaspoon
Cayenne		A pinch
Canned minced clams	2	6½-ounce cans
Dry white wine	1	cup
Fresh parsley, minced	½	cup
Dry sherry	2	tablespoons
Unbleached flour	2	tablespoons
Dried spaghettini	12	ounces
Parmesan cheese, finely grated	¼	cup
Lemon wedges	1	per person

In a stockpot, bring several quarts of water to a boil for the pasta. Meanwhile, put bell pepper, onion, and garlic in a large skillet with ¼ cup water. Bring to the steaming stage over medium heat and stir and sauté for 3 minutes. Most of the liquid will evaporate. Stir in the mushrooms, salt, and cayenne, then add the juice from the canned clams and the white wine. Bring to a simmer, reduce heat, and cook, uncovered, 5 minutes. Stir in the clams, parsley, and sherry and bring back to a simmer. In a small jar with a tight-fitting lid, shake the flour with ¼ cup cold water until flour is dissolved. Pour into the sauce in a thin stream, whisking constantly. Cook and stir about 3 more minutes, until the sauce thickens.

Meanwhile, cook the pasta in the boiling water until al dente. Drain well and toss with the sauce in a warmed serving bowl. Serve very hot, passing the Parmesan and the lemon wedges.

Recommended companion dishes: **Roasted Garlic Bread (page 58) and Basil Balsamic Salad (page 67)**

Each serving provides:

515	Calories	0.2 g	Omega-3
24 g	Protein	6 g	Fat
77 g	Carbohydrate		9% of calories from fat
261 mg	Sodium		2 g saturated fat
62 mg	Cholesterol		1 g polyunsaturated fat
			1 g monounsaturated fat

Fusilli with Grilled Scallops in Sweet Red Pepper Sauce

The scallops take on a smoky flavor from the grill which gives this pasta dish its unique flavor. The presentation is spectacular—the red pepper sauce showcases the scallops in the center of the plate, with the noodles forming a border.

Yield: 4 servings

Red bell peppers	2	medium
Sea scallops	1	pound
Clam juice	1	8-ounce bottle
Dry white wine	¼	cup
Dried basil	1	teaspoon
Unsalted butter	2	tablespoons
Vermouth	2	tablespoons
Dried pasta spirals (fusilli)	8	ounces
Olive oil	2	teaspoons

Soak about 12 wooden skewers in water for 30 minutes. Preheat a coal or gas grill to medium-high (see page 340).

Place the peppers on the grill and roast for about 5 minutes until the skin is black. Turn and roast the other sides. Remove to a paper bag, fold over to seal, and allow to cool for 15 minutes.

Meanwhile, in a stockpot, bring several quarts of water to a boil for the pasta. Rinse the scallops and drain. For easy turning, thread two parallel skewers through each scallop, leaving about ½ inch of space between the scallops. You should be able to fit four or five scallops on each pair of skewers. Place the skewered scallops on a platter and refrigerate.

When the pepper is cool enough to handle, remove the skin and seeds. Chop coarsely and place in a food processor or blender; puree until smooth. Add the clam juice, wine, and basil, and puree. Transfer to a medium skillet and bring to a simmer over medium heat. Simmer 15 minutes, stirring occasionally, to reduce by one-fourth. Stir in the butter and vermouth during the last 2 minutes.

Meanwhile, cook the pasta until al dente. Drain well and transfer to a warm serving bowl and toss with the olive oil. While the pasta is cooking, place the scallops on the grill and cook 3 minutes. Turn and cook about 2 minutes longer, until scallops are opaque all the way through. Evenly distribute the red pepper sauce on warmed serving plates and place the scallops on top of the sauce. Arrange the pasta around the outer rim of the plates and serve immediately.

Recommended companion dishes: steamed green beans (see page 64), Roasted Garlic Bread (page 58), and Honey Mustard Salad (page 76)

Each serving provides:

369	Calories	0.2 g	Omega-3
28 g	Protein	7 g	Fat
46 g	Carbohydrate		15% of calories from fat
330 mg	Sodium		2 g saturated fat
94 mg	Cholesterol		2 g polyunsaturated fat
			2 g monounsaturated fat

Fettuccine with Basil Pesto and Grilled Orange Roughy

ALMOST INSTANT

This dish tastes rich and succulent. It will soon become one of your favorite Almost Instant Italian specialties.

Yield: 4 servings

Pine nuts	2	**tablespoons**
Orange roughy fillets	1	**pound**
Dried fettuccine	8	**ounces**
Plain nonfat yogurt	½	**cup**
Basil Pesto (see page 41)	3	**tablespoons**
Dry white wine	2	**cups**
Garlic	2	**cloves, minced**

In a stockpot, bring several quarts of water to a boil for the pasta. Toast the pine nuts (see page 34).

Rinse the fish and pat dry. Preheat the broiler for 5 minutes. Broil the fish 4 inches from the flame 4 minutes. Turn and continue to cook 3 minutes, depending on the thickness of the fish. Fish is done when mostly opaque but still barely translucent at the very center. Remove from the broiler and set aside. When just cool enough to handle, cut into bite-size pieces and cover with foil to keep warm.

Cook the pasta in the boiling water until al dente. Meanwhile, just before pasta is done, combine the yogurt, pesto, wine, and garlic in a small saucepan and heat through. Drain the pasta well and place in a warmed serving bowl. Toss with the sauce and arrange the fish on top. Sprinkle with the pine nuts and serve immediately.

Recommended companion dishes: Basil Balsamic Salad (page 67) and Roasted Garlic Bread (page 58)

Each serving provides:

506	Calories	0.02 g	Omega-3
28 g	Protein	8 g	Fat
45 g	Carbohydrate		17% of calories from fat
142 mg	Sodium		1 g saturated fat
78 mg	Cholesterol		2 g polyunsaturated fat
			5 g monounsaturated fat

Linguine with Tomatoes, Olives, and Anchovy Bread Crumb Topping

ALMOST INSTANT

This is an unusual and addictive dish. The flavor of the anchovies is completely undetectable in the finished dish, but they add a wonderful and mysterious rich flavor to the topping. In Italy, this would almost certainly be served with grated Parmesan or Pecorino Romano cheese, but we find it quite delicious without it.

Yield: 4 servings

Sourdough French bread, slightly stale	2	ounces
Fresh parsley, minced	¼	cup
Olive oil	2	tablespoons
Garlic	3	cloves, minced
Canned anchovy fillets	5	
Dried red chili flakes	¼	teaspoon
Fresh pear tomatoes	1	pound
Dried oregano	1	teaspoon
Salt		A pinch
Calamata olives, coarsely chopped	¼	cup
Balsamic vinegar	2	tablespoons
Dried linguine	12	ounces

In a stockpot, bring several quarts of water to a boil for the pasta. Meanwhile, tear the bread into large chunks and process with the parsley in a food processor to a coarse crumb consistency. Heat the olive oil over medium-low heat in a small cast-iron skillet. Add the garlic, anchovies, and chili flakes and stir constantly as you break the anchovies up with a wooden spoon. Within a few minutes, the anchovies will have incorporated into the oil. Add the bread crumb mixture and stir constantly for about five minutes, as the bread crumbs dry and crisp. It is all right for the crumbs to brown considerably, but be careful not to let them burn. If they start to blacken, remove the pan from the heat, and when cooled off, return to the stove over lower heat. When crumbs are crisp and browned, set them aside in a bowl.

Drop the tomatoes into the boiling water and blanch, peel, and seed them (see page 35), then return the water to a boil for the pasta. Coarsely chop the tomatoes and place in a skillet over medium heat with the oregano and salt. Bring to a simmer and cook just long enough for the tomatoes to release most of their juices—no longer than 5 minutes. Remove from the heat and stir in the olives and vinegar.

Meanwhile, cook the pasta until al dente. Drain well and toss with the tomato sauce in a warmed serving dish. Top with the crumb mixture and serve hot.

Recommended companion dishes: **steamed carrots (see page 64) and Basil Balsamic Salad (page 67)**

Each serving provides:

500	Calories	0.1 g	Omega-3
16 g	Protein	15 g	Fat
77 g	Carbohydrate		26% of calories from fat
625 mg	Sodium		2 g saturated fat
85 mg	Cholesterol		2 g polyunsaturated fat
			9 g monounsaturated fat

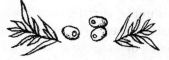

Mussels in Orange Basil
Tomato Sauce and Linguine

Inexpensive mussels are succulent and flavorful if prepared properly. For this recipe, we remove the meat from most of the steamed mussels, but save a few in their shells for a more dramatic presentation.

Yield: 4 servings

Low-sodium crushed tomatoes	1	**28-ounce can**
Fresh-squeezed orange juice	½	**cup**
Dry sherry	¼	**cup**
Dried basil	1	**tablespoon**
Fresh orange peel, minced	1	**heaping teaspoon**
Garlic	2	**cloves, minced**
Salt	¼	**teaspoon**
Pepper		**Several grinds**
Bay leaves	2	
Peppercorns	1	**teaspoon**
Fresh orange	2	**slices**
Live mussels in their shells	2	**pounds**
Dried linguine	12	**ounces**

In a medium saucepan, combine the tomatoes, orange juice, sherry, basil, orange peel, garlic, salt, and pepper. Bring to a simmer over medium-high heat, then reduce heat to low, cover, and simmer 30 minutes, stirring occasionally. In a stockpot, bring several quarts of water to a boil for the pasta.

Bring four cups of water to a boil in a large pot with the bay leaves, peppercorns, and orange slices. Meanwhile, carefully scrub the shells of the mussels. Gently tug at the beard with your fingers or pliers to remove it. Any mussels that are not tightly closed after scrubbing should be discarded. Also discard any mussels with cracked or broken shells. Place the cleaned mussels in the boiling orange water, cover, and cook 2 to 3 minutes. Mussels will pop open when done. Discard any mussels that do not open. When the mussels are cooked, reserve 8 in their shells. Scoop the meat from the remaining shells and stir into the tomato sauce, along with ¼ cup of the mussel cooking liquid. (Strain the remainder of the cooking liquid and save in the refrigerator for another use, such as soup stock or broth for risotto.) Cook the sauce another minute or two, to just heat through.

Meanwhile, cook the pasta until al dente. Drain well and toss with the hot sauce. Portion out into 4 warmed shallow bowls, and garnish each portion with 2 mussels in their shells and a thin strip of orange peel, if you wish.

Recommended companion dishes: **Roasted Garlic Bread (page 58) and Honey Mustard Salad (page 76)**

Each serving provides:

467	Calories	0.4 g	Omega-3
24 g	Protein	6 g	Fat
77 g	Carbohydrate		12% of calories from fat
418 mg	Sodium		1 g saturated fat
105 mg	Cholesterol		2 g polyunsaturated fat
			2 g monounsaturated fat

Linguine with Scallops and Oregano Tomato Coulis

ALMOST INSTANT

The dried tomatoes add a wonderful intense flavor, which infuses the scallops as they cook in this delicious sauce.

Yield: 4 servings

Dried tomatoes, minced	3	tablespoons
Sea scallops	¾	pound
Olive oil	1	tablespoon
Dry sherry	1	tablespoon
Garlic	2	cloves, minced
Green onions	4,	minced
Dried oregano	2	teaspoons
Low-sodium chopped tomatoes	1	28-ounce can
Dried linguine	8	ounces

Reconstitute the tomatoes if they are too dry to mince (see page 37). In a stockpot, bring several quarts of water to boil for the pasta.

Meanwhile, rinse the scallops and slice them crosswise to create ¼-inch disks. Pat dry and set aside in the refrigerator. Heat the oil and sherry in a large skillet over medium heat and add the garlic, onions, and oregano. Sauté 1 minute, then add the canned tomatoes along with their juice. Stir in the dried tomatoes and simmer 15 minutes over medium-high heat, until the sauce reduces to a thick consistency. Add the scallops, lower the heat to medium, and continue to cook 5 minutes.

Meanwhile, cook the pasta in the boiling water until al dente. Drain and divide among warmed shallow serving bowls. Top with the tomato coulis and serve immediately.

Recommended companion dishes: **Basil Balsamic Salad (page 67) and sweet French bread**

Each serving provides:

407	Calories	0.2 g	Omega-3
23 g	Protein	5 g	Fat
65 g	Carbohydrate		11% of calories from fat
159 mg	Sodium		0.7 g saturated fat
24 mg	Cholesterol		1 g polyunsaturated fat
			3 g monounsaturated fat

---

dfish and Calamata Olives Rigatoni

ALMOST INSTANT

This dish combines many flavors of the Mediterranean. It is simple to prepare and delicious and will appear on your table often.

Yield: 4 servings

Swordfish steak	½	pound
Olive oil	1	tablespoon plus ½ teaspoon
Fresh pear tomatoes	1	pound
Garlic	3	cloves, minced
Yellow onion	½	medium, diced
Green bell pepper	½	medium, chopped
Calamata olives, chopped	¼	cup, loosely packed
Capers, drained and minced	2	tablespoons
Fresh oregano leaves, minced	1	tablespoon
Dried rigatoni	10	ounces
Reduced-fat feta cheese, crumbled	2	ounces (½ cup)

In a stockpot, bring several quarts of water to a boil for the pasta. Meanwhile, rinse the fish and pat dry. Lightly oil both sides of the fish with ½ teaspoon of the olive oil. Preheat the broiler for 5 minutes; broil the fish 4 inches from the heat for 3 minutes. Turn and cook about 4 more minutes, depending on the thickness of the fish. Fish is done when mostly opaque but still barely translucent at the very center. Remove any skin and bones and slice the fish into strips. Cover with foil and set aside in a warm place.

Without peeling them, coarsely chop the tomatoes. Place the remaining 1 tablespoon of oil in a skillet and add the garlic, onion, and bell pepper. Sauté over medium heat for 2 minutes, then add the tomatoes, olives, capers, and oregano. Increase heat to medium-high and simmer to reduce the tomato liquid to a thick sauce consistency, about 5 minutes.

Meanwhile, cook the pasta in the boiling water until al dente. Drain well and distribute among warmed shallow serving bowls. Arrange the cooked fish over the pasta and top with the sauce. Sprinkle with the feta cheese and serve at once.

Recommended companion dishes: **Basil Balsamic Salad (page 67) and steamed green beans (see page 64)**

Each serving provides:

482	Calories	0.4 g	Omega-3
25 g	Protein	16 g	Fat
61 g	Carbohydrate		29% of calories from fat
575 mg	Sodium		4 g saturated fat
102 mg	Cholesterol		2 g polyunsaturated fat
			8 g monounsaturated fat

Prawns and Pasta with Lemon Caviar Cream

ALMOST INSTANT

This spectacular dish is fit for your most elegant dinner party. It is beautiful as well as delectable—particularly if you follow our suggestion and use a green spinach pasta. Best of all, it's quite simple to prepare.

Yield: 6 servings

Light sour cream	¾	cup
Fresh-squeezed lemon juice	1	teaspoon
Dijon mustard	1	teaspoon
Lemon zest	½	teaspoon
Green onions	4,	minced
Pepper		Several grinds
Golden lumpfish caviar	2	ounces
Dried spinach fettuccine	12	ounces
Shelled peas, fresh or frozen	1	cup
Peeled and deveined raw prawns*	¾	pound
Dry white wine	½	cup
Garlic	2	cloves, minced
Lemon wedges	1	per serving

In a stockpot, bring several quarts of water to a boil for the pasta. Meanwhile, stir together the sour cream, lemon juice, mustard, lemon zest, green onions, and pepper until well combined. Stir in the caviar, reserving 2 tablespoons, and set aside in a warm place.

*If you purchase unpeeled raw shrimp or prawns, break away the shells and cut a shallow slit along the back so you can remove the dark vein.

Cook the pasta in the boiling water until al dente, adding the peas for the last 2 minutes of cooking time. Meanwhile, combine the prawns with the white wine and garlic in a sauté pan over medium heat. When liquid begins to steam, stir and sauté for 2 to 3 minutes, until all the prawns have turned bright pink.

Drain the pasta and peas well. Toss the prawns and their pan juices with the cooked pasta in a warmed serving bowl, then toss with the sauce. Sprinkle the reserved caviar over the top and grind on some black pepper. Serve immediately, with a lemon wedge at each plate.

***Recommended companion dishes:* bread sticks and Honey Mustard Salad (page 76)**

Each serving provides:

317	Calories	0.3 g	Omega-3
22 g	Protein	7 g	Fat
37 g	Carbohydrate		21% of calories from fat
145 mg	Sodium		3 g saturated fat
135 mg	Cholesterol		1 g polyunsaturated fat
			1 g monounsaturated fat

reamy Crab and Tarragon Fettuccine

ALMOST INSTANT

When you hunger for a rich, creamy-tasting meal, turn to this recipe. The fat content is very reasonable, so enjoy it guiltlessly. Tarragon adds a delightful sweetness to the sauce.

Yield: 4 servings

"No Yolks" egg noodles	8	ounces
Dry sherry	2	tablespoons
Garlic	3	cloves, minced
Red bell pepper	½	medium, minced
Unsalted butter	2	teaspoons
Unbleached flour	2	teaspoons
Lowfat milk	½	cup
Light sour cream	½	cup
Dried tarragon	½	teaspoon
Crab meat*	8	ounces (about 1½ cups)

In a stockpot, bring several quarts of water to a boil for the pasta. Assemble the ingredients, but do not begin the sauce until the pasta is added to the water. When water comes to a boil, cook the pasta until al dente. Meanwhile, put the sherry in a large skillet over medium heat. Add the garlic and bell pepper and sauté for 2 minutes. Push the vegetables to the edges of the pan and place the butter in the center to melt. Stir the flour into

---

*If purchasing cooked whole crab, ask for 2 pounds of crab. Have your fish-monger crack and clean it. Pick all the meat from the shell, being careful to discard all the bits of shell and cartilage. If using canned lump crab meat, rinse and drain well before using.

the butter and cook for a minute, then gradually add the milk, stirring to incorporate the other ingredients as it thickens. Stir in the sour cream, tarragon, and crab. Heat through for 2 to 3 minutes. Drain the pasta well, and distribute it among warmed shallow serving bowls. Top with the sauce and serve immediately.

Recommended companion dishes: **Honey Mustard Salad (page 76), steamed asparagus (see page 64), and Roasted Garlic Bread (page 58)**

Each serving provides:

320	Calories	0.2 g	Omega-3
17 g	Protein	7 g	Fat
38 g	Carbohydrate		21% of calories from fat
187 mg	Sodium		3 g saturated fat
45 mg	Cholesterol		1 g polyunsaturated fat
			1 g monounsaturated fat

mon, Capers, and Basil
with Angel Hair Pasta

ALMOST INSTANT

This dish is a delicate combination of flavors, a perfect match for the angel hair pasta.

Yield: 4 servings

Salmon fillet	½	pound
Unsalted butter	2	tablespoons
Unbleached flour	2	tablespoons
Nonfat milk	1¼	cups
Dry white wine	¼	cup
Fresh basil leaves, minced	2	tablespoons
Capers, drained and minced	2	tablespoons
Dried angel hair pasta	12	ounces

In a stockpot, bring several quarts of water to boil for the pasta. Meanwhile, preheat the broiler 5 minutes. Rinse the salmon, pat it dry, and broil 4 inches from the flame 4 minutes, then turn and cook about 3 minutes longer, depending on its thickness. Fish is done when mostly opaque but still barely translucent at the very center. Remove from the broiler and set aside.

Melt the butter over medium-low heat in a large skillet and add the flour. Stir constantly for several seconds to cook the flour mixture slightly, then gradually whisk in the milk. Cook, whisking often, until mixture is slightly thickened, about 5 minutes. Add the wine, basil, and capers to the sauce. Flake the salmon into the sauce and stir. Heat through for a minute or two.

Meanwhile, cook the pasta in the boiling water until al dente. Drain well and distribute evenly among warmed shallow serving bowls. Top with the sauce and serve immediately.

***Recommended companion dishes:* Roasted Garlic Bread (page 58) and Honey Mustard Salad (page 76)**

Each serving provides:

489	Calories	0.6 g	Omega-3
26 g	Protein	9 g	Fat
71 g	Carbohydrate		18% of calories from fat
148 mg	Sodium		4 g saturated fat
47 mg	Cholesterol		2 g polyunsaturated fat
			3 g monounsaturated fat

Scallops, Mushrooms, and Tarragon Sauce over Noodles

ALMOST INSTANT

The tarragon flavor is infused into the mushrooms, with delicious results. The sauce has the consistency of heavy cream, but is actually made with lowfat milk. Another healthy indulgence.

Yield: 4 servings

Sea scallops	¾	pound
Dry white wine	1	cup
Fresh tarragon, minced	1	tablespoon
Small mushrooms	½	pound, quartered
Salt	¼	teaspoon
Pepper		Several grinds
"No Yolks" egg noodles	8	ounces
Unbleached flour	2	tablespoons
Lowfat milk	1	cup
Light sour cream	½	cup

In a stockpot, bring several quarts of water to a boil for the pasta. Rinse the scallops and slice them crosswise to create ¼-inch disks. Pat dry and set aside in the refrigerator.

In a large skillet over medium-high heat, combine the white wine, tarragon, mushrooms, salt, and pepper. Bring to a simmer and cook 10 minutes. The liquid should reduce by about half. Turn off the heat and remove the mushrooms with a slotted spoon. Set them aside in a warm spot.

Cook the pasta in the boiling water until al dente. Meanwhile, pour the mushroom liquid into a small jar that has a tight-fitting lid. Add the flour and shake vigorously until dissolved. Return to the skillet and cook over medium-low heat, stirring constantly, until a thick sauce develops. Gradually add the milk to the sauce, whisking with each addition to incorporate. Stir the sour cream into the sauce, then add the scallops and mushrooms and heat about 5 minutes, stirring frequently.

Drain the noodles and distribute evenly among warmed shallow serving bowls. Top with the scallops and mushroom sauce. Garnish with fresh tarragon, if you wish.

Recommended companion dishes: Basil Balsamic Salad (page 67) and Roasted Garlic Bread (page 58)

Each serving provides:

332	Calories	0.2 g	Omega-3
22 g	Protein	5 g	Fat
40 g	Carbohydrate		18% of calories from fat
302 mg	Sodium		1 g saturated fat
26 mg	Cholesterol		1 g polyunsaturated fat
			2 g monounsaturated fat

Broiled Swordfish and Vegetables with Smoked Cheese and Noodles

ALMOST INSTANT

The vegetables are slightly charred in the broiler, so they pair well with the flavor of smoked Gouda. You can play with the quantity of cayenne pepper to suit your taste. We enjoy the exotic crunch added by toasted pumpkin seeds, but the dish is also delicious without them.

Yield: 6 servings

Raw pumpkin seeds (optional)	2	tablespoons
Swordfish steak	¾	pound
Crookneck squash	2	medium
Red bell pepper	1	small
Yellow onion	1	medium
Nonfat milk	1½	cups
Unsalted butter	1	tablespoon
Garlic	3	cloves, minced
Chili powder	2	teaspoons
Unbleached flour	1	tablespoon
Smoked Gouda, grated	2	ounces (⅓ cup)
Fresh cilantro, minced	⅓	cup
Tomato paste	1	tablespoon
Salt	¼	teaspoon
Cayenne		To taste
"No Yolks" egg noodles	12	ounces
Balsamic vinegar	2	tablespoons

In a stockpot, bring several quarts of water to a boil for the pasta. Toast the pumpkin seeds (see page 34), mince, and set aside.

Preheat the broiler 5 minutes. Rinse the swordfish and pat dry. Trim the ends off the squashes and slice lengthwise into eighths. Cut the bell pepper lengthwise into 8 strips, discarding the stem and seeds. Peel the onion and cut crosswise into

½-inch-thick slices. Broil the fish and vegetables 4 inches from the heat 4 minutes. Turn everything and broil an additional 3 to 4 minutes, depending on the thickness of the fish. Fish is done when mostly opaque but still barely translucent at the very center. If the vegetables are not yet limp, remove the swordfish and continue broiling the vegetables, turning if necessary, until they are charred in spots and tender, but not overly soft (this should take no more than a few minutes longer). When fish is cool enough to handle, remove any skin and bones and break up into bite-size pieces. When vegetables are done, coarsely chop them and set aside with the fish in a warm spot, covered with foil.

Meanwhile, heat the milk until steaming in a small saucepan over low heat. Melt the butter in a medium saucepan over medium heat and sauté the garlic and chili powder for 1 minute, then add the flour and cook, stirring constantly, for 2 minutes. Whisk in the hot milk, then the cheese, cilantro, tomato paste, salt, and cayenne. Cook, whisking frequently, for about ten minutes, until smooth and slightly thickened.

Meanwhile, cook the noodles in the boiling water until al dente. Drain briefly and toss with the balsamic vinegar in a warmed serving bowl. Top the noodles with the fish, vegetables, and sauce and toss to combine well. If the dish is gummy, add two tablespoons or so of nonfat milk and toss again until smooth. Serve very hot, passing the toasted pumpkin seeds.

Recommended companion dish: **Southwest Salad (page 70)**

<hr>

Each serving provides:

352	Calories	0.4 g	Omega-3
23 g	Protein	9 g	Fat
46 g	Carbohydrate		23% of calories from fat
281 mg	Sodium		3 g saturated fat
32 mg	Cholesterol		1 g polyunsaturated fat
			2 g monounsaturated fat

<hr>

Smoked Salmon Ravioli
with Sherry Cream Sauce

*Wonton wrappers are available at most supermarkets in the produce
section. They are a real time saver for making ravioli, though you
may make fresh pasta dough, if you wish. We use a "light" French
version of feta cheese for this dish—look for it at your local market.
If it isn't available, request that your grocer stock it for you.*

Yield: 6 servings

Wonton wrappers	12	**ounces**
The filling		
Smoked salmon	3	**ounces**
Reduced-fat feta cheese, crumbled	4	**ounces (1 cup)**
Plain nonfat yogurt	¾	**cup**
Garlic	3	**cloves, minced**
Green onions	2,	**minced**
Pickled green peppercorns, drained	1	**teaspoon, minced**
The sauce		
Dry sherry	1	**tablespoon**
Green onion	1,	**minced**
Garlic	1	**clove, minced**
Light sour cream	½	**cup**

Bring the wonton wrappers to room temperature. Flake or
mince the salmon and set it aside. Place the feta, yogurt, garlic,
green onions, and peppercorns in a bowl and mix until well com-

bined. The mixture will be lumpy because of the cheese chunks. Gently fold in the salmon, mixing to incorporate.

Enlist a helper to assist in filling the ravioli. Have the filling, the wrappers, and a small bowl of water close at hand. Lay a wrapper flat on a plate and use your fingers to moisten all around the edges of the dough with water. Place a rounded teaspoon of filling in the center of the wrapper and top with another square. Pinch the edges together to seal tightly, pressing out the trapped air as you go. Wrap the filled ravioli in a lightly floured tea towel so they do not dry out. Allow to set up for 30 minutes to 1 hour.

In a stockpot, bring several quarts of water to a boil. Gently drop in the ravioli. Cook 4 minutes. Remove the cooked ravioli from the water with a slotted spoon and drain well.

Meanwhile, put the sherry in a small saucepan and add the onion and garlic. Cook over medium heat 1 minute, then stir in the sour cream. Cook for 1 to 2 minutes longer, to just heat through. Distribute the ravioli evenly among warmed, shallow serving bowls. Drizzle with the sauce and serve immediately.

***Recommended companion dishes:* Basil Balsamic Salad (page 67), steamed carrots (see page 64), and Roasted Garlic Bread (page 58)**

Each serving provides:

161	Calories	0.1 g	Omega-3
11 g	Protein	5 g	Fat
18 g	Carbohydrate		28% of calories from fat
367 mg	Sodium		1 g saturated fat
28 mg	Cholesterol		1 g polyunsaturated fat
			1 g monounsaturated fat

Steamed Shrimp Dumplings with Spicy Dipping Sauce

*You cannot make too many of these scrumptious shrimp wontons—
every last one will disappear. They can be served at room temperature as part of an appetizer buffet or hot with rice and stir-fried
vegetables as a dinner entrée.*

Yield: 6 servings

Wonton wrappers	1	**pound**
The sauce		
Sake	3	**tablespoons**
Dry sherry	2	**tablespoons**
Rice wine vinegar	2	**tablespoons**
Low-sodium soy sauce	1	**tablespoon**
Dark sesame oil	1	**teaspoon**
Chili oil	½	**teaspoon**
Garlic	1	**clove, minced**
The filling		
Peeled and deveined raw shrimp°	1	**pound**
Water chestnuts, finely minced	⅓	**cup**
Green onions	4,	**minced**
Dry sherry	2	**tablespoons**
Fresh ginger, grated	1	**tablespoon**
Garlic	3	**cloves, minced**
Low-sodium soy sauce	2	**teaspoons**
Dark sesame oil	1	**teaspoon**
Canola oil	1	**teaspoon**

°If you purchase unpeeled raw shrimp or prawns, break away the shells and
cut a shallow slit along the back so you can remove the dark vein.

Bring the wonton wrappers to room temperature. Meanwhile, whisk the dipping sauce ingredients together, and set aside at room temperature. Rinse the shrimp and pat dry. Use a very sharp knife to mince the shrimp meat finely, or mince in a food processor. Stir in the remaining ingredients, except the canola oil, until very well combined.

Meanwhile, enlist a helper to assist in making the wontons. Have the filling, the wrappers, and a small bowl of water close at hand. Lay a wrapper flat on a plate and place a rounded tea- spoon of filling in the center. Use your fingers to moisten the corners of the wrapper. Bring two opposite corners together and pinch tightly to seal. Bring the remaining two corners together and seal again to create a tight bundle.

Place a steaming rack over a couple of inches of boiling water in a large pot. Put half the canola oil in the palm of your hand and lightly rub half the dumplings with oil as you place them on the steaming rack. Steam for 12 minutes. Remove and keep warm. Repeat with the remaining dumplings. You may need to add a little more water to the pot—be sure to bring it to boiling before adding the dumplings. Serve immediately or refrigerate for several hours, but reheat or bring to room tem- perature before serving—they are not as tasty when cold. Por- tion out a small amount of dipping sauce to serve in a tiny bowl at each plate, or simply place the sauce in the center of the table where everyone can reach it.

Recommended companion dishes: **Steamed Brown Rice (page 46) and stir-fried vegetables**

Each serving provides:

220	Calories	0.4 g	Omega-3
19 g	Protein	5 g	Fat
22 g	Carbohydrate		21% of calories from fat
293 mg	Sodium		1 g saturated fat
141 mg	Cholesterol		2 g polyunsaturated fat
			1 g monounsaturated fat

Crab and Spinach Pasta Pillows with Roasted Red Bell Pepper Coulis

These stuffed pasta morsels with their bright red topping are delectable. You can find round potsticker wrappers in most large supermarkets—check the produce section or ask your grocer. You may make homemade pasta dough if you have the time. We also use a commercial variety of roasted red bell peppers here, though you may roast your own, if you wish.

Yield: 4 servings

Potsticker wrappers	14	**ounces**
The sauce		
Roasted red bell peppers	1	**cup**
Red onion, minced	¼	**cup**
Apple juice	2	**tablespoons**
Brandy	1½	**tablespoons**
Fresh dill, minced	1	**tablespoon**
Garlic	1	**clove, minced**
Dried red chili flakes	¼	**teaspoon**
Ground cloves	⅛	**teaspoon**
Salt	⅛	**teaspoon**

The filling

Fresh spinach	2	bunches (about 1½ pounds)
Crab meat*	5	ounces (about 1 cup)
Raw, unsalted walnut pieces	¼	cup, toasted and minced
Fresh dill, minced	1	tablespoon
Garlic	2	cloves, minced
Lemon zest	1	teaspoon
Salt	⅛	teaspoon
Pepper		Several grinds

Bring the potsticker wrappers to room temperature. Meanwhile, combine all sauce ingredients in a blender or food processor. Puree to a thick and smooth consistency. Set aside at room temperature so the flavors can blend.

Carefully wash the spinach and remove the thickest stems. Without drying them, pile the leaves into a stockpot. Cover and cook over medium heat 5 minutes, or until spinach wilts. Remove to a colander to drain. When cool enough to handle, squeeze as much water as possible from the spinach (you may want to save the juice for a soup stock). Finely chop the spinach. Chop the crab meat very fine and toss with the spinach and the remaining filling ingredients until well combined.

In a stockpot, bring several quarts of water to a boil for the pasta. Meanwhile, enlist a helper to assist in stuffing the pillows. Have the filling, the wrappers, and a small bowl of water close at hand. Lay a wrapper flat on a plate and use your fingers to moisten all around the edge of the dough with water. Place a rounded teaspoon of filling in the center of the wrapper and fold

*If purchasing cooked whole crab, ask for 1¾ pounds of crab. Have your fishmonger crack and clean it. Pick all the meat from the shell, being careful to discard all the bits of shell and cartilage. If using canned lump crab meat, rinse and drain well before using.

the wrapper over so the edges meet to create a half-moon shape. Pinch the edges together firmly to tightly seal the pillow.

Gently drop the pasta pillows into the boiling water and cook for 10 minutes, stirring occasionally. Meanwhile, warm the sauce in a small covered saucepan over low heat, or in a microwave. You want it hot, but don't let it simmer. Remove the cooked pasta pillows from the water with a slotted spoon and drain well. Distribute evenly among four warmed serving plates, arranging in a pinwheel pattern. Spoon equal portions of the sauce over the center of each plate, where the pillows meet. Garnish with a few fresh dill sprigs, if you have some. Serve very hot, or you may allow the pasta and sauce to cool to room temperature and serve as an appetizer.

Recommended companion dishes: Roasted Garlic Bread (page 58) and Buttermilk Cucumber Salad (page 68)

Each serving provides:

274	Calories	0 g	Omega-3
20 g	Protein	7 g	Fat
36 g	Carbohydrate		22% of calories from fat
666 mg	Sodium		1 g saturated fat
47 mg	Cholesterol		4 g polyunsaturated fat
			1 g monounsaturated fat

Sautés and Stir-Fry Dishes

This chapter presents our favorite seafood sautés and stir-fry dishes, which are all quick to prepare as well as delicious. Typically, some oil is used to prevent sticking and the ingredients are bound together in a light sauce. A simple grain side dish is the perfect accompaniment and brings the overall fat picture into balance.

Most of these recipes call for olive oil, with its characteristic fruity flavor. In our Asia-inspired dishes, however, we use dark sesame oil, pressed from toasted sesame seeds. It has a smoky flavor that pairs well with ginger, garlic, soy sauce, and other traditional seasonings.

Once you become familiar with this easy cooking method, you will enjoy creating your own favorite combinations of vegetables, seafood, and seasonings.

Tools . . .

- A large Chinese wok and/or heavy-bottomed skillet or sauté pan.
- Wooden and metal spoons and spatulas for stirring and tossing.
- Heavy-handled wire whisk for blending sauce ingredients.

. . . and Tips

- Dredging is a method whereby fish is immersed in flour or seasonings to lightly coat the surface. Larger pieces are more easily dredged on a plate. Small chunks of fish or shrimp are more easily dredged by tossing in a bag with the coating mixture.
- Stir-frying is best done in a large, round-bottomed, high-walled wok in which ingredients can be continually tossed as they cook over high heat.

- Sautés and stir-fry dishes usually begin with a little oil. Don't add ingredients until the oil is hot enough to sizzle a drop of water. Foods placed in unheated oil tend to absorb more of it.

- Transfer the food from the pan to a serving dish immediately when done, so it doesn't continue cooking.

Sautéed Sea Bass and Vegetables Niçoise

ALMOST INSTANT

This is a simple yet stunning dish. The anchovies lend an intense, mysterious flavor to the sauce. It is almost buttery in its richness.

Yield: 4 servings

Sea bass fillets	1	**pound**
Red potatoes	½	**pound**
Fresh green beans	¾	**pound**
Red bell pepper	1	**medium**
Dijon mustard	1	**tablespoon**
Garlic	3	**cloves, minced**
Canned anchovy fillets	2	
Dry white wine	½	**cup**
Capers, drained and minced	1	**tablespoon**
Pepper		**A few grinds**
Fresh parsley, minced	2	**tablespoons**

Rinse the fish and pat dry. Trim off any skin and remove any bones, using tweezers or pliers, if necessary. Chop coarsely into 2-inch pieces. Set aside in the refrigerator. Without peeling them, dice the potatoes into ½-inch cubes. Trim the ends from the green beans and cut into 1-inch pieces. Remove the seeds and stem from the bell pepper, and cut into thin 2-inch strips.

In a heavy-bottomed sauté pan or skillet over medium heat, combine the mustard, garlic, and anchovies, breaking up with a wooden spoon. Cook for 2 to 3 minutes, until anchovies have dissolved into the mustard. Add the potatoes and stir and sauté about 2 minutes, until they are well coated with the seasonings. Add the wine and ½ cup water and bring to a simmer. Add the green beans and bell pepper, cover, reduce heat to medium-low, and cook for 10 minutes, or until the potato is fork tender. Use a fork or wooden spoon to mash about half of the potato pieces—this will thicken the sauce. Stir in the sea bass, capers, and pepper. Replace the lid and cook 5 to 8 minutes, depending on the thickness of the fish. Fish is done when it is mostly opaque but still barely translucent at the very center. Stir in the parsley and serve very hot.

***Recommended companion dishes:* Mediterranean Pasta (page 52) and bread sticks**

Each serving provides:

210	Calories	0.7 g	Omega-3
25 g	Protein	3 g	Fat
17 g	Carbohydrate		12% of calories from fat
223 mg	Sodium		1 g saturated fat
48 mg	Cholesterol		1 g polyunsaturated fat
			1 g monounsaturated fat

Lobster Broccoli Stir-Fry with Ginger and Fermented Black Beans

ALMOST INSTANT

The pungent flavor of fermented black beans is unique and delicious. They are sold at Asian markets and sometimes in major super-markets. This Cantonese-style dish is an authentic representation of that region's cooking. For a true feast, serve this with the Steamed Shrimp Dumplings with Spicy Dipping Sauce (page 226) and—of course—steamed rice.

Yield: 4 servings

Dry sherry	⅓	**cup**
Fermented black beans, minced	3	**tablespoons**
Arrowroot powder or cornstarch	1½	**tablespoons**
Fresh ginger, grated	2	**teaspoons**
Dark sesame oil	2	**teaspoons**
Garlic	4	**cloves, minced**
Dried red chili flakes	½	**teaspoon**
Red or yellow bell pepper	1	**medium, sliced thin**
Fresh broccoli, chopped	4	**cups**
Green onions	4,	**in 1-inch pieces**
Lobster meat*	¾	**pound**

Stir together the sherry, black beans, arrowroot powder, and ginger and set aside. In a wok or large skillet, heat the oil over medium heat. Sauté the garlic and chili flakes 2 minutes, then add the bell pepper, broccoli, and green onions. Sauté, stirring frequently, 5 minutes. Add the lobster meat and stir well, then

*If purchasing lobster tails, ask for 1¼ pounds.

add ¾ cup water and cook about 3 minutes, stirring frequently, until simmering. Lobster meat should be opaque and broccoli fork tender. Stir the black bean mixture and add to the wok, stirring for a moment or two, just until the sauce thickens. Transfer to a warmed serving dish and serve immediately.

Recommended companion dishes: **Steamed Brown Rice (page 46) and Asian Salad (page 74)**

Each serving provides:

200	Calories	0.3 g	Omega-3
22 g	Protein	5 g	Fat
16 g	Carbohydrate		21% of calories from fat
649 mg	Sodium		1 g saturated fat
60 mg	Cholesterol		2 g polyunsaturated fat
			1 g monounsaturated fat

Sauté of Oysters, Mushrooms, and Sweet Red Pepper

ALMOST INSTANT

If you like oysters, this will become a favorite dish. It has a comfort food quality, and the serving size is generous.

Yield: 4 servings

Fresh oysters, shucked	1	10-ounce jar
Unsalted butter	1	tablespoon
Dry vermouth	4	tablespoons
Worcestershire sauce	1	teaspoon
Mushrooms	1	pound
Red bell pepper	1	medium, chopped
Yellow onion	1	medium, chopped
Dried thyme	½	teaspoon
Salt	¼	teaspoon
Pepper		Several grinds
Unbleached flour	2	tablespoons
Lowfat milk	½	cup
Fresh parsley, minced	¼	cup
Parmesan cheese, finely grated	3	tablespoons

Drain the oysters, reserving their liquid. Cut them in halves or thirds, depending on their size, to create bite-size pieces. Set aside. Melt the butter in a large sauté pan or skillet over medium-high heat. Add the vermouth, Worcestershire sauce, and oysters. Sauté, stirring occasionally, until the oysters' edges curl, about 3 minutes. Reduce heat to medium, remove the oysters with a slotted spoon, and set them aside in a warm spot.

Retain their cooking liquid in the pan and add the mushrooms, bell pepper, onion, thyme, salt, and pepper. Increase heat to medium-high, cover, and sauté 5 minutes. Remove the lid and cook for an additional 5 minutes, stirring frequently. Reduce heat to medium; spoon 3 tablespoons of the cooking liquid into a jar that has a tight-fitting lid. Add the reserved oyster liquid and the flour and shake vigorously to dissolve. Stir this into the skillet, then gradually add the milk, stirring constantly. Cook 5 minutes, until sauce thickens, then add the cooked oysters and parsley. Heat through. Serve immediately, passing the Parmesan.

***Recommended companion dishes:* Garlic Mashed Potatoes (page 56), steamed carrots (see page 64), and Buttermilk Cucumber Salad (page 68)**

Each serving provides:

196	Calories	0.5 g	Omega-3
14 g	Protein	7 g	Fat
19 g	Carbohydrate		31% of calories from fat°
253 mg	Sodium		3 g saturated fat
49 mg	Cholesterol		1 g polyunsaturated fat
			2 g monounsaturated fat

°Health experts recommend that we derive no more than 30 percent of our overall calories from fat. When served with our recommended companion dishes or on an otherwise lowfat day, this recipe fits the bill.

Sautéed Salmon with Asparagus and Fresh Dill

ALMOST INSTANT

Beautiful, aromatic, and delicious—this dish has all the prerequisites of a very special meal.

Yield: 6 servings

Red onion	½	medium
Red potatoes	2	medium (about ¾ pound)
Fresh asparagus	1	pound
Fresh-squeezed lemon juice	2	tablespoons
Salmon steaks	1	pound
Olive oil	1	tablespoon
Garlic	4	cloves, minced
Salt	¼	teaspoon
Pepper		A few grinds
Fresh dill, minced	¼	cup
Lemon wedges	1	per person

Cut the onion in half lengthwise and slice thinly. Scrub the potatoes and dice them; do not peel. Snap off and discard the tough stem ends of the asparagus and cut the stalks at a slant into 2-inch lengths. Heat ¾ cup water and the lemon juice to a boil in a skillet that has a tight-fitting lid. Rinse the salmon and place into the boiling water. Cover, reduce heat to low, and poach for 4 minutes, then turn, cover, and cook 3 to 5 minutes longer, depending on the thickness of the fish. Fish is done when mostly opaque but still barely translucent at the very center. Remove from the water and set aside on a tea towel.

Heat the olive oil in a large sauté pan or skillet over medium heat. Add the garlic and stir for a moment or two, then add the onion and potatoes and sauté 7 minutes, stirring frequently. Add the asparagus, salt, and pepper and sauté, stirring frequently, 7 minutes more, until asparagus is fork tender. Meanwhile, remove any skin and bones from the salmon and break up into bite-size pieces. Add to the skillet along with the fresh dill, toss to combine well, and heat through for one minute. Serve very hot, passing the lemon wedges.

Recommended companion dishes: **Steamed Basmati Rice (page 45) and raw cucumber sticks**

Each serving provides:

182	Calories	0.5 g	Omega-3
19 g	Protein	6 g	Fat
13 g	Carbohydrate		28% of calories from fat
140 mg	Sodium		1 g saturated fat
56 mg	Cholesterol		1 g polyunsaturated fat
			3 g monounsaturated fat

Prawn Scampi with Anise Liqueur

ALMOST INSTANT

The anise flavor is very refreshing in this dish. It is easy to prepare, yet a starring attraction!

Yield: 4 servings

Peeled and deveined raw prawns*	1	pound
Unbleached flour	2	tablespoons
Olive oil	1	tablespoon
Ouzo (or other Anise liqueur)	¼	cup
Anise seed	1	teaspoon, crushed
Green onions	3,	minced
Garlic	3	cloves, minced
Fresh-squeezed lemon juice	2	tablespoons
Dry white wine	¼	cup

Rinse the prawns and pat them dry. Put the flour into a paper bag, add the prawns, and shake to coat. Combine the oil and liqueur in a large sauté pan or skillet over medium-high heat. Add the anise seed, green onions, garlic, lemon juice, and wine

*If you purchase unpeeled raw shrimp or prawns, break away the shells and cut a shallow slit along the back so you can remove the dark vein.

and cook 3 minutes. Stir in the prawns and cook 2 to 4 minutes, stirring frequently, until they have all turned bright pink. Serve immediately.

Recommended companion dishes: **Steamed Basmati Rice (page 45), steamed cauliflower (see page 64), sweet French bread, and Buttermilk Cucumber Salad (page 68)**

Each serving provides:

193	Calories	0.6 g	Omega-3
24 g	Protein	5 g	Fat
7 g	Carbohydrate		26% of calories from fat
172 mg	Sodium		1 g saturated fat
175 mg	Cholesterol		1 g polyunsaturated fat
			3 g monounsaturated fat

Lobster Scampi with Basil Pesto and Fresh Lemon

ALMOST INSTANT

This dish maximizes the succulent flavor of lobster with pesto and lemon. Steamed rice is a necessary accompaniment for balancing the fat content of the meal. Quick to prepare, this is perfect for a spontaneous dinner party that will dazzle your guests.

Yield: 4 servings

Lobster meat*	¾	pound
Unbleached flour	2	tablespoons
Olive oil	1	tablespoon
White onion, diced	¼	cup
Garlic	2	cloves, minced
Dry white wine	⅓	cup
Basil pesto (see page 41)	3	tablespoons
Lemon wedges	1	per serving

Rinse the lobster meat, pat dry, and cut into bite-size pieces. Put the flour into a paper bag, add the lobster chunks, and shake to coat. Heat the olive oil in a large sauté pan or skillet over medium heat and add the onion and garlic. Sauté 2 minutes, stirring often, then stir in the wine. Increase the heat to

*If purchasing lobster tails, ask for 1¼ pounds.

medium-high, add the lobster, and cook 2 minutes, stirring frequently, until the lobster is opaque. Stir in the pesto, cook another minute to just heat through, and serve immediately with the lemon wedges.

Recommended companion dishes: Steamed Basmati Rice (page 45), sourdough French bread, and Basil Balsamic Salad (page 67)

Each serving provides:

179	Calories	0.3 g	Omega-3
16 g	Protein	8 g	Fat
7 g	Carbohydrate		41% of calories from fat*
172 mg	Sodium		1.5 g saturated fat
51 mg	Cholesterol		1 g polyunsaturated fat
			5 g monounsaturated fat

---

*Health experts recommend that we derive no more than 30 percent of our overall calories from fat. When served with our recommended companion dishes or on an otherwise lowfat day, this recipe fits the bill.

Stir-Fry of Scallops, Shiitake, Ginger, and Cilantro

ALMOST INSTANT

This colorful mélange utilizes fresh shiitake mushrooms, which are often available in gourmet produce markets. If you can't find shiitakes, you may substitute standard mushrooms for a different, but still delicious, variation. Miso is a fermented soybean paste available at natural food stores or Asian markets.

Yield: 4 servings

Sea scallops	1	pound
Green onions	4	
Carrots	½	pound
Snow peas	½	pound
Fresh shiitake mushrooms	¼	pound
Dark sesame oil	1	tablespoon
Dry sherry	2	tablespoons
Fresh-squeezed lemon juice	3	tablespoons
Garlic	2	cloves, minced
Fresh ginger, grated	1	tablespoon
White miso	1	tablespoon
Low-sodium soy sauce	1	teaspoon
Fresh cilantro, minced	¼	cup

Rinse the scallops, pat dry, and slice crosswise to create ¼-inch disks. Set aside in the refrigerator. Cut the green onions into 1-inch pieces, including some of the green portion. Peel the carrots and cut into julienne strips. String the snow peas and cut in half crosswise at a slant. Carefully wash and slice the mushrooms.

Place the oil, sherry, and lemon juice in a wok or large skillet over medium heat. Add the garlic and ginger, cook for

1 minute, then add the onions and carrots. Sauté 5 minutes, stirring frequently. Meanwhile, whisk 5 tablespoons of water with the miso and soy sauce, then stir into the pan. Add the snow peas and mushrooms, continue to stir and cook 5 minutes. Stir in the scallops and cook for about 4 minutes, until they are opaque. Stir in the cilantro and serve immediately.

Recommended companion dishes: Steamed Brown Rice (page 46), Asian Salad (page 74), and bread sticks

---

Each serving provides:

228	Calories	0.2 g	Omega-3
19 g	Protein	5 g	Fat
20 g	Carbohydrate		18% of calories from fat
282 mg	Sodium		1 g saturated fat
32 mg	Cholesterol		2 g polyunsaturated fat
			1 g monounsaturated fat

Shrimp and Snow Pea Stir-Fry in Ginger Peanut Sauce

ALMOST INSTANT

The peanut butter adds a distinctive rich touch to this pretty dish.
It comes together very quickly, so it is a good choice for a delicious
meal after a busy day.

Yield: 4 servings

Basmati rice, uncooked	1	**cup**
Mirin	2	**tablespoons**
Low-sodium soy sauce	1	**tablespoon**
Arrowroot powder or cornstarch	1	**tablespoon**
Creamy peanut butter	1	**tablespoon**
Fresh ginger, grated	2	**teaspoons**
Garlic	2	**cloves, minced**
Snow peas	½	**pound**
Fresh shiitake mushrooms	¼	**pound**
Green onions	4	
Dark sesame oil	1	**tablespoon**
Peeled deveined raw shrimp*	1	**pound**
Fresh cilantro, minced	¼	**cup**

In a medium saucepan, bring 2 cups water to a boil over high heat. Stir in the rice, reduce heat to low, cover, and cook 25 minutes.

Meanwhile, whisk ½ cup water with the mirin, soy sauce, and arrowroot powder, then whisk in the peanut butter, ginger,

---

*If you purchase unpeeled raw shrimp or prawns, break away the shells and cut a shallow slit along the back so you can remove the dark vein.

and garlic. Set aside. String the snow peas and cut in half cross-wise. Carefully wash the mushrooms and thickly slice them. Cut the green onions into 1-inch pieces, including some of the green tops. Heat the oil in a wok or large skillet over medium-high heat and add the peas, mushrooms, and onions. Cook for 4 minutes, stirring frequently. Add the ginger peanut sauce and the shrimp. Stir and cook 4 to 5 minutes until all the shrimp have turned bright pink. Stir in the cilantro. Divide the rice equally among warmed individual serving plates. Spoon the hot shrimp mixture over the top and serve immediately.

Recommended companion dishes: **Steamed Basmati Rice (page 45) and Asian Salad (page 74)**

Each serving provides:

229	Calories	0.6 g	Omega-3
26 g	Protein	7 g	Fat
12 g	Carbohydrate		30% of calories from fat
340 mg	Sodium		1 g saturated fat
172 mg	Cholesterol		2 g polyunsaturated fat
			2 g monounsaturated fat

Swordfish Stir-Fry with Feta and Tomatoes

ALMOST INSTANT

All the classic flavors of Greece come together in this delicious stir-fry. If your garden is overloaded with tomatoes, you may wish to use 1½ pounds—blanched, peeled, and seeded—in place of the canned variety.

Yield: 4 servings

Low-sodium pear tomatoes	1	**14½-ounce can**
Fresh green beans	½	**pound**
Swordfish steaks	1	**pound**
Garlic	3	**cloves, minced**
Pepper		**Several grinds**
Dried oregano	2	**teaspoons**
Calamata olives, chopped	¼	**cup**
Reduced-fat feta cheese, crumbled	2	**ounces (about ½ cup)**

Chop the canned tomatoes, retaining their juice. String the beans and cut into 1-inch pieces. Steam them for several minutes, until barely tender.

Rinse the fish and pat dry. Trim off any skin and remove any bones, using tweezers or pliers, if necessary. Cut into ¾-inch cubes and set aside in the refrigerator. In a wok or large skillet over medium heat, combine the tomatoes with their juice, green beans, garlic, pepper, and oregano. Increase heat to medium-high and cook 5 minutes, stirring frequently. Add the fish and cook 5 to 7 minutes, depending on the thickness of the fish. It is done when mostly opaque, but still barely translucent at the very center. Stir often. Stir in the olives and heat through. Transfer to a warmed serving dish and sprinkle the feta cheese evenly over the top. Serve hot.

Recommended companion dishes: steamed Brussels sprouts (see page 64) and Steamed Bulgur (page 49)

Each serving provides:

237	Calories	1 g	Omega-3
27 g	Protein	10 g	Fat
11 g	Carbohydrate		36% of calories from fat°
556 mg	Sodium		2 g saturated fat
44 mg	Cholesterol		2 g polyunsaturated fat
			4 g monounsaturated fat

°Health experts recommend that we derive no more than 30 percent of our overall calories from fat. When served with our recommended companion dishes or on an otherwise lowfat day, this recipe fits the bill.

Shark and Sweet
Red Pepper Fajitas

Marinating shark in a jalapeño, garlic, and citrus concoction trans-
forms its trademark firm texture to melt-in-your-mouth tenderness.
This easy dish is a real treat for those who like their food hot and
spicy!

Yield: 6 servings

Fresh-squeezed lime juice	3	**tablespoons**
Fresh-squeezed lemon juice	2	**tablespoons**
Garlic	3	**cloves, minced**
Pickled jalapeño, seeded		
and minced	2	**tablespoons**
Salt		**A pinch**
Fresh cilantro, minced	¼	**cup**
Shark steaks	1¼	**pounds**
Flour tortillas	12	
Olive oil	2	**tablespoons**
Mushrooms	½	**pound, coarsely chopped**
White onion	1	**large, thinly sliced**
Red and/or yellow bell peppers	2	**large, seeded and diced**
Salsa Fresca (see page 40)	1½	**cups**

In a shallow dish, combine the lime and lemon juices with the
garlic, jalapeño, salt, and cilantro. Rinse the shark and pat dry.
Trim off any skin and remove any bones, using tweezers or pli-

ers, if necessary. Chop coarsely into 1-inch pieces. Stir the shark pieces into the juice mixture and set aside in the refrigerator for an hour or so.

Just before serving time, wrap the tortillas in a damp towel and place in a warm oven for 15 minutes or so. Heat the olive oil briefly in a heavy-bottomed sauté pan or skillet over medium-high heat. Add the mushrooms, onion, and bell peppers and sauté, stirring frequently, 10 minutes, until the vegetables are beginning to go limp. Add the shark and its marinade and stir and sauté 4 to 6 minutes, until the fish is mostly opaque but still barely translucent at the very center.

Immediately place the fish mixture in its skillet on the table, along with the warm tortillas and the salsa. Allow everyone to fill their own tortillas and top with salsa.

Recommended companion dishes: Seasoned Black Beans (page 50) and Spanish Rice (page 47)

Each serving provides:

408	Calories	1 g	Omega-3
28 g	Protein	13 g	Fat
46 g	Carbohydrate		29% of calories from fat
402 mg	Sodium		3 g saturated fat
48 mg	Cholesterol		3 g polyunsaturated fat
			7 g monounsaturated fat

Steamed, Poached, and Braised Dishes

Steaming, poaching, and braising are all moist-heat, stovetop cooking methods. They work well with quick-cooking fish and seafood and eliminate the risk of the fish drying out. No fat is added for steaming or poaching, and minimal fat is required in braised dishes. Poaching, in particular, is a favorite technique of ours because it requires no added fat or advance preparation, allowing us to put a healthy, delicious meal on the table in minutes.

Our recipes draw on various ethnic traditions for inspiration but are our own unique inventions. We think we've included something for every taste. Enjoy!

Tools . . .

- Large stockpot with a tight-fitting lid for steaming shellfish.
- Shallow skillet with a tight-fitting lid for poaching.
- Large saucepan or dutch oven with a tight-fitting lid for braising.
- Slotted spoons or large slotted spatula for removing fish from steaming or poaching liquid.

. . . and Tips

- Steaming and poaching utilize a considerable amount of liquid, sometimes with seasonings added, that can be saved for a day or two in the refrigerator, or frozen for longer periods, and reused as broth for soups or risotto.
- Poaching liquid should be hot when fish is added. Place the fish in the pan, add liquid to cover, then remove the fish while bringing the liquid to a boil.

Thyme and Dill Steamed Littleneck Clams

ALMOST INSTANT

Be sure to choose small clams that are tightly shut. If your fish-monger puts them in a plastic bag, transfer them to a bowl in the refrigerator, loosely covered with a damp cloth or paper towel. The clams need to breathe to stay alive. This recipe makes a delicious broth—serve a fresh, crusty bread to sop it up.

Yield: 4 servings

Dry white wine	1	**cup**
Fresh parsley, coarsely chopped	1	**cup**
Celery	2	**ribs, sliced**
Yellow onion	½	**medium, chopped**
Pimiento, chopped	1	**2-ounce jar**
Fresh dill, chopped	¼	**cup**
Unsalted butter	1	**tablespoon**
Dried thyme	1	**teaspoon**
Live littleneck clams in their shells	4	**pounds**

In a large stockpot, combine 6 cups of water with all of the ingredients except the clams. Cover, bring to a boil over high heat, reduce heat to medium-high, and simmer 10 minutes. Meanwhile, scrub the clams. Any clams that are not tightly closed after scrubbing should be discarded. Also discard any clams with cracked or broken shells. Place the scrubbed clams in a steamer rack. Lower them into the simmering pot, increase heat to high, cover tightly, and cook 3 to 5 minutes, until they have popped open. Discard any clams that have not opened. Transfer the clams to warmed shallow serving bowls. Strain the broth and pour ½ cup into each bowl. Reserve any remaining broth for another use, such as soup stock.

***Recommended companion dishes:* Honey Mustard Salad (page 76) and baguettes with muenster cheese**

Each serving provides:

267	Calories	0.4 g	Omega-3
32 g	Protein	6 g	Fat
11 g	Carbohydrate		20% of calories from fat
169 mg	Sodium		2 g saturated fat
90 mg	Cholesterol		1 g polyunsaturated fat
			1 g monounsaturated fat

Mussels in Spicy Tomatillo Sauce with Soft Cheese Polenta

The contrasts in texture, flavor, and color achieved in this dish are wonderful and surprising. Any supermarket with a well-stocked Mexican food section will have the canned tomatillos. If your grocer doesn't carry them, make a request.

Yield: 4 servings

Tomatillos, packed in water	2	14-ounce cans, drained
White onion, minced	¼	cup
Fresh cilantro, minced	¼	cup
Fresh-squeezed lime juice	1	tablespoon
Pickled jalapeño, seeded and minced	1	tablespoon
Garlic	2	cloves, minced
Salt	¼	teaspoon
Live mussels in their shells	1½	pounds
Low-sodium vegetable broth cube	½	large
Chili powder	1½	teaspoon
Granulated garlic	¼	teaspoon
Coarse cornmeal	1¼	cups
Part-skim ricotta cheese	½	cup

In a blender or food processor, combine the tomatillos with the onion, cilantro, lime juice, jalapeño, garlic, and salt and puree to a smooth consistency. Set aside.

Scrub the mussels and gently tug at the beard with your fingers or pliers to remove it. Any mussels that are not tightly closed after scrubbing should be discarded. Also discard any mussels with cracked or broken shells. Set cleaned mussels aside in the refrigerator in a bowl loosely covered with a damp cloth or paper towel.

Put the tomatillo sauce in a heavy-bottomed sauté pan or dutch oven that has a tight-fitting lid. Bring to a boil over medium-high heat, then reduce heat to very low, and simmer 15 minutes. Pile the mussels into the pot, and cover tightly. Cook 4 to 5 minutes, until most of the mussels have popped open. Remove the pot from the heat and discard any mussels that have not opened.

Meanwhile, bring 3 cups of water to a boil in a heavy-bottomed saucepan, along with the vegetable broth cube, chili powder, and granulated garlic. Reduce heat to medium-low and pour the cornmeal into the water in a slow, steady stream, whisking constantly. Continue to whisk until mixture begins to pull away from the sides of the pan, about 5 minutes. Add 1 cup cold water and whisk to incorporate. Bring back to a bubble, whisking frequently. When bubbling again, whisk constantly until mixture again begins to pull away from the sides of the pan. Whisk in an additional ½ cup cold water. When the mixture bubbles a third time, stir in the ricotta and remove from the heat to a warmed serving bowl. Spoon some soft polenta into each of 4 warmed shallow bowls. Divide the mussels in their shells evenly among the bowls, and spoon the tomatillo sauce over the polenta and into the mussel shells. Serve very hot, with plenty of napkins.

Recommended companion dishes: **Seasoned Black Beans (page 50) and Southwest Salad (page 70)**

Each serving provides:

341	Calories	0.5 g	Omega-3
23 g	Protein	6 g	Fat
48 g	Carbohydrate		16% of calories from fat
664 mg	Sodium		2 g saturated fat
41 mg	Cholesterol		1 g polyunsaturated fat
			2 g monounsaturated fat

Poached Red Snapper with
Dried Tomato and Ginger Sauce

ALMOST INSTANT

This dish is simple and quick to prepare. If you serve it with steamed couscous and a simple salad, you can put an impressive dinner on the table within a half hour.

Yield: 4 servings

Dried tomatoes, minced	**¼**	**cup**
Garlic	**2**	**cloves, minced**
Pepper		**Several grinds**
Red snapper fillets	**1**	**pound**
Nonfat milk	**½**	**cup**
Dry sherry	**2**	**tablespoons**
Fresh ginger, grated	**2**	**teaspoons**
Salt	**⅛**	**teaspoon**
Unbleached flour	**1½**	**tablespoons**
Green onions	**2,**	**minced**

Reconstitute the tomatoes if they are too tough to mince (see page 37). In a medium skillet over medium heat, bring ¾ cup water to a boil, along with the garlic and pepper. Meanwhile, rinse the fish and pat dry. Reduce heat to low and add the fish in a single layer. Cover and cook 3 minutes. Turn the fish over, replace the lid, and cook about 2 to 4 minutes longer, depending on the thickness of the fish. Fish is done when it is mostly opaque but still barely translucent at the very center. Remove from the liquid, drain well, cover with foil, and set aside in a warm spot.

Turn the heat under the skillet up to medium-high and simmer, whisking frequently, 5 minutes to reduce the liquid by about half. Whisk in the milk, tomatoes, sherry, ginger, and salt and bring back to a simmer. Meanwhile, in a small jar with a tight-fitting lid, vigorously shake the flour with ¼ cup water until dissolved. Pour this mixture in a thin stream into the skillet, whisking constantly. Cook and whisk about 3 minutes, until the sauce has thickened. Drain off any liquid that has accumulated on the fish platter, pour the sauce evenly over the fish, and sprinkle the green onions over the top. Serve very hot.

Recommended companion dishes: **Steamed Couscous (page 51) and Asian Salad (page 74)**

Each serving provides:

200	Calories	0.4 g	Omega-3
26 g	Protein	2 g	Fat
12 g	Carbohydrate		8% of calories from fat
178 mg	Sodium		0.4 g saturated fat
42 mg	Cholesterol		0.5 g polyunsaturated fat
			0.3 g monounsaturated fat

Salmon Poached in Champagne with Capers and Tarragon

ALMOST INSTANT

The champagne adds a unique hint of flavor; however, water or fish stock could be substituted. The recommended Mustard Tarragon Sauce really completes the dish, but you could substitute another favorite sauce.

Yield: 4 servings

Salmon fillets	1¼	pounds
Champagne	2	cups
Fresh-squeezed lemon juice	¼	cup
Yellow onion	½	medium, sliced
Capers	1	tablespoon
Fresh tarragon	4	5-inch sprigs
Pepper		Several grinds

Rinse the fillets and place in a shallow pan large enough to hold them in one layer. Add the champagne, lemon juice, and enough water to just cover the fillets. Remove the fish and bring poaching liquid to a boil. Lay the fish back in the pan in a single layer and top with the onion slices, capers, tarragon, and pepper. Reduce heat to low, cover, and simmer 4 to 6 minutes, depending on the thickness of the fish. Fish is done when mostly opaque but still barely translucent at the very center. Remove fish from the liquid, along with onions, capers, and tarragon. Drain well and serve immediately on warmed plates.

Recommended companion dishes: **Mustard Tarragon Sauce (page 62), Wild Rice Pilaf (page 48), and Basil Balsamic Salad (page 67)**

Each serving provides:

256	Calories	0.9 g	Omega-3
29 g	Protein	5 g	Fat
5 g	Carbohydrate		19% of calories from fat
102 mg	Sodium		1 g saturated fat
105 mg	Cholesterol		1 g polyunsaturated fat
			3 g monounsaturated fat

Halibut Poached with Sherry and Thyme

ALMOST INSTANT

This is a wonderfully easy main course. It pairs perfectly with the quick-to-prepare Yogurt Thyme Sauce (page 63), or use no sauce at all, if you prefer.

Yield: 4 servings

Halibut steaks	1¼	pounds
Dry sherry	½	cup
Fresh-squeezed lemon juice	¼	cup
Olive oil	1	tablespoon
Dried thyme	1	teaspoon
Yellow onion	½	cup, coarsely chopped
Celery	1	rib, thickly sliced
Garlic	2	cloves, sliced
Bay leaves	2	

Rinse the halibut and place in a shallow pan large enough to hold it in a single layer. Add the sherry, lemon juice, olive oil, and enough water to just cover the fish. Remove the fish and bring the poaching liquid to a boil. Add the thyme, onion, celery, garlic, and bay leaves to the poaching liquid and bring back to a boil over high heat. Lay the halibut back in the pan in a single layer. Cover the pan and return to a boil, reduce heat to low, and simmer for 3 to 5 minutes, depending on the thickness of the fish. Fish is done when it is mostly opaque but still barely translucent at the very center. Remove fish from the pan, draining well, and serve immediately.

Recommended companion dishes: **Yogurt Thyme Sauce (page 63), Steamed Couscous (page 51), and Honey Mustard Salad (page 76)**

Each serving provides:

236	Calories	0.5 g	Omega-3
30 g	Protein	6 g	Fat
5 g	Carbohydrate		26% of calories from fat
87 mg	Sodium		1 g saturated fat
45 mg	Cholesterol		1 g polyunsaturated fat
			3 g monounsaturated fat

Curried Poached Sole

ALMOST INSTANT

This dish fills the house with wonderful, exotic aromas, and you will be pleased by its fast and easy preparation. Make your companion dishes before you begin to cook the sole, since it comes together so quickly.

Yield: 4 servings

Sole fillets	1¼	**pounds**
Ground turmeric	½	**teaspoon**
Chili powder	½	**teaspoon**
Ground cumin	½	**teaspoon**
Ground cinnamon	⅛	**teaspoon**
Ground cloves		**A pinch**
Whole coriander	1	**teaspoon**
Mustard seed	1	**teaspoon**
Lemon wedges	1	**per serving**

Rinse the fillets and place in a shallow pan large enough to hold them in a single layer. Add enough water to just cover the fish. Remove the fish from the pan and add the turmeric, chili powder, cumin, cinnamon, and cloves to the liquid. Grind the coriander and mustard seed with a mortar and pestle or small food processor and add them to the liquid. Bring the poaching liquid to a boil over high heat. Return the fish to the pan in a single layer. Reduce heat to medium, cover, and simmer 2 to 3 minutes, depending on the thickness of the fish. Fish is done when opaque all the way through. Carefully remove the fillets, draining off as much liquid as possible, and serve immediately on warm plates with the lemon wedges.

Recommended companion dishes: **Mango Chutney (page 42), nonfat yogurt, and golden raisins as condiments; Steamed Couscous (page 51); and Middle East Salad (page 72)**

Each serving provides:

143	Calories	0.3 g	Omega-3
27 g	Protein	2 g	Fat
2 g	Carbohydrate		14% of calories from fat
120 mg	Sodium		0.4 g saturated fat
68 mg	Cholesterol		0.5 g polyunsaturated fat
			0.6 g monounsaturated fat

Poached Red Snapper with Pineapple Jalapeño Chutney

ALMOST INSTANT

This hot/sweet dance of flavors and aromas is quite delectable. Serve it as the centerpiece of a Southwestern dinner party. The juice from the canned unsweetened pineapple is used to flavor the poaching liquid.

Yield: 4 servings

Mustard seed	1½	**teaspoons**
Cumin seed	1	**teaspoon**
Unsweetened crushed pineapple	1	**8-ounce can**
Red onion, minced	3	**tablespoons**
Pickled jalapeño, seeded and minced	1½	**tablespoons**
Raw unsalted pumpkin seeds	2	**tablespoons**
Red snapper fillets	1¼	**pounds**
Garlic	2	**cloves, minced**
Fresh-squeezed lime juice	2	**teaspoons**

Toast the mustard and cumin seeds (see page 34) and grind them with a mortar and pestle or small food processor to a coarse meal consistency. Drain the pineapple well, reserving the juice. Combine the cumin and mustard seeds with the pineapple, red onion, and jalapeño and set the resulting chutney aside at room temperature. Toast the pumpkin seeds (see page 34), mince, and set aside.

Rinse the fish and pat dry. Place in a skillet large enough to hold the fillets in a single layer and add the pineapple juice and enough water to just cover the fish. Remove the fish from the pan, add the garlic, and bring to a boil over high heat. Return the fish to the pan in a single layer, cover, reduce heat to medium, and poach 3 to 4 minutes, depending on the thickness of the fillets. Fish is done when mostly opaque but still barely translucent at the very center.

Remove the fish from the pan, draining off as much liquid as possible, and place on a warmed platter. Stir the lime juice into the pineapple chutney and spoon evenly over the fish. Sprinkle with the toasted pumpkin seeds and serve immediately.

Recommended companion dishes: **Seasoned Black Beans (page 50) and Southwest Salad (page 70)**

Each serving provides:

194	Calories	0.5 g	Omega-3
30 g	Protein	4 g	Fat
9 g	Carbohydrate		18% of calories from fat
139 mg	Sodium		1 g saturated fat
52 mg	Cholesterol		1 g polyunsaturated fat
			1 g monounsaturated fat

Poached Mahimahi with Pear, Coconut, and Mint

ALMOST INSTANT

*Paradise on a plate, this succulent dish transports us to the tropics.
It's a wonderful pairing of flavors, and it's very simple to prepare.*

Yield: 4 servings

Fresh pears	3	**large**
Fresh-squeezed lime juice	¼	**cup**
Ground cardamom	½	**teaspoon**
Cayenne		**A pinch**
Mahimahi steaks or fillets	1¼	**pounds**
Unsweetened shaved coconut	2	**tablespoons**
Fresh mint leaves, minced	2	**tablespoons**

Peel the pears and grate them into a pan. Add 2 tablespoons of the lime juice, ¼ cup water, cardamom, and cayenne and cook over medium heat, stirring occasionally, 15 minutes. Mixture will have a thick sauce consistency.

Meanwhile, rinse the fish and pat dry. Place in a skillet large enough to hold it in a single layer and add enough water to just cover the fish. Remove the fish and set aside. Add the remaining 2 tablespoons lime juice to the pan and bring to a boil over high heat. Reduce heat to medium and lay the fish into the liquid in a single layer. Cover and cook 3 to 4 minutes, depending on the thickness of the fish. Fish is done when mostly opaque but still barely translucent at the very center.

Meanwhile, toast the coconut chips in a heavy-bottomed skillet over very low heat, shaking or stirring frequently, until chips are tan around the edges, about 3 minutes. Remove from the pan and set aside.

The Best 125 Lowfat Fish and Seafood Dishes

Use a slotted spoon to transfer the fish to a warmed serving platter. Pour off any liquid that accumulates on the platter, and spoon the topping over the fish. Distribute the coconut and mint evenly over the top and serve immediately.

Recommended companion dishes: Steamed Basmati Rice (page 45) and Southwest Salad (page 70)

Each serving provides:

222	Calories	0.2 g	Omega-3
27 g	Protein	3 g	Fat
22 g	Carbohydrate		13% of calories from fat
132 mg	Sodium		0.3 g saturated fat
103 mg	Cholesterol		0.4 g polyunsaturated fat
			0.3 g monounsaturated fat

Poached Orange Roughy with Hot Tomato Orange Marmalade

This unconventional combination of seasonings is intriguing and delicious. The fish cooks almost instantly, so begin the marmalade first. You may even prepare it several hours ahead of time and reheat it quickly in a small saucepan or microwave oven just before serving it on the hot fish.

Yield: 4 servings

Fresh tomatoes	1½	pounds (about 3 medium)
White onion, grated	3	tablespoons
Salt	⅛	teaspoon
Orange marmalade	¼	cup
Brandy	2	tablespoons
Whole coriander	2	teaspoons, crushed
Ground cinnamon	½	teaspoon
Cayenne		A pinch
Orange roughy fillets	1¼	pounds
Lemon wedges	1	per serving

Cut the unpeeled tomatoes in half crosswise, squeeze out the seed pockets, and cut out the stem ends. Dice the tomatoes and place in a saucepan with the onion and salt. Cook over medium heat, 5 minutes, stirring occasionally. Add the marmalade and brandy and continue to cook, 5 minutes, stirring frequently. Add the coriander, cinnamon, and cayenne and cook 5 minutes longer, stirring frequently.

Meanwhile, rinse the fish. Place it in a skillet large enough to hold it in a single layer and add enough water to just cover the fish. Remove the fish and set aside. Bring the water to a boil over high heat, reduce heat to medium, and add the fish in a single layer. Bring back to a simmer, cover, and poach 3 to 5 minutes, depending on the thickness of the fish. Fish is done when mostly opaque but still barely translucent at the very center. Remove from the poaching liquid, draining off as much water as possible. Place on a platter and drain again. Pour the hot tomato orange marmalade over the fish, garnish with lemon wedges, and serve immediately.

Recommended companion dishes: **Steamed Couscous (page 51) and raw vegetable sticks**

Each serving provides:

259	Calories	0.03 g	Omega-3
22 g	Protein	2 g	Fat
20 g	Carbohydrate		10% of calories from fat
182 mg	Sodium		0.2 g saturated fat
28 mg	Cholesterol		0.3 g polyunsaturated fat
			1.5 g monounsaturated fat

Braised Shark with Sauerkraut and Carrots

ALMOST INSTANT

We invented this dish to satisfy our occasional craving for sauerkraut.
It is absolutely succulent and delicious, not at all harsh in flavor.

Yield: 6 servings

Red onions	2	**medium**
Carrots	1	**pound**
Unsalted butter	1	**tablespoon**
Paprika	1½	**teaspoons**
Dill seed	1	**teaspoon**
Garlic	2	**cloves, minced**
Salt		**A pinch**
Pepper		**A few grinds**
Sauerkraut, drained	2	**cups**
Shark steaks	1	**pound**
Dry sherry	½	**cup**

Coarsely chop the onions. Halve the carrots lengthwise then cut into 1-inch lengths. In a large high-walled saucepan or dutch oven with a tight-fitting lid, melt the butter over medium-high heat. Stir in the paprika and dill seed, then add the onions, carrots, garlic, salt, and pepper. Sauté, stirring frequently, about 15 minutes, until carrots are fork tender. Meanwhile, rinse the fish and pat it dry. Remove any skin and bones, using tweezers or pliers, if necessary. Chop the fish into 1-inch chunks. Stir the sauerkraut, sherry, and ⅓ cup water into the pan and bring to a simmer, then nestle the shark pieces into the mixture. Cover, reduce heat to medium-low, and cook 3 minutes. Stir the mixture, replace the cover, and simmer an additional 2 to 4 minutes, depending on the thickness of the fish. Fish is done when mostly opaque but still barely translucent at the very center. Transfer to a warmed platter, sprinkle a little more paprika on top, and serve very hot.

Recommended companion dishes: **Garlic Mashed Potatoes (page 56) and Buttermilk Cucumber Salad (page 68)**

Each serving provides:

226	Calories	0.6 g	Omega-3
18 g	Protein	7 g	Fat
17 g	Carbohydrate		28% of calories from fat
648 mg	Sodium		3 g saturated fat
48 mg	Cholesterol		1 g polyunsaturated fat
			2 g monounsaturated fat

Fennel Braised Halibut with Calamata Olives

ALMOST INSTANT

This dish provides a wonderful blending of flavors—a little sweet and a little spicy. It is special enough for company, yet quick and simple to prepare.

Yield: 6 servings

Olive oil	2	teaspoons
Red onions	2	medium, chopped
Bell peppers	2	medium, chopped
Garlic	3	cloves, minced
Fennel seed	1	tablespoon
Dried red chili flakes	½	teaspoon
Low-sodium crushed tomatoes	1½	cups
Dry red wine	½	cup
Halibut steaks	1½	pounds
Calamata olives, minced	3	tablespoons
Fresh parsley, minced	¼	cup

In a large, high-walled saucepan or dutch oven with a tight-fitting lid, heat the oil over medium heat. When hot, add the onions, peppers, garlic, fennel seed, and chili flakes. Stir and sauté 5 minutes. You want the vegetables to brown a little. Stir in the tomatoes and wine and bring to a simmer. Cover and simmer 10 minutes, removing the lid and stirring once midway through. Simmer 5 minutes with the lid off to reduce the sauce slightly.

Arrange the halibut steaks in the pan, spooning some sauce over them. Replace the lid and cook 8 to 10 minutes, depending on the thickness of the fish. Fish is done when mostly opaque but still barely translucent at the very center. Transfer the fish to a platter and remove all skin and bones, breaking it up into large pieces. Stir the olives and parsley into the hot sauce and spoon the sauce over the halibut. Serve very hot.

Recommended companion dishes: **Mediterranean Pasta (page 52) and Basil Balsamic Salad (page 67)**

Each serving provides:

190	Calories	0.4 g	Omega-3
22 g	Protein	6 g	Fat
10 g	Carbohydrate		26% of calories from fat
221 mg	Sodium		1 g saturated fat
31 mg	Cholesterol		1 g polyunsaturated fat
			3 g monounsaturated fat

Braised Sea Bass and Carrots with Lentils and Ginger

ALMOST INSTANT

As unlikely as it may sound, mashed potatoes are the perfect accompaniment to this hearty dish. The ginger/lentil/yogurt combination makes a delicious gravy.

Yield: 6 servings

Dried lentils	½	cup
Bay leaf	1	
Carrots	2	large
Olive oil	2	teaspoons
Red onions	2	medium
Dried thyme	1½	teaspoons
Salt	¼	teaspoon
Dried red chili flakes	¼	teaspoon
Fresh ginger, grated	1½	tablespoons
Fresh parsley, minced	¼	cup
Sea bass fillets	1¼	pounds
Plain nonfat yogurt	¾	cup
Lemon wedges	1	per person

Put the lentils and bay leaf in a saucepan with 2 cups of hot water. Bring to a boil, reduce heat to low, and simmer, uncovered, 15 minutes.

Meanwhile, halve the carrots lengthwise and cut into 2-inch lengths. Coarsely chop the onions. Heat the oil over medium-high heat in a large, high-walled saucepan or dutch oven with a tight-fitting lid. Sauté the onions, carrots, thyme, salt, and chili flakes, stirring frequently, 5 minutes. Add lentils, along with their cooking liquid. Stir in the ginger and parsley and bring to a simmer.

Rinse the fish and pat dry. Lay it on top of the simmering lentil mixture, cover, and cook 4 minutes. Turn the fish over, replace the lid, and cook 2 to 4 minutes longer, depending on the thickness of the fish. Fish is done when mostly opaque but still barely translucent at the very center. Turn off the heat. Remove the fish to a platter, cover with foil, and set aside in a warm spot.

Whisk a few tablespoons of the sauce into the yogurt, then a few more tablespoons, until the yogurt is slightly warmed. Stir the yogurt into the lentil mixture and heat for only a moment over a tiny flame. Pour the sauce over the sea bass and arrange the lemon wedges around the edge of the plate. Serve very hot.

Recommended companion dishes: Garlic Mashed Potatoes (page 56) and Middle East Salad (page 72)

Each serving provides:

456	Calories	1 g	Omega-3
24 g	Protein	7 g	Fat
71 g	Carbohydrate		13% of calories from fat
130 mg	Sodium		2 g saturated fat
33 mg	Cholesterol		2 g polyunsaturated fat
			2 g monounsaturated fat

Fish and Seafood
en Papillote

Tightly wrapped in parchment paper and baked briefly, fish and vegetables are tender, moist, and infused with flavor. The paper packets are easy to assemble and fun to serve, and the aroma that bursts from the packets when they are opened at the table is irresistible. As steam builds up inside the packets, they puff up, trapping nutrients as well as the aromas inside, so these dishes deliver optimum nutrition.

This technique is said to have originated centuries ago in France, hence the French name. However, it suits our modern-day needs for lowfat, quick cuisine perfectly. We often prepare the contents and wrap the packets ahead of time, setting them aside in the refrigerator until we're ready to bake. Add

2 minutes to the cooking time if you are taking the packets directly from the refrigerator to the oven.

En papillote preparation lends itself equally well to casual dining and elegant presentations. It is a great technique for single people to master, since our recipes can be easily adapted for single portions. Conversely, they can be multiplied for large crowds.

Tools . . .

- Invest in an inexpensive oven thermometer and test the accuracy of your oven. You can adjust temperatures and cooking times accordingly.
- Be sure to preheat the oven at least 10 minutes to achieve the proper temperature before inserting the packets.
- The parchment paper called for in our recipes is available in the paper goods section of any well-stocked supermarket or gourmet cookware store.
- Baking sheets, such as those used for cookies, are ideal for holding the packets in the oven.
- An inexpensive small rubber spatula is very handy for spreading seasonings on the fish before wrapping the packets.

. . . and Tips

- Clear off a large working surface so you can set up an assembly line for the packets. This is quicker and easier than preparing them one by one.
- Paper packets will brown considerably in the oven. This is no cause for concern.
- See individual recipes for specific filling and wrapping instructions.

Halibut with Carrots and Ginger en Papillote

ALMOST INSTANT

Enoki mushrooms, also known as snow puff mushrooms, are readily available at Asian markets, and also in many well-stocked super-markets. You may substitute sliced button mushrooms, if necessary.

Yield: 4 servings

Low-sodium soy sauce	1	tablespoon
Mirin	1	tablespoon
Rice wine vinegar	1	tablespoon
Fresh ginger, grated	1	teaspoon
Dry mustard	½	teaspoon
Fresh-squeezed lemon juice	2	tablespoons
Dark sesame oil	2	teaspoons
Carrots	½	pound
Halibut steaks	1	pound
Green onions	4,	minced
Fresh enoki mushrooms	3½	ounces
Fresh cilantro, minced	¼	cup
Parchment paper for baking	4	12 × 16-inch pieces

Preheat the oven to 350 degrees F. Whisk together the soy sauce, mirin, vinegar, ginger, mustard, lemon juice, and oil. Set aside. Cut the carrots into matchsticks and steam them for several minutes, until barely tender. Rinse the fish and pat dry. Trim off any skin and remove any bones, using tweezers or pliers, if necessary. Cut into 4 equal-size servings.

Fold each piece of parchment in half and crease to create 8 × 12-inch rectangles. Use scissors to cut each rectangle into a half-heart shape. Open out the hearts and distribute the carrots equally among them, positioning near the center of each crease. Lay a portion of fish on each bed of carrots. Cut the green onions into 1-inch sections and arrange them over the fish. Divide the mushrooms and cilantro equally among the packets. Drizzle a quarter of the soy sauce mixture over the contents of each packet. Close the heart so the edges of the paper meet. Beginning at the round end, fold over about ½ inch of the paper and crease sharply. Work your way around the shape of the heart, folding in the edges and creasing sharply in overlapping pleats. Twist the pointy end to seal everything tightly in the paper packet. Repeat this process with the remaining packets.

Place the packets in a single layer on a baking sheet and bake 20 minutes if steaks are an inch or less thick, 25 minutes if thicker. Place each packet on a warmed serving plate and instruct your guests to pinch and tear the paper to release the aromatic steam. The contents can then be lifted out onto the plate and the paper removed from the table and discarded.

Recommended companion dishes: **Asian Salad (page 74), Steamed Brown Rice (page 46), and sweet French bread**

Each serving provides:

196	Calories	0.4 g	Omega-3
25 g	Protein	5 g	Fat
11 g	Carbohydrate		25% of calories from fat
232 mg	Sodium		1 g saturated fat
36 mg	Cholesterol		2 g polyunsaturated fat
			2 g monounsaturated fat

Tex-Mex Orange Roughy, Zucchini, and Peppers en Papillote

ALMOST INSTANT

Succulent orange roughy is particularly delicious cooked in parchment paper. Here it is seasoned Tex-Mex style with chili powder, cilantro, and lime.

Yield: 6 servings

Red bell peppers	3	large
Fresh Anaheim chilies	3	medium
Corn oil	1	tablespoon
Fresh-squeezed lime juice	1	tablespoon
Chili powder	2	teaspoons
Dried oregano	½	teaspoon
Granulated garlic	¼	teaspoon
Salt		A pinch
Zucchini	3	medium
Orange roughy fillets	1½	pounds
Fresh cilantro, minced	2	tablespoons
Parchment paper for baking	6	12 × 16-inch pieces

Using tongs to turn them, roast the red bells and the Anaheim chilies over the open flame of a gas burner until their skin is charred black all over (alternatively, peppers may be broiled or grilled until charred). While still hot, place the charred peppers in a paper bag and close tightly to trap the steam. When all the peppers are in the bag, set aside for at least 10 minutes.

Meanwhile, stir together the oil, lime juice, chili powder, oregano, garlic, and salt. Trim the ends from the zucchini, cut in half lengthwise, and slice each half into long, thin strips.

Rinse the fish and pat it dry. Trim off any skin and remove any bones, using tweezers or pliers, if necessary. Cut fish into 12 equal-size pieces.

Preheat the oven to 450 degrees F. Remove peppers from the bag and, when cool enough to handle, rub the charred skin off under a thin stream of running water. Remove the stems and seeds and slice the peppers into long, thin strips.

Fold each piece of parchment in half and crease to create 8 × 12-inch rectangles. Use scissors to cut each rectangle into a half-heart shape. Open out the hearts and place 2 pieces of fish near the center of each crease. Coat each portion of fish with a sixth of the oil mixture. Distribute the zucchini and pepper strips equally among the 6 packets and sprinkle each with minced cilantro. Close the heart so the edges of the paper meet. Beginning at the round end, fold over about ½ inch of the paper and crease sharply. Work your way around the shape of the heart, folding in the edges and creasing sharply in overlapping pleats. Twist the pointy end to seal everything tightly in the paper packet. Repeat this process for the remaining packets.

Place the packets in a single layer on baking sheets and bake 12 minutes. Place each packet on a warmed serving plate and instruct your guests to pinch and tear the paper to release the aromatic steam. The contents can then be lifted out onto the plate and the paper removed from the table and discarded.

Recommended companion dishes: **Southwest Salad (page 70) and Spanish Rice (page 47)**

Each serving provides:

199	Calories	0.02 g	Omega-3
19 g	Protein	4 g	Fat
8 g	Carbohydrate		25% of calories from fat
121 mg	Sodium		0.5 g saturated fat
23 mg	Cholesterol		1.5 g polyunsaturated fat
			2 g monounsaturated fat

Tuna and Leeks en Papillote with Paprika, Feta, and Fresh Dill

ALMOST INSTANT

The flavors and aromas of Eastern Europe are wrapped up in paper envelopes and released at the table for your guests to enjoy.

Yield: 4 servings

Paprika	2	teaspoons
Granulated garlic	½	teaspoon
Pepper		A few grinds
Salt		A pinch
Reduced-fat feta cheese, crumbled	1½	ounces (⅓ cup)
Fresh dill, minced	3	tablespoons
Leeks	4	large
Tuna steaks	1¼	pounds
Parchment paper for baking	4	12 × 16-inch pieces

Preheat the oven to 450 degrees F. Combine the paprika, garlic, pepper, and salt in a small dish. Toss the feta with the minced dill in another small dish. Cut all but 2 inches of the green from the leeks. Trim off the root ends and cut in half lengthwise. Rinse well to remove any dirt lodged between the layers. Cut the leeks into 3-inch lengths. Rinse the fish and pat dry. Trim off any skin and remove any bones, using tweezers or pliers, if necessary. Cut the tuna into even-size strips.

Fold each piece of parchment in half and crease to create 8 × 12-inch rectangles. Use scissors to cut each rectangle into a half-heart shape. Open out the hearts and distribute the fish strips in a single layer evenly among them, positioning near the center of each crease. Distribute the leeks equally, laying them alongside the fish. Rub a quarter of the paprika mixture on the tuna in each packet. Sprinkle the contents of each packet evenly with the feta and dill mixture. Close the heart so the edges of the paper meet. Beginning at the round end, fold over about ½ inch of the paper and crease sharply. Work your way around the shape of the heart, folding in the edges and creasing sharply in overlapping pleats. Twist the pointy end to seal everything tightly in the paper packet. Repeat this process with the remaining packets.

Place the packets in a single layer on a baking sheet and bake 18 minutes. Place each packet on a warmed serving plate and instruct your guests to pinch and tear the paper to release the aromatic steam. The contents can then be lifted out onto the plate and the paper removed from the table and discarded.

Recommended companion dishes: **Steamed Couscous (page 51), steamed carrots (see page 64), and Buttermilk Cucumber Salad (page 68)**

Each serving provides:

271	Calories	1.6 g	Omega-3
32 g	Protein	7 g	Fat
19 g	Carbohydrate		25% of calories from fat
246 mg	Sodium		2 g saturated fat
45 mg	Cholesterol		2 g polyunsaturated fat
			2 g monounsaturated fat

Mahimahi and Asparagus
en Papillote with Thai Seasonings

ALMOST INSTANT

Thai food is famous for its combination of sweet and pungent season-
ings. It lends itself well to baking in parchment paper, where the
aromas are trapped inside the packets until they arrive on the table.

Yield: 4 servings

Fresh asparagus	1	**pound**
Unsweetened coconut milk	3	**tablespoons**
Fresh cilantro, minced	3	**tablespoons**
Fresh-squeezed lemon juice	1	**teaspoon**
Garlic	2	**cloves, minced**
Low-sodium soy sauce	½	**teaspoon**
Fresh ginger, grated	1	**teaspoon**
Cayenne pepper		**A pinch**
Mahimahi steaks or fillets	1¼	**pounds**
Parchment paper for baking	4	**12 × 16-inch pieces**

Preheat the oven to 250 degrees F. Wash the asparagus and
break off the tough ends. In a small bowl, stir together the
coconut milk, cilantro, lemon juice, garlic, soy sauce, ginger, and
cayenne. Rinse the fish and pat dry. Trim off any skin and
remove any bones, using tweezers or pliers, if necessary. Cut the
fish into 8 equal-size strips. Fold each piece of parchment in half
and crease to create 8 × 12-inch rectangles. Use scissors to cut
each rectangle into a half-heart shape. Open out the hearts and
distribute the asparagus spears evenly among them, positioning
near the center of each crease. Place two strips of fish on top of
the asparagus on each piece of paper. Spread the sauce evenly

The Best 125 Lowfat Fish and Seafood Dishes

over the fish. Close the heart so the edges of the paper meet. Beginning at the round end, fold over about ½ inch of paper and crease sharply. Work your way around the shape of the heart, folding the edges and creasing sharply in overlapping pleats. Twist the pointy end to seal everything tightly in the paper packet. Repeat this process for the remaining packets.

Place the packets in a single layer on a baking sheet and bake for 12 minutes if fish is an inch or less thick, 18 minutes if thicker. Place each packet on a warmed serving plate and instruct your guests to pinch and tear the paper to release the aromatic steam. The contents can then be lifted out onto the plate and the paper removed from the table and discarded.

Recommended companion dishes: **Steamed Basmati Rice (page 45) and cucumber sticks**

Each serving provides:

171	Calories	0.2 g	Omega-3
30 g	Protein	4 g	Fat
3 g	Carbohydrate		20% of calories from fat
166 mg	Sodium		2 g saturated fat
103 mg	Cholesterol		0.4 g polyunsaturated fat
			0.3 g monounsaturated fat

Fish and Seafood en Papillote

Curried Calamari en Papillote

ALMOST INSTANT

Calamari is so often overcooked that it has a reputation of being tough. This oven-steaming method cooks it and the vegetables perfectly.

Yield: 4 servings

Dry sherry	2	tablespoons
Fresh-squeezed lemon juice	3	tablespoons
Curry powder	2	teaspoons
Cauliflower	¼	pound
Green beans	¼	pound
Yellow bell pepper	½	medium
Calamari steak	1	pound
Parchment paper for baking	4	12 × 16-inch pieces

Preheat the oven to 425 degrees F. Whisk together the sherry, lemon juice, and curry powder. Set aside. Cut the cauliflower into small florets and slice the beans at an angle into 1-inch pieces. Slice the bell pepper thinly. Rinse the calamari steaks and pat dry. Slice into 1-inch strips. Fold each piece of parchment in half and crease to create 8 × 12-inch rectangles. Use scissors to cut each rectangle into a half-heart shape. Open out the hearts and distribute equal amounts of each vegetable near the center of each crease. Place a quarter of the calamari strips in a single layer on top of the vegetables on each piece of paper. Spread a quarter of the curry mixture evenly over the contents of each packet. Close the heart so the edges of the paper meet. Beginning at the round end, fold over about ½ inch of paper and crease sharply. Work your way around the shape of the heart, folding the edges and creasing sharply in overlapping pleats. Twist the pointy end to seal everything tightly in the paper packet. Repeat this process for the remaining packets.

Place the packets in a single layer on a baking sheet and bake 20 minutes. Place each packet on a warmed serving plate and instruct your guests to pinch and tear the paper to release the aromatic steam. The contents can then be lifted out onto the plate and the paper removed from the table and discarded.

***Recommended companion dishes:* Mango Chutney (page 42) and nonfat yogurt as condiments; Middle East Salad (page 72), Steamed Basmati Rice (page 45), and bread sticks**

Each serving provides:

132	Calories	0.5 g	Omega-3
19 g	Protein	2 g	Fat
10 g	Carbohydrate		13% of calories from fat
56 mg	Sodium		0.4 g saturated fat
264 mg	Cholesterol		0.6 g polyunsaturated fat
			0.2 g monounsaturated fat

Catfish, Sweet Potatoes, and Hot Honey Mustard en Papillote

This meal in a packet delivers the taste and aroma of Southern cooking. It is satisfying enough for big appetites.

Yield: 6 servings

Dijon mustard	2	**tablespoons**
Honey	2	**teaspoons**
Pickled jalapeño, seeded and minced	1	**tablespoon**
Garlic	2	**cloves, minced**
Sweet potatoes	2	**medium**
Catfish fillets	1¼	**pounds**
Parchment paper for baking	6	**12 × 16-inch pieces**

Thoroughly combine the mustard, honey, jalapeño, and garlic and set aside. Scrub the sweet potatoes and, without peeling, slice crosswise into ¼-inch-thick disks, then into thin matchsticks.

Preheat the oven to 425 degrees F. Rinse the fish and pat dry. Remove any bones with tweezers or pliers, if necessary. Cut into 12 equal-size pieces. Fold each piece of parchment in half and crease to create 8 × 12-inch rectangles. Use scissors to cut each rectangle into a half-heart shape. Open out the hearts and distribute equal amounts of fish near the center of each crease. Use a small rubber spatula or knife to spread a sixth of the mustard mixture evenly over each portion of fish. Mound a sixth of the potato matchsticks on top of each portion. Close the heart so the edges of the paper meet. Beginning at the round end, fold over about ½ inch of paper and crease sharply. Work your way around the shape of the heart, folding the edges and creasing sharply in overlapping pleats. Twist the pointy end to seal everything tightly in the paper packet. Repeat this process for the remaining packets.

Place in a single layer on a baking sheet and bake for 15 minutes. Place each packet on a warmed serving plate and instruct your guests to pinch and tear the paper to release the aromatic steam. The contents can then be lifted out onto the plate and the paper removed from the table and discarded.

***Recommended companion dishes:* Southwest Salad (page 70) and steamed corn on the cob (see page 64)**

Each serving provides:

163	Calories	0.3 g	Omega-3
18 g	Protein	4 g	Fat
12 g	Carbohydrate		25% of calories from fat
152 mg	Sodium		1 g saturated fat
54 mg	Cholesterol		1 g polyunsaturated fat
			2 g monounsaturated fat

Sole en Papillote with Couscous, Green Beans, and Red Pesto

ALMOST INSTANT

The pesto comes together quickly using a commercial variety of roasted red bell peppers, and from there this dish gets even easier. It is a truly simple and scrumptious discovery! If you have an aversion to anchovies, leave them out of the pesto.

Yield: 4 servings

Dried tomatoes, minced	2	tablespoons
Roasted red bell peppers	½	cup
Fresh parsley, minced	¼	cup
Canned anchovy fillets	2	
Parmesan cheese, finely grated	1	tablespoon
Dried basil	1	tablespoon
Brandy	1	tablespoon
Garlic	2	cloves, minced
Pepper		Several grinds
Sole fillets	1¼	pounds
Dried couscous	¾	cup
Fresh green beans	½	pound
Parchment paper for baking	4	12 × 16-inch pieces

Reconstitute the tomatoes if they are too dry to mince (see page 37). In a food processor or blender, combine the dried tomatoes, bell peppers, parsley, anchovies, Parmesan, basil, brandy, garlic, and pepper. Puree to a smooth paste consistency.

Preheat the oven to 425 degrees F. Rinse the fish and pat dry. Remove any bones, using tweezers or pliers, if necessary.

Cut into 8 equal-size pieces. Fold each piece of parchment in half and crease to create 8 × 12-inch rectangles. Use scissors to cut each rectangle into a half-heart shape. Open out the hearts and place 3 tablespoons of couscous in a neat, flattened pile near the center of each crease. Place a quarter of the fish on each pile of couscous. Use a small rubber spatula or knife to spread a quarter of the pesto over each portion of fish. Arrange a quarter of the beans on top of each portion.

Close the heart so the edges of the paper meet. Beginning at the round end, fold over about ½ inch of paper and crease sharply. Work your way around the shape of the heart, folding the edges and creasing sharply in overlapping pleats. Twist the pointy end to seal everything tightly in the paper packet. Repeat this process for the remaining packets.

Place in a single layer on a baking sheet and bake for 15 minutes. Place each packet on a warmed serving plate and instruct your guests to pinch and tear the paper to release the aromatic steam. The contents can then be lifted out onto the plate and the paper removed from the table and discarded.

Recommended companion dish: **Basil Balsamic Salad (page 67)**

Each serving provides:

325	Calories	0.3 g	Omega-3
35 g	Protein	3 g	Fat
38 g	Carbohydrate		8% of calories from fat
230 mg	Sodium		0.8 g saturated fat
71 mg	Cholesterol		0.7 g polyunsaturated fat
			0.6 g monounsaturated fat

Fish and Seafood en Papillote

Salmon Misoyaki with Mushrooms en Papillote

This is a hands-down favorite among our recipe testers. The flavors are clean and fresh and the texture of the salmon is absolutely buttery.

Yield: 4 servings

Raw sesame seeds	2	**teaspoons**
White miso	2	**tablespoons**
Sake	1	**tablespoon**
Granulated sugar	2	**teaspoons**
Granulated garlic	¼	**teaspoon**
Mushrooms	¾	**pound**
Green onions	8	
Salmon steaks	1¼	**pounds**
Parchment paper for baking	4	**12 × 16-inch pieces**

Toast the sesame seeds (see page 34). In a small bowl, mash together the miso, sake, sugar, and granulated garlic until you have achieved a smooth paste consistency. Clean any loose dirt particles from the mushrooms and slice them thickly. Trim root ends from the green onions, along with all but 2 inches of the green portion.

Preheat the oven to 450 degrees F. Rinse the fish and pat dry. Cut into 4 equal-size pieces. Fold each piece of parchment in half and crease to create 8 × 12-inch rectangles. Use scissors to cut each rectangle into a half-heart shape. Open out the hearts and place a quarter of the fish near the center of each crease. Use a small rubber spatula or knife to spread a quarter of the miso mixture evenly over each portion of fish. Arrange a quarter of the mushrooms and whole green onions alongside each portion of fish. Sprinkle the contents of each packet with a quarter of the sesame seeds.

Close the heart so the edges of the paper meet. Beginning at the round end, fold over about ½ inch of paper and crease sharply. Work your way around the shape of the heart, folding the edges and creasing sharply in overlapping pleats. Twist the pointy end to seal everything tightly in the paper packet. Repeat this process for the remaining packets.

Place in a single layer on a baking sheet and bake for 12 minutes. Place each packet on a warmed serving plate and instruct your guests to pinch and tear the paper to release the aromatic steam. The contents can then be carefully lifted out onto the plate and the paper removed from the table and discarded.

Recommended companion dishes: **Steamed Brown Rice (page 46) and Asian Salad (page 74)**

Each serving provides:

227	Calories	1.1 g	Omega-3
33 g	Protein	8 g	Fat
8 g	Carbohydrate		30% of calories from fat
413 mg	Sodium		1 g saturated fat
73 mg	Cholesterol		3 g polyunsaturated fat
			2 g monounsaturated fat

Fish and Seafood en Papillote

Trout and Fennel en Papillote with Lemon Caper Cream

ALMOST INSTANT

Since trout is available cleaned and filleted all year at our fish markets, we have grown to love it. This is a favorite flavor combination, light yet distinctive. Lemon extract—often used in desserts—is available in large supermarkets near the vanilla extract.

Yield: 4 servings

Fresh fennel bulb	1	**medium**
Carrot	1	**large**
Green onions	4	
Fresh whole trout°	4	**medium (about 4 pounds)**
Granulated garlic	¾	**teaspoon**
Plain nonfat yogurt	¼	**cup**
Light sour cream	¼	**cup**
Capers, drained and minced	1	**tablespoon**
Lemon extract	½	**teaspoon**
Paprika	½	**teaspoon**
Pepper		**Several grinds**
Parchment paper for baking	4	**12 × 16-inch pieces**

Slice the fennel bulb and carrot into thin julienne strips. Discard all but about 2 inches of the green portion of the onions and sliver lengthwise, then cut into 2-inch lengths.

Preheat the oven to 425 degrees F. Fold each piece of parchment in half and crease to create 8 × 12-inch rectangles.

°Purchase boned and butterflied trout (heads and bones removed but skin intact).

Use scissors to cut each rectangle into a half-heart shape. Open out the hearts and place a trout near the center of each crease. Sprinkle ½ teaspoon of the granulated garlic evenly over the interior of each fish. Evenly distribute the fennel, carrot, and green onions among them, filling the cavities. Close the heart so the edges of the paper meet. Beginning at the round end, fold over about ½ inch of paper and crease sharply. Work your way around the shape of the heart, folding the edges and creasing sharply in overlapping pleats. Twist the pointy end to seal everything tightly in the paper packet. Repeat this process for the remaining packets. Place in a single layer on a baking sheet and bake for 20 minutes.

Meanwhile, whisk together the yogurt, sour cream, capers, lemon extract, paprika, remaining ¼ teaspoon granulated garlic, and pepper. Just before removing the fish from the oven, warm the sauce over very low heat on the stovetop or in a microwave oven until barely heated. Keep warm. Place each packet on a warmed serving plate, and instruct your guests to pinch and tear the paper to release the aromatic steam. The contents can then be lifted out onto the plate and the paper removed from the table and discarded. Pass the sauce to spoon over the fish.

Recommended companion dishes: Steamed Basmati Rice (page 45) and Buttermilk Cucumber Salad (page 68)

Each serving provides:

458	Calories	2 g	Omega-3
73 g	Protein	13 g	Fat
8 g	Carbohydrate		27% of calories from fat
151 mg	Sodium		3 g saturated fat
198 mg	Cholesterol		4 g polyunsaturated fat
			4 g monounsaturated fat

Swordfish en Papillote
with Fermented Black Beans

ALMOST INSTANT

The flavors in this dish will surprise and delight you. Fermented black beans are available at Asian markets or well-stocked supermarkets.

Yield: 4 servings

Fresh spinach	1	bunch (about ¾ pound)
Fermented black beans	2	tablespoons
Garlic	2	cloves, minced
Dry sherry	2	tablespoons
Dried red chili flakes	¼	teaspoon
Swordfish steaks	1½	pounds
Parchment paper for baking	4	12 × 16-inch pieces

Preheat the oven to 425 degrees F. Carefully wash the spinach, removing the thickest stems. Place it in a large pot with the water that is still clinging to its leaves, cover, and steam over medium-high heat for about 5 minutes, until it wilts. Meanwhile, finely mince the black beans and mix with the garlic, sherry, and chili flakes in a small bowl. Set aside.

Rinse the swordfish and pat dry. Trim off any skin and remove any bones, using tweezers or pliers, if necessary. Cut into 4 equal-size servings. Drain the spinach in a colander, pressing with a wooden spoon to remove as much water as possible. Chop the spinach.

Fold each piece of parchment in half and crease to create 8 × 12-inch rectangles. Use scissors to cut each rectangle into a half-heart shape. Open out the hearts and lay a quarter of the spinach near the center of each crease. Lay a portion of fish in a single layer on top of each bed of spinach. Sprinkle evenly with the black bean mixture.

Close the heart so the edges of the paper meet. Beginning at the round end, fold over about ½ inch of paper and crease sharply. Work your way around the shape of the heart, folding the edges and creasing sharply in overlapping pleats. Twist the pointy end to seal everything tightly in the paper packet. Repeat this process for the remaining packets. Place in a single layer on a baking sheet and bake for 12 minutes. Place each packet on a warmed serving plate, and instruct your guests to pinch and tear the paper to release the aromatic steam. The contents can then be lifted out onto the plate and the paper removed from the table and discarded.

***Recommended companion dishes:* Steamed Brown Rice (page 46), Asian Salad (page 74), and sesame bread sticks**

Each serving provides:

213	Calories	0.9 g	Omega-3
32 g	Protein	6 g	Fat
5 g	Carbohydrate		28% of calories from fat
196 mg	Sodium		2 g saturated fat
55 mg	Cholesterol		2 g polyunsaturated fat
			2 g monounsaturated fat

Entrées from the Oven

The baked dishes presented in this chapter encompass a wide variety of styles, from lightly sauced dishes to hearty, composed casseroles to not-quite-traditional fish sticks. None of these dishes requires attention while baking, so they free up the cook to relax for a few minutes before completing the meal. Indeed, some of these creations are labeled Almost Instant, since the preparation and baking times are so short.

Many people associate baked goods with cold weather, since the heat from the oven warms the kitchen and the house fills with tantalizing aromas. We find, however, that many of our lighter baked dishes are welcome year round.

Tools . . .

- A selection of glass and ceramic casserole dishes in various sizes, some with lids.
- Oven mitts for retrieving hot dishes from the oven and heat-proof trivets to protect table or counter surfaces.
- Spatulas or large spoons for serving.

. . . and Tips

- Invest in an inexpensive oven thermometer and test the accuracy of your oven. You can adjust temperatures and cooking times accordingly.
- Be sure to preheat the oven at least 10 minutes to achieve the proper temperature before inserting the dish.
- Never transfer a baking dish directly from the refrigerator to the oven, as the sudden change in temperature can crack the dish.
- Where an oiled dish is called for, a fraction of a teaspoon of oil is all that is needed. Use a pastry brush, paper towel, or your fingers to oil the surface.

Cod Baked with Green Bell Pepper and Tomatoes

ALMOST INSTANT

This is a quick and easy way to prepare cod. The tomatoes and bell pepper enhance the sweetness of the fish.

Yield: 4 servings

Olive oil	1	**tablespoon plus ¼ teaspoon**
Garlic	2	**cloves, minced**
White onion, minced	¼	**cup**
Low-sodium stewed tomatoes	1	**14½-ounce can**
Green bell pepper	1	**medium**
Cod fillets	1¼	**pounds**

Preheat the oven to 425 degrees F. Put 1 tablespoon of the olive oil in a large skillet over medium heat. Add the garlic and onion and sauté 2 minutes. Drain the tomatoes, coarsely chop them, and add to the skillet. Continue to cook for 12 minutes, until the liquid has evaporated and a chunky sauce develops. Meanwhile, slice the bell pepper into thin strips. Rinse the cod and pat dry. Trim off any skin and remove any bones, with tweezers or pliers, if necessary. Rub the bottom of a 3-quart baking dish with the remaining ¼ teaspoon of oil and arrange the cod in a single layer. Spoon the tomato mixture over the fish and top with the bell pepper slices. Bake, covered, for 15 minutes, until fish is opaque all the way through. Serve immediately.

Recommended companion dishes: **Basil Balsamic Salad (page 67), Mediterranean Pasta (page 52), and steamed broccoli (see page 64)**

Each serving provides:

196	Calories	0.3 g	Omega-3
27 g	Protein	5 g	Fat
11 g	Carbohydrate		22% of calories from fat
118 mg	Sodium		1 g saturated fat
52 mg	Cholesterol		1 g polyunsaturated fat
			3 g monounsaturated fat

Huachanango with Pickled Jalapeños

This is a favorite Mexican seafood preparation. Our version adds pickled jalapeño peppers for an extra flavor burst. Rather than smothering the snapper with cheese, as in the traditional version, we use a small amount so the dish comes across light and fresh-tasting.

Yield: 8 servings

Red snapper fillets	2	pounds
Fresh-squeezed lemon juice	½	cup
Salt	¼	teaspoon
Pepper		Several grinds
Canola oil	1	tablespoon
Yellow onion	1	medium, diced
Low-sodium whole tomatoes	1	28-ounce can
Diced green chilies	1	7-ounce can
Dry white wine	½	cup
Pickled jalapeño, seeded and diced	1	tablespoon
Capers, drained and minced	1	tablespoon
Monterey Jack cheese, shredded	1	cup (3 ounces)

Rinse the fish and pat it dry. Trim off any skin and remove any bones, using tweezers or pliers, if necessary. Arrange the fish in a 9 × 13-inch baking dish, pour the lemon juice over it, and sprinkle with the salt and pepper. Set aside in the refrigerator for 20 minutes.

Meanwhile, put the oil in a large skillet over medium heat. Add the onion and sauté 2 minutes. Drain the juice from the tomatoes, dice them, and add to the skillet, along with the green chilies, wine, pickled jalapeño, and capers. Increase heat to medium-high and simmer 20 minutes, stirring frequently. Drain the lemon juice from the fish and top with the tomato sauce. Cover and bake for 20 minutes. Fish is done when it breaks apart easily when a fork is inserted and twisted in the thickest part. Remove from the oven and carefully drain off the liquid that has accumulated in the bottom of the dish during cooking. Be careful not to disturb the tomato sauce. Top with the cheese, return to the oven for 2 minutes or until cheese melts, and serve immediately.

***Recommended companion dishes:* Southwest Salad (page 70), Spanish Rice (page 47), and warm tortillas**

	Each serving provides:		
211	Calories	0.3 g	Omega-3
27 g	Protein	7 g	Fat
8 g	Carbohydrate		29% of calories from fat
245 mg	Sodium		3 g saturated fat
51 mg	Cholesterol		1 g polyunsaturated fat
			1 g monounsaturated fat

Squid Baked with Zucchini and Mushrooms in Tomato Sauce

Squid (also called calamari) is easiest to deal with if you buy it already cleaned. In its cleaned state, it is often sold as "squid tubes." This dish is hearty Italian fare, a perfect match for Mediterranean Pasta and crusty rolls for soaking up the wonderful sauce.

Yield: 6 servings

Low-sodium stewed tomatoes	1	14½-ounce can
Garlic	2	cloves, minced
Bay leaves	2	
Dried basil	1	teaspoon
Honey	1	tablespoon
Zucchini	3	medium (about 1 pound)
Olive oil	1	tablespoon
White onion	1	medium, diced
Mushrooms	½	pound, sliced
Squid tubes	1	pound, sliced
Parmesan cheese, finely grated	¼	cup

Combine the tomatoes and their juice, garlic, bay leaves, basil, and honey in a medium saucepan. Bring to a boil over medium-high heat, reduce heat to medium-low, and simmer, stirring occasionally, about 40 minutes to reduce the sauce. Preheat the oven to 375 degrees F.

Meanwhile, trim the ends off the zucchini, cut in half lengthwise, and cut crosswise into ¼-inch slices. Put the olive oil in a large skillet over medium heat and add the zucchini, onion, and mushrooms. Sauté for 20 minutes, stirring occasionally. Rinse the squid, pat it dry, and cut into strips. Remove the bay leaves from the tomato sauce and spoon half of it into a 3-quart baking dish. Lay in the squid strips, then the zucchini mixture. Top with the remaining tomato sauce. Sprinkle with the Parmesan cheese and bake, uncovered, 20 minutes.

***Recommended companion dishes:* Basil Balsamic Salad (page 67), Mediterranean Pasta (page 52), and crusty rolls**

Each serving provides:

155	Calories	0.4 g	Omega-3
15 g	Protein	5 g	Fat
13 g	Carbohydrate		28% of calories from fat
122 mg	Sodium		1 g saturated fat
179 mg	Cholesterol		1 g polyunsaturated fat
			2 g monounsaturated fat

Catfish, Greens, and Black-Eyed Peas with Smoked Cheddar and Tomatoes

A flight of fancy inspired by spicy Louisiana cuisine, this showy casserole is full-bodied, full-flavored, and really quite easy to make. The rinsing of the rice is essential to the texture of this dish—otherwise, it will be too sticky. If mustard greens are unavailable, you may substitute chard.

Yield: 6 servings

Cooked black-eyed peas	1½	cups
Stewed tomatoes	1	14½-ounce can
Dry white wine	¾	cup
Garlic	4	cloves, minced
Dried thyme	½	teaspoon
Tabasco sauce	1	teaspoon
Olive oil	¼	teaspoon
White rice, uncooked*	1	cup
Mustard greens	1	pound, washed and chopped
Catfish fillets	1	pound
Lowfat cultured buttermilk	¾	cup
Smoked cheddar cheese, grated	¾	cup (2¼ ounces)
Granulated garlic	¼	teaspoon
Paprika	½	teaspoon

*Do not use "converted" rice for this dish.

Cook the peas according to the instructions on page 36, or drain and rinse canned beans. Preheat the oven to 375 degrees F.

In a medium saucepan over medium heat, combine the tomatoes, peas, wine, garlic, thyme, and ¾ teaspoon of the Tabasco sauce. Heat to a strong simmer, then turn off the heat, but keep warm. Use the olive oil to rub down a 2-quart casserole dish. Rinse the rice in a bowl of water several times, swirling around and pouring off the cloudy water, until water is fairly clear. Drain. Spread the rice evenly over the bottom of the casserole dish. Layer the chopped greens over the rice and pour the tomato sauce evenly over the greens. Cover and bake for 25 minutes.

Meanwhile, rinse the fish and pat dry. When casserole has finished cooking, lay the fish fillets in an even layer over the casserole. Mix together the buttermilk, cheese, granulated garlic, and remaining ¼ teaspoon Tabasco sauce. Spread evenly over the fish. Sprinkle the paprika evenly over the casserole, replace the lid, and bake 10 minutes. Remove the lid and bake an additional 5 to 7 minutes, until fish is opaque all the way through. Allow to sit about 10 minutes with the lid on before serving.

Recommended companion dishes: Southwest Salad (page 70) and Cornbread (page 57)

Each serving provides:

370	Calories	0.3 g	Omega-3
26 g	Protein	9 g	Fat
42 g	Carbohydrate		22% of calories from fat
456 mg	Sodium		4 g saturated fat
60 mg	Cholesterol		1 g polyunsaturated fat
			3 g monounsaturated fat

Clam and Leek Frittata with Potatoes, Dried Tomatoes, and Oregano

This dish is very filling and the flavors are wonderful. Serve it for a casual dinner or weekend brunch. It is delicious right out of the oven or at room temperature.

Yield: 8 servings

Dried tomatoes, minced	2	tablespoons
Leeks	3	large
Russet potato	½	pound
Minced clams	2	6½-ounce cans
Olive oil	1	tablespoon
Dry sherry	1	tablespoon
Red bell pepper	1	large, diced
Whole eggs	4	medium
Egg whites	2	medium
Plain nonfat yogurt	½	cup
Fresh parsley, minced	⅓	cup
Dried oregano	1	teaspoon
Black pepper		Several grinds

Reconstitute the dried tomatoes if they are too dry to mince (see page 37). Preheat the oven to 350 degrees F. Trim off the root end and the tough green tops of the leeks. Slice the leeks in half lengthwise, carefully wash them to remove all of the dirt caught in the layers, then thinly slice them. Peel and dice the potato. Drain the clams, reserving the liquid.

Heat the olive oil, sherry, and clam juice over medium heat in a large ovenproof skillet. Add the leeks, potato, and bell pepper and cook 25 minutes, stirring occasionally. Remove from the heat, stir in the clams and dried tomatoes, and set aside. Beat the eggs with the additional egg whites, then beat in the yogurt. Stir in the parsley, oregano, and pepper. Pour this evenly over the leek potato mixture. Bake 30 minutes; cool for 5 minutes before serving. Serve hot or at room temperature.

***Recommended companion dishes:* steamed pea pods (see page 64), Buttermilk Cucumber Salad (page 68), and sweet French bread**

Each serving provides:

143	Calories	0 g	Omega-3
10 g	Protein	5 g	Fat
16 g	Carbohydrate		30% of calories from fat
91 mg	Sodium		1 g saturated fat
133 mg	Cholesterol		1 g polyunsaturated fat
			2 g monounsaturated fat

Sole Florentine with Nutmeg and Paprika

This wonderful, rich-tasting dish is suitable for company. Its flavors are subtle yet distinctive, and the presentation is elegant if you use a pretty casserole dish or individual baking dishes.

Yield: 4 servings

Fresh spinach	2	bunches (about 1½ pounds)
Nonfat milk	¾	cup
Unsalted butter	1	tablespoon
Garlic	2	cloves, minced
Unbleached flour	1	tablespoon
Dry sherry	1	tablespoon
Freshly grated nutmeg	½	teaspoon
Salt	⅛	teaspoon
Pepper		A few grinds
Sole fillets	1	pound
Parmesan cheese, finely grated	2	tablespoons
Paprika	1	teaspoon
Fresh lemon wedges	1	per serving

Carefully wash the spinach and remove the thickest stems. Without drying them, place the leaves in a stockpot and cover. Heat over medium heat about 5 minutes, or until spinach wilts. Drain in a colander. When cool enough to handle, squeeze with your hands to remove as much water as possible. Finely chop the spinach and set aside.

Meanwhile, heat the milk over very low heat until steaming and keep hot. Heat the butter in a saucepan over medium heat and sauté the garlic for a few moments. Add the flour and stir 2 minutes to cook it slightly. Whisk in the hot milk in a steady stream and cook 3 to 4 minutes, whisking frequently, until thickened. Stir in the spinach, sherry, nutmeg, salt, and pepper, and stir and cook for 2 more minutes, to just heat through.

Meanwhile, preheat the broiler 5 minutes. Rinse the fish and pat dry. Remove any bones, using tweezers or pliers, if necessary. Broil 4 inches from the flame for 3 to 4 minutes, depending on the thickness of the fish. Fish is done when opaque all the way through. Remove to a warmed plate and set aside.

Preheat the oven to 425 degrees F. Make a layer of the creamed spinach on the bottom of a 1-quart shallow casserole dish, individual baking dishes, or a pie plate. Drain off any liquid that has been released from the sole, and arrange the broiled fish in a single layer on the bed of spinach. Sprinkle the Parmesan and paprika evenly over the fish and bake 10 minutes, until cheese is melted and lightly browned. Garnish with lemon wedges, and serve.

Recommended companion dishes: Steamed Basmati Rice (page 45) and Honey Mustard Salad (page 76)

Each serving provides:

217	Calories	0.2 g	Omega-3
30 g	Protein	6 g	Fat
12 g	Carbohydrate		25% of calories from fat
373 mg	Sodium		3 g saturated fat
66 mg	Cholesterol		1 g polyunsaturated fat
			1 g monounsaturated fat

Baked Orange Roughy in Grapefruit Oregano Sauce

This dish is very aromatic, calling to mind scenes of Mexico. The fish is delicate and receives the flavors perfectly.

Yield: 4 servings

Orange roughy fillets	1¼	pounds
Unbleached flour	3	tablespoons
Canola oil	¼	teaspoon
Fresh-squeezed pink grapefruit juice	1	cup
Ground cumin	1	teaspoon
Chili powder	½	teaspoon
Granulated garlic	½	teaspoon
Fresh oregano leaves, minced	1	tablespoon

Preheat the oven to 350 degrees F. Rinse the fish and pat it dry. Remove any bones, using tweezers or pliers, if necessary. Place the flour on a plate and dredge the fish to lightly coat each side. Rub a 9 × 13-inch glass baking dish with the oil and add the fish in a single layer. Combine the grapefruit juice, cumin, chili powder, granulated garlic, and oregano. Pour this over the fish, cover, and bake 30 minutes, until fish is opaque all the way through. Serve immediately.

Recommended companion dishes: **Wild Rice Pilaf (page 48), Southwest Salad (page 70), and hot rolls**

Each serving provides:

234	Calories	0.03 g	Omega-3
22 g	Protein	2 g	Fat
12 g	Carbohydrate		14% of calories from fat
95 mg	Sodium		0.3 g saturated fat
28 mg	Cholesterol		0.3 g polyunsaturated fat
			1.4 g monounsaturated fat

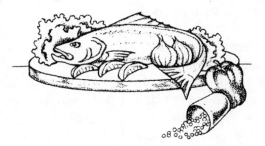

Halibut Baked in Coconut Lime Sauce

ALMOST INSTANT

The sweetness of the coconut milk is nicely balanced by the lime juice, and the halibut melts in your mouth.

Yield: 4 servings

Halibut steaks	1¼	pounds
Unbleached flour	2	tablespoons
Unsweetened coconut milk	¼	cup
Fresh-squeezed lime juice	3	tablespoons
Granulated garlic	¼	teaspoon
Ground cinnamon	⅛	teaspoon
Ground coriander	⅛	teaspoon
Freshly grated nutmeg	⅛	teaspoon
Salt	⅛	teaspoon
Pepper		Several grinds
Fresh cilantro, minced	¼	cup

Preheat the oven to 425 degrees F. Rinse the fish and pat dry. Trim off any skin and remove any bones, using tweezers or pliers, if necessary. Cut into 4 equal portions. Place the flour on a plate and dredge the fish to lightly coat each side. Whisk together the coconut milk, lime juice, granulated garlic, cinnamon, coriander, nutmeg, salt, and pepper. Pour into a 1½-quart baking dish and lay the fish on top. Turn to coat the reverse side, then sprinkle the cilantro evenly over the fish. Cover and bake

10 minutes, until the fish is mostly opaque but still barely translucent at the very center. Serve immediately, spooning some of the coconut lime sauce over each portion.

Recommended companion dishes: **Honey Mustard Salad (page 76), Steamed Brown Rice (page 46), and Seasoned Black Beans (page 50)**

Each serving provides:

217	Calories	0.5 g	Omega-3
31 g	Protein	7 g	Fat
5 g	Carbohydrate		32% of calories from fat°
154 mg	Sodium		3 g saturated fat
45 mg	Cholesterol		1 g polyunsaturated fat
			1 g monounsaturated fat

°Health experts recommend that we derive no more than 30 percent of our overall calories from fat. When served with our recommended companion dishes or on an otherwise lowfat day, this recipe fits the bill.

Baked Sole with Capers and Mushrooms

Creamy without being fat-laden, this dish fits our definition of comfort food. It comes together in a snap and will appear on your table frequently.

Yield: 4 servings

Olive oil	1	tablespoon plus ¼ teaspoon
Dry sherry	1	tablespoon
Mushrooms	½	pound, sliced
Green onions	3,	minced
Sole fillets	1¼	pounds
Dry white wine	½	cup
Unbleached flour	2	tablespoons
Plain nonfat yogurt	⅔	cup
Capers, drained and minced	2	tablespoons
Fresh parsley, minced	¼	cup

Preheat the oven to 350 degrees F. Heat 1 tablespoon of the oil and the sherry in a large skillet over medium heat and add the mushrooms and onions. Sauté 10 minutes, stirring frequently.

Meanwhile, rinse the fish and pat dry. Remove any bones, using tweezers or pliers, if necessary. Oil a 10 × 10-inch baking dish with the remaining ¼ teaspoon oil, then arrange the fish in the dish in a single layer.

Put the wine and flour in a small jar that has a tight-fitting lid. Shake to dissolve. Gradually add this to the mushrooms in the skillet, stirring constantly as it thickens. Turn off the heat.

Stir a few tablespoons of hot sauce into the yogurt to warm it a bit. Stir the yogurt and capers into the sauce, then pour this mixture over the fish and top with the parsley. Cover and bake 25 minutes, until fish is opaque all the way through.

Recommended companion dishes: Poppy Seed Noodles (page 53) and Honey Mustard Salad (page 76)

Each serving provides:

239	Calories	0.3 g	Omega-3
31 g	Protein	7 g	Fat
8 g	Carbohydrate		24% of calories from fat
209 mg	Sodium		1 g saturated fat
69 mg	Cholesterol		1 g polyunsaturated fat
			3 g monounsaturated fat

Halibut Baked in a
Wine Oregano Marinade

ALMOST INSTANT

*When baked in this marinade, the halibut comes out so succulent
it melts in your mouth. The aroma that permeates the kitchen is
wonderful, too.*

Yield: 4 servings

Halibut steaks	**1¼**	**pounds**
Dry white wine	**¼**	**cup**
Fresh-squeezed lemon juice	**2**	**tablespoons**
Olive oil	**1**	**tablespoon**
Green onions	**2,**	**minced**
Garlic	**2**	**cloves, minced**
Dried oregano	**1**	**teaspoon**
Salt	**⅛**	**teaspoon**
Pepper		**Several grinds**

Preheat the oven to 400 degrees F. Rinse the fish and pat dry.
Trim off any skin and remove any bones, using tweezers or
pliers, if necessary. Cut into 4 equal-size servings. In a bowl,
stir together the wine, lemon juice, oil, onions, garlic, oregano,

salt, and pepper. Place the fish in an 8 × 8-inch baking dish. Top with the marinade, cover, and bake 20 minutes, until fish is mostly opaque but still barely translucent at the very center.

Recommended companion dishes: Basil Balsamic Salad (page 67), Wild Rice Pilaf (page 48), and steamed carrots (see page 64)

Each serving provides:

192	Calories	0.5 g	Omega-3
30 g	Protein	6 g	Fat
2 g	Carbohydrate		27% of calories from fat
158 mg	Sodium		1 g saturated fat
45 mg	Cholesterol		2 g polyunsaturated fat
			3 g monounsaturated fat

Baked Sole Almondine
with Lime and Thyme

ALMOST INSTANT

The flavor combination of lime, thyme, and almond is unique and quite delicious.

Yield: 4 servings

Raw unsalted slivered almonds	¼	cup
Sole fillets	1	pound
Olive oil	1	tablespoon
Fresh-squeezed lime juice	¼	cup
Grated lime peel	1	teaspoon
Garlic	2	cloves, minced
Dried thyme	½	teaspoon
Pepper		Several grinds
Fresh parsley, chopped	¼	cup

Toast the almond slivers (see page 34). Preheat the oven to 375 degrees F. Rinse the fillets and pat them dry. Remove any bones, using tweezers or pliers, if necessary. Place the fillets in a single layer in a 9 × 13-inch baking dish. Whisk together the oil, lime juice, lime peel, garlic, thyme, and pepper. Pour evenly over the fish, turning once to coat. Sprinkle the almonds over the fish. Bake, uncovered, 8 to 10 minutes, until the fish is opaque all the way through. Top with the parsley and serve.

Recommended companion dishes: **steamed green beans (see page 64), Garlic Mashed Potatoes (page 56), and Buttermilk Cucumber Salad (page 68)**

Each serving provides:

191	Calories	0.2 g	Omega-3
24 g	Protein	8 g	Fat
6 g	Carbohydrate		38% of calories from fat°
95 mg	Sodium		1 g saturated fat
55 mg	Cholesterol		1 g polyunsaturated fat
			5 g monounsaturated fat

°Health experts recommend that we derive no more than 30 percent of our overall calories from fat. When served with our recommended companion dishes or on an otherwise lowfat day, this recipe fits the bill.

Stuffed Orange Roughy Sicilian Style

*Orange roughy fillets are usually fairly large. For this dish, purchase
2 large fillets or 4 smaller ones, keeping the total weight around 1¼
pounds. This lovely main course is easy to prepare ahead and refrigerate until just before you bake it.*

Yield: 4 servings

The stuffing
Orange roughy fillets	1¼	pounds
Fine dry bread crumbs	½	cup
Golden raisins	¼	cup, chopped
Fresh parsley, minced	¼	cup
Capers, drained and minced	2	tablespoons
Pine nuts, chopped	2	tablespoons
Garlic	3	cloves, minced
Olive oil	1	tablespoon
Fresh-squeezed lemon juice	2	tablespoons

The sauce
Low-sodium pear tomatoes	1	14½-ounce can
Dried basil	1	teaspoon
Capers, drained and minced	1	tablespoon
Green onions	2,	minced

Preheat the oven to 350 degrees F. Rinse the fillets and pat dry.
Remove any bones, using tweezers or pliers, if necessary. Combine the bread crumbs, raisins, parsley, capers, pine nuts, and
garlic and toss. Add the olive oil and lemon juice and stir to
moisten. Evenly distribute the bread crumb mixture among the

fillets, patting it on the fish. Roll each one up jelly-roll fashion and wrap securely in foil. You will have two or four packets, depending on the size of the fillets. Put on a baking sheet, place in the oven, and bake 25 minutes.

Meanwhile, drain, seed, and chop the tomatoes. Combine with the basil, capers, and onions and heat over medium-high heat 5 minutes to reduce any moisture. Stir frequently. Spoon the sauce into a serving dish. Remove the foil from the orange roughy and serve immediately. If you used larger fillets, slice the rolls into individual servings. Pass the sauce.

Recommended companion dishes: **Mediterranean Pasta (page 52) and Basil Balsamic Salad (page 67)**

Each serving provides:

356	Calories	0.03 g	Omega-3
26 g	Protein	8 g	Fat
29 g	Carbohydrate		25% of calories from fat
296 mg	Sodium		1 g saturated fat
28 mg	Cholesterol		2 g polyunsaturated fat
			4.5 g monounsaturated fat

Lemon Sole Stuffed
with Olives and Tarragon

The olives and tarragon showcase the mild flavor and delicate texture of the sole. This dish is creamy but very low in fat.

Yield: 4 servings

Sole fillets	1	pound
Dry white wine	¼	cup
Fresh-squeezed lemon juice	¼	cup
Green onions	2,	minced
Garlic	2	cloves, minced
Dried tarragon	1	teaspoon
Plain nonfat yogurt	1	cup
Black olives, chopped	3	tablespoons
Fine dry bread crumbs	1	cup

Rinse the fillets and pat them dry. Remove any bones, using tweezers or pliers, if necessary. Set aside in the refrigerator. Preheat the oven to 450 degrees F. Put the wine and lemon juice in a skillet over medium-high heat and add the onions, garlic, and tarragon. Simmer, stirring constantly, about 5 minutes, until the liquid has almost totally evaporated. Turn off the heat and stir in the yogurt and olives. Remove ½ cup of the resulting sauce and set aside. Stir the bread crumbs into the remaining sauce and spread this evenly over each fillet. Roll them up jelly-roll fashion and place seam side down in a loaf pan. Pour the reserved sauce over the top. Cover and bake 30 minutes.

Recommended companion dishes: **Honey Mustard Salad (page 76), Parsley Potatoes (page 55), and steamed broccoli (see page 64)**

Each serving provides:

262	Calories	0.2 g	Omega-3
28 g	Protein	4 g	Fat
26 g	Carbohydrate		13% of calories from fat
413 mg	Sodium		1 g saturated fat
56 mg	Cholesterol		1 g polyunsaturated fat
			2 g monounsaturated fat

Entrées from the Oven

Oven-Baked Fish Sticks

Kids (and the kids in us) still love fish sticks. Here is a lighter version that is baked rather than fried. Tartar sauce is a delightful addition, though you may choose to serve them with lemon wedges or catsup instead.

Yield: 4 servings

Canola oil	**1½ tablespoons**
Ling cod fillets°	**1 pound**
Nonfat milk	**⅓ cup**
Fine dry bread crumbs	**½ cup**

Preheat the oven to 550 degrees F. Rub a 10 × 15-inch baking dish with a scant drizzle of oil. Rinse the fish and pat dry. Remove any bones, using tweezers or pliers, if necessary. Cut the fillets into 1 × 3-inch fingers. Place the milk and bread crumbs in separate shallow bowls. Dip each piece of fish in milk, then roll in the bread crumbs. Arrange in the baking dish, leaving an inch between them. With a pastry brush, dab the remaining oil

°Purchase fillets that are ½ to 1 inch thick.

evenly onto the fish sticks. Place the dish in the upper third of the oven and bake 12 to 15 minutes. They are done when the fish flakes easily with a fork and the crumbs are golden brown.

***Recommended companion dishes:* Tartar Sauce (page 61), steamed carrots (see page 64), Garlic Mashed Potatoes (page 56), and Basil Balsamic Salad (page 67)**

Each serving provides:

197	Calories	0.2 g	Omega-3
22 g	Protein	7 g	Fat
10 g	Carbohydrate		33% of calories from fat°
169 mg	Sodium		1 g saturated fat
59 mg	Cholesterol		2 g polyunsaturated fat
			1 g monounsaturated fat

°Health experts recommend that we derive no more than 30 percent of our overall calories from fat. When served with our recommended companion dishes or on an otherwise lowfat day, this recipe fits the bill.

Baked Crab with Red Potatoes, Pearl Onions, and Garlic

Guy Hadler prepared this crab feast for us one Christmas Eve and it was a sumptuous treat—simple to prepare, yet so delicious! Allow about 1 hour and 20 minutes to cook. You will have ample time to visit with your guests during the cooking time. Serve it with lots of napkins and a good Chardonnay.

Yield: 4 servings

Whole crabs*	4	pounds
Baby red potatoes	1	pound
Olive oil	2	tablespoons
Salt	⅛	teaspoon
Pepper		Several grinds
Pearl onions	10	ounces
Garlic	2	bulbs
Fresh parsley, minced	2	tablespoons
Lemon wedges	1	per serving

Preheat the oven to 400 degrees F. Rinse the crabs under cold water and break the legs into 2-inch pieces. Using kitchen shears, cut the body of the crab into 2-inch pieces. Do not remove the crab meat from the shells. Set aside. Wash the potatoes and cut them in half. Place 1 tablespoon of the olive oil in a 9 × 13-inch baking pan. Add the potatoes, salt, and pepper, then toss to coat with oil. Place in the oven, uncovered, and bake 30 minutes. Remove at the halfway point and toss to ensure even cooking.

*Purchase cooked whole crabs—with large claws, if possible—and have your fishmonger crack and clean them.

Meanwhile, peel the onions. Break the garlic bulbs into individual cloves and peel, but leave them whole. At the end of the initial 30 minutes of baking time, add the onions and garlic to the potatoes, along with the remaining oil. Toss to combine and continue to bake 30 minutes, removing at the halfway point to toss. Add the crab, toss again, and bake 20 minutes. Again, remove at the halfway point, toss, and return to the oven.

Remove from the oven, toss with the parsley, and transfer to a large, warmed serving platter. Set in the middle of the table and allow everyone to serve themselves. If you have small cocktail forks, set them out and use them to remove the meat from the shells. Otherwise, dinner forks will work. Pass the lemon wedges.

***Recommended companion dishes:* Basil Balsamic Salad (page 67) and Roasted Garlic Bread (page 58)**

Each serving provides:

295	Calories	0.3 g	Omega-3
25 g	Protein	8 g	Fat
31 g	Carbohydrate	25% of calories from fat	
414 mg	Sodium	1 g saturated fat	
67 mg	Cholesterol	1 g polyunsaturated fat	
		5 g monounsaturated fat	

Red Snapper and Zucchini Enchiladas with Green Sauce

Enchiladas are, by nature, time-consuming to prepare—a labor of love. You may make the tomatillo salsa ahead of time to make things simpler at the dinner hour, or use a commercial variety of green enchilada sauce (you will need 2 cups).

Yield: 6 servings

Tomatillo salsa

Fresh tomatillos	¾	pound
Diced green chilies	2	3-ounce cans
Fresh-squeezed orange juice	¼	cup
Fresh cilantro, minced	¼	cup
Red onion, minced	¼	cup
Garlic	3	cloves, minced
Honey	1	teaspoon
Salt	¼	teaspoon

The enchiladas

Light sesame oil	1	tablespoon
Fresh corn tortillas	12	
Red snapper fillets	1¼	pounds
Zucchini	3	medium
Red onion	1	medium, diced
Garlic	2	cloves, minced
Dried oregano	1	teaspoon
Cumin seed	½	teaspoon
Salt		A pinch
Cayenne		A pinch
Dry sherry	¼	cup

Part-skim mozzarella cheese,
grated   1½ cups (4 ounces)

Optional condiments: Salsa Fresca (page 40), light
sour cream, minced green onions

Up to a day or two ahead of time, prepare the salsa. If holding longer than a few hours, keep in the refrigerator, but bring back to room temperature before using.

For the tomatillo salsa, remove and discard the tomatillos' stems and papery skins. Place the tomatillos under a hot broiler until they soften and turn from bright to dull green in color—this will take about 8 minutes. Turn them over once midway through the cooking time. In a blender or food processor, combine them with the remaining salsa ingredients and puree to a thick sauce consistency. Set aside.

When you are ready to prepare the enchiladas, heat the salsa in a small saucepan over very low heat so it is hot when you assemble the casserole. Heat ¼ teaspoon oil in a large heavy-bottomed skillet over medium heat. When pan is very hot, add a tortilla and twirl it around with your fingers. Quickly turn it over and allow to cook for about 1 minute. The tortilla will puff and brown just a little; do not let it get crisp. Proceed with the remaining tortillas, adding ¼ teaspoon oil for each one. Keep the cooked tortillas warm in a tea towel.

Meanwhile, rinse the fish fillets and pat dry. Remove any bones, using tweezers and pliers, if necessary. Chop the fish into bite-size chunks and set aside. Cut the zucchini in fourths lengthwise, then crosswise into ¼-inch wedges. When all the tortillas have been cooked, reduce the heat to low and add the onion, garlic, oregano, and cumin seed to the pan. Stir, then add the zucchini, salt, cayenne, and 2 tablespoons of the sherry. Stir and sauté 5 minutes, then stir in the fish and remaining 2 tablespoons sherry and cook, stirring frequently, 4 minutes only; it will finish cooking in the oven. Use a slotted spoon to remove the resulting fish filling to a bowl, stirring any liquid remaining in the pan into the tomatillo salsa.

Set up an assembly line with the tortillas, fish filling, and cheese close at hand. Ladle a little tomatillo salsa into a 9 × 13-inch baking dish or 6 individual oblong baking dishes and spread around—use just enough to coat the bottom of the dish(es). Holding a tortilla in the palm of your hand, spoon a few tablespoons of filling along one side of it, sprinkle on ¹⁄₁₂ of the cheese, and roll up as tightly as possible. Place seam side down in the baking dish. Proceed with the remaining tortillas, taking care to distribute the ingredients as evenly as possible to create twelve equal-size enchiladas. If using the larger baking dish, wedge the enchiladas together snugly. If using smaller dishes, place two in each dish. Ladle the remaining tomatillo salsa evenly over the top and bake, uncovered, 25 minutes. Allow to cool 5 minutes before serving. Pass the condiments.

***Recommended companion dishes:* Salsa Fresca (page 40), Spanish Rice (page 47), and Southwest Salad (page 70)**

Each serving provides:

408	Calories	0.3 g	Omega-3
31 g	Protein	9 g	Fat
41 g	Carbohydrate		20% of calories from fat
401 mg	Sodium		3 g saturated fat
46 mg	Cholesterol		3 g polyunsaturated fat
			2 g monounsaturated fat

Broiled, Grilled, and Skewered Dishes

Broiling and grilling both utilize dry heat at high temperatures. The close contact with a hot flame slightly chars the surface of foods, lending a characteristic flavor that is the basis of the recipes in this chapter. These are good lowfat cooking methods, since any fat that is released from the fish drips away.

Every stove is equipped with a broiler function—it is the very hottest oven setting. Broilers preheat quickly and cook foods almost instantly, so never leave the broiler unattended.

Grilling has long been synonymous with summer. Many modern kitchens, however, are equipped with indoor grills, making this method a year-round option. It is particularly suitable for fish and seafood, since the fish cooks quickly and is easily penetrated by the flavors of a basting liquid.

There is a mystique surrounding grilling, but this cooking method has been around since the discovery of fire. Become familiar with the unique features of your particular grill, stay close at hand so food is not overcooked, and you'll soon have the skill mastered.

Grilling times are affected by air temperature, wind, condition of the coals, and the distance of the cooking surface from the heat source. Our recipes were tested on a gas grill with the cooking surface 5 inches from the heat. Consider all the above factors, and adjust grilling times accordingly. Fish is done when mostly opaque but still barely translucent at the very center.

Tools . . .

- A vast assortment of grill units—both gas and coal varieties—are available for purchase. Read the brochures and talk with friends before deciding which grill is right for your purposes.

- Gas grills utilize refillable propane canisters. For coal grills, we prefer natural lump charcoal to charcoal briquettes, which contain large quantities of chemical lighter fluid. Lump charcoal is available in different hardwoods, such as alder, hickory, and mesquite. It starts quicker, burns hotter, and smells better than briquettes. You will need only about half as much lump charcoal as you would briquettes to achieve the desired temperature.

- Hardwood chips, which add unique flavors, are available for use with gas or charcoal grills. Soak them in water 15 minutes before adding to the fire.

- A handy, inexpensive grill chimney is a chemical-free way to ignite lump charcoal or briquettes. Ask for one at your hardware store. Charcoal lighter fluid emits harmful pollutants that damage air quality, and we discourage their use.
- Large, shallow glass dishes to hold fish in a single layer for marinating.
- Long-handled basting brushes in various widths.
- Insulated mitts for handling grill parts.
- Skewers can be either wooden or metal. Wooden ones need to be soaked for a half hour before using to avoid burning on the grill. Metal skewers, obviously, need not be soaked, but they become quite hot on the grill. Be careful to use mitts when handling them.
- Cooking bricks or tiles, positioned to hold the ends of the skewers, prevent them from burning, and hold the kabobs in place.
- Long-handled tongs and spatulas are perfect for turning foods on the grill and removing them when they are done. Inexpensive drywall trowels or knives are excellent alternatives.
- Stiff wire brush for cleaning the grill.

. . . and Tips

- Some safety tips: Set up the grill in an open area away from the house, and don't attempt to move a hot grill. Do not cook on a charcoal fire in high winds. Avoid wearing flowing garments when cooking on a grill. Never squirt charcoal lighter fluid directly into a fire. Use long-handled utensils and wear heavy-duty mitts. Make sure ashes are completely cold before discarding.

- The grill is easiest to clean when hot. Scrape with a stiff wire brush to remove any charred food particles before the next use.
- Unless fish has been marinated or had oil applied directly to it, brush the grill with a bit of oil.
- To preheat a coal grill, prepare the charcoal at least 15 to 20 minutes before cooking begins so the proper temperature can be achieved in time. Preheat a gas grill at least 10 minutes or according to the manufacturer's specific directions.
- A grill that is too hot will dry out the fish. Learn to visually judge the temperature of a coal grill. A high-temperature fire has a bright red glow with a small amount of visible white ash. A medium-temperature fire has an orange glow with a coating of gray ash. Gas grills are equipped with a dial for setting the appropriate temperatures.
- Thin fish fillets are delicate—they will cook adequately without turning.

Broiled Orange Roughy
with Ginger Miso Gravy

This exotic miso gravy is wonderful over plain steamed rice, or you can serve it with potatoes if potatoes and gravy is comfort food for you. If you can't find yellow and red bell peppers, you may substitute green ones—though you will sacrifice the visual beauty of the dish.

Yield: 6 servings

Dried shiitake mushrooms	1	**ounce**
Raw sesame seeds	1	**tablespoon**
Mustard greens	1	**bunch (about 1 pound)**
Fresh-squeezed lemon juice	2	**tablespoons**
Yellow bell peppers	2	**medium**
Red bell peppers	2	**medium**
Orange roughy fillets	1½	**pounds**
White miso	3	**tablespoons**
Sake	2	**tablespoons**
Mirin	2	**tablespoons**
Dark sesame oil	2	**teaspoons**
Fresh ginger, grated	1	**teaspoon**
Granulated garlic	⅛	**teaspoon**
Cayenne		**A pinch**
Arrowroot powder	1½	**teaspoons**
Low-sodium soy sauce (optional)		

Soak mushrooms in 1½ cups hot water for half an hour or so. Strain the soaking liquid through a paper coffee filter and reserve 1 cup of it. Carefully wash the mushrooms under a thin stream of running water to remove any grit clinging to the membranes under the caps. Leave the mushrooms whole, but remove and discard their tough stems.

Meanwhile, toast the sesame seeds (see page 34). Wash the mustard greens, discarding the thick stem portions. Tear the leaves into coarse pieces and, without drying them, pile them into a pot that has a tight-fitting lid. Heat over medium heat 7 to 10 minutes, until greens are wilted. Drain the greens and toss them with the lemon juice and toasted sesame seeds. Cover with foil and set aside in a warm spot.

Preheat the broiler 5 minutes. Cut the bell peppers lengthwise into eighths, discarding the stems and seeds. Broil the peppers and mushroom caps 4 inches from the flame 2 minutes, then add the orange roughy and broil 4 minutes longer. Turn the fish and vegetables over and broil an additional 3 to 4 minutes, depending on the thickness of the fish. Fish is done when mostly opaque but still barely translucent at the very center. Mushrooms and peppers should be soft and charred in spots.

Meanwhile, whisk together the reserved mushroom soaking liquid, miso, sake, mirin, oil, ginger, garlic, and cayenne in a small saucepan. Bring to a boil over medium heat. Shake the arrowroot powder with ¼ cup cold water in a tightly covered jar. When miso mixture is bubbling, whisk in the arrowroot mixture and immediately remove from the heat. Whisk a moment, until sauce is thickened and smooth.

Remove the fish and vegetables from the broiler and arrange on a warmed serving platter, leaving a space in the center. Heap the cooked greens in the center and drizzle the gravy evenly over the fish and vegetables. Serve very hot, passing soy sauce if you wish.

Recommended companion dishes: Steamed Brown Rice (page 46) and carrot sticks

---

Each serving provides:

221	Calories	0.02 g	Omega-3
20 g	Protein	4 g	Fat
12 g	Carbohydrate		24% of calories from fat
391 mg	Sodium		0.5 g saturated fat
23 mg	Cholesterol		1.5 g polyunsaturated fat
			2 g monounsaturated fat

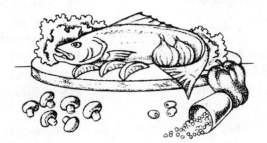

Broiled Sea Bass and Peppers with Green Olive Tomato Topping

This is a showy dish, with the red and yellow peppers flanking the fish. Don't substitute green ones—the flavor and color balance will suffer too much. It is served at room temperature and can be prepared up to two hours ahead of time.

Yield: 6 servings

Low-sodium tomato puree	½	cup
Fresh-squeezed lemon juice	2	tablespoons
Balsamic vinegar	2	tablespoons
Dried oregano	2	teaspoons
Salt		A pinch
Pepper		A few grinds
Green onions	4,	minced
Pitted green olives, water-packed	¾	cup, whole
Garlic	2	cloves, chopped
Yellow bell peppers	1	pound
Red bell peppers	1	pound
Sea bass fillets	1½	pounds

Whisk together the tomato puree, lemon juice, vinegar, oregano, salt, and pepper. Stir in the green onions. In a food processor, combine the olives and garlic and pulse briefly to mince. Stir this mixture into the tomato mixture. Set aside at room temperature.

Preheat the broiler 5 minutes. Remove the stems and seeds from the peppers and cut them lengthwise into inch-thick strips. Broil 4 inches from the flame 5 minutes, then turn and broil another 3 to 5 minutes. It is fine if the peppers blacken in spots—you want them to get limp and take on a roasted flavor. Remove the peppers to a platter, arranging the red strips on one side and the yellow strips on the other.

Rinse the fish and pat dry. Broil 4 inches from the flame 4 minutes, then turn and broil 3 to 5 minutes longer, depending on the thickness of the fish. Fish is done when mostly opaque but still barely translucent at the very center. Arrange the fish on the platter between the yellow and red pepper strips. When fish is cool enough to handle, carefully remove any skin and bones and break up into large pieces. Drain any liquid that has collected on the platter into the tomato sauce and stir to incorporate. Spoon the sauce over the fish and serve warm or at room temperature. You may prepare this dish up to 2 hours before serving time. Hold it at room temperature, loosely covered with a dry tea towel.

Recommended companion dishes: **Mediterranean Pasta (page 52), Honey Mustard Salad (page 76), and bread sticks**

Each serving provides:

164	Calories	0.7 g	Omega-3
20 g	Protein	5 g	Fat
12 g	Carbohydrate		24% of calories from fat
551 mg	Sodium		1 g saturated fat
40 mg	Cholesterol		1 g polyunsaturated fat
			2 g monounsaturated fat

Broiled Swordfish with Sweet Red Pepper Sauce

ALMOST INSTANT

This delicious dish comes together quickly and looks pretty on the plate.

Yield: 4 servings

Unsalted butter	1	tablespoon
Garlic	2	cloves, minced
Salt		A scant pinch
Dry white wine	1	cup
Red bell pepper	1	large, diced
Nonfat milk	¼	cup
Paprika	½	teaspoon
Swordfish steaks	1	pound
Granulated garlic	1	teaspoon

Preheat the broiler 5 minutes. Place the butter in a small skillet over medium heat and add the garlic and salt. Stir and sauté 1 minute, then add the wine and bell pepper. Bring to a simmer over medium-high heat and cook until the wine evaporates, about 15 minutes. Transfer to a blender or small food processor, add the milk and paprika, and process until smooth.

Meanwhile, rinse the steaks and pat them dry. Rub both sides with granulated garlic. Broil the fish 4 inches from the flame 4 minutes, then turn and broil an additional 3 to 4 minutes, depending on the thickness of the fish. Fish is done when mostly opaque but still barely translucent at the very center.

Meanwhile, return the sauce to the pan over very low heat to just heat through. Distribute the fish among warmed serving plates and top with the sauce.

Recommended companion dishes: **Wild Rice Pilaf (page 48), steamed green beans (see page 64), and Buttermilk Cucumber Salad (page 68)**

Each serving provides:

183	Calories	0.7 g	Omega-3
20 g	Protein	5 g	Fat
4 g	Carbohydrate		25% of calories from fat
152 mg	Sodium		2 g saturated fat
40 mg	Cholesterol		1 g polyunsaturated fat
			2 g monounsaturated fat

Skewered Shark Marinated in Green Olive Balsamic Vinaigrette

Not counting the marinating time, this dish comes together very quickly. It is hearty and delicious—perfect for nourishing ourselves after a day of physical exertion in the garden. This recipe calls for broiling the marinated shark skewers, but you can grill them if you prefer.

Yield: 6 servings

Low-sodium crushed tomatoes	1	14½-ounce can
Red wine	½	cup
Pitted green olives, water-packed, drained, and minced	3	tablespoons
Balsamic vinegar	2	tablespoons
Olive oil	2	teaspoons
Garlic	3	cloves, minced
Dried oregano	2	teaspoons
Pepper		Several grinds
Shark steaks	2	pounds
Mushrooms	½	pound
Zucchini	3	medium

Soak 12 wooden skewers in water for 30 minutes.

Meanwhile, combine the tomatoes, wine, olives, vinegar, oil, garlic, oregano, and pepper in a large bowl or soufflé dish. Rinse the shark steaks and pat dry. Trim off any skin and remove any bones, using tweezers or pliers, if necessary. Cut the fish into 1-inch pieces. Immerse the fish in the marinade, cover the dish, and set aside in the refrigerator. Marinate 1 to 2 hours, stirring the fish at least once during this time.

Meanwhile, brush the loose dirt particles from the mushrooms. Trim the ends from the zucchini and cut crosswise into 1-inch slices. When shark has finished marinating, remove the fish but retain the marinade. Thread the fish cubes onto the skewers, alternating with the whole mushrooms and zucchini slices, piercing the zucchini through the skin sides. Fill all 12 skewers in this manner.

Preheat the broiler 5 minutes. Pour the marinade into a small saucepan, bring to a boil over medium-high heat, reduce heat to low, and simmer 10 to 15 minutes, stirring occasionally, until reduced to a thick sauce consistency. Meanwhile, broil the skewers 4 inches from the flame 4 minutes, then turn and broil 3 to 5 minutes longer. Fish is done when mostly opaque but still barely translucent at the very center. Arrange the cooked skewers on warmed serving plates, two to a serving, and spoon a little of the sauce over them. Serve immediately.

***Recommended companion dishes:* Steamed Basmati Rice (page 45) and Basil Balsamic Salad (page 67)**

Each serving provides:

272	Calories	1.3 g	Omega-3
34 g	Protein	9 g	Fat
10 g	Carbohydrate		31% of calories from fat°
227 mg	Sodium		2 g saturated fat
76 mg	Cholesterol		3 g polyunsaturated fat
			4 g monounsaturated fat

°Health experts recommend that we derive no more than 30 percent of our overall calories from fat. When served with our recommended companion dishes or on an otherwise lowfat day, this recipe fits the bill.

Skewered Ginger Prawns and Eggplant with Spicy Teriyaki Sauce

These wonderful ginger- and soy-infused prawns have never failed to win rave reviews. Medium to large prawns (not jumbo ones) are best for this dish, as the flavors of the marinade will penetrate all the way through.

Yield: 4 servings

Peeled and deveined raw prawns°	1	**pound**
Sake	⅓	**cup**
Mirin	⅓	**cup**
Low-sodium soy sauce	1½	**tablespoons**
Dark sesame oil	2	**teaspoons**
Fresh ginger, grated	1	**tablespoon**
Cayenne pepper		**A pinch**
Japanese eggplants	2	**medium**
Arrowroot powder	2	**teaspoons**

Rinse the prawns and pat dry. Whisk together the sake, mirin, soy sauce, oil, ginger, and cayenne. Pour over the prawns in a shallow dish and place in the refrigerator to marinate for 2 to 3 hours. Stir the prawns at least once during this time. About half an hour before grilling time, wash and dry the eggplants and cut crosswise into 1-inch-thick rounds. Add to the prawns, stirring well to coat with marinade, and return to the refrigerator until needed. Soak 8 wooden skewers in cold water for 30 minutes.

°If you purchase unpeeled raw shrimp or prawns, break away the shells and cut a shallow slit along the back so you can remove the dark vein.

Preheat a coal or gas grill to medium high (see page 340). Just before grilling, distribute the eggplant slices among four skewers, piercing the skin sides of the eggplant. Grill 10 minutes, turning once midway through. On 4 separate skewers, thread the prawns, piercing both ends to secure on the skewer. Grill 2 to 3 minutes, then turn and grill 2 to 3 minutes longer, depending on their size. Prawns are done when bright pink and their flesh is opaque all the way through.

Meanwhile, bring the marinade to a boil in a small saucepan over medium-high heat. Dissolve the arrowroot in ¼ cup cold water and whisk into the simmering sauce. Sauce will thicken almost immediately; don't overcook as it will turn gummy. Serve each person two skewers, one of prawns, the other of eggplant, passing the hot sauce to spoon over.

Recommended companion dishes: **Wild Rice Pilaf (page 48) and Asian Salad (page 74)**

Each serving provides:

238	Calories	0.6 g	Omega-3
25 g	Protein	4 g	Fat
13 g	Carbohydrate		17% of calories from fat
416 mg	Sodium		1 g saturated fat
175 mg	Cholesterol		2 g polyunsaturated fat
			1 g monounsaturated fat

Skewered Calamari Steaks with Grilled Papaya and Tomato

This summer show stopper is a beautiful combination of flavors and colors—you may wish to garnish the plate with fresh mint sprigs for a touch of green. Papayas are sometimes sold green at the markets. Be sure to shop for them a few days ahead of time so they can finish ripening on your kitchen counter. When ready, they will be mostly yellowish-orange and will yield slightly to pressure, like a ripe avocado.

Yield: 4 servings

Calamari steaks	1¼	pounds
Mirin	¼	cup
Low-sodium soy sauce	2	teaspoons
Dark sesame oil	1	teaspoon
Fresh ginger, grated	1	teaspoon
Granulated garlic	1	teaspoon
Fresh whole papayas	2	medium
Tomatoes	2	medium
Canola oil	½	teaspoon

Soak 8 wooden skewers in water for 30 minutes.

Meanwhile, rinse the calamari and cut into long 1-inch-wide strips. Whisk the mirin with ¼ cup water, the soy sauce, sesame oil, ginger, and garlic. Pour it into a shallow dish. Lay in the strips of calamari, turn to coat, and marinate in the refrigerator for 30 minutes to 1 hour.

Preheat a coal or gas grill to medium-high (see page 340). Remove the calamari from the marinade, reserving the marinade, and loosely thread strips on the bamboo skewers in a lazy-S pattern. Cut the papayas into quarters lengthwise and discard the seeds, but do not peel. Cut the tomatoes in half from stem to point. Coat your hands with a little of the oil and rub the papaya quarters, then the tomato halves to lightly coat. Add more of the oil to your hands as needed. You should need no more than ½ teaspoon total oil. Place the papayas skin side down on the grill and cook 4 minutes. Simultaneously, place the tomato halves skin side down and lay the skewers of calamari on the grill.

Cook the tomatoes 2 minutes, then flip them to their cut side and cook an additional 8 minutes. Spoon the remaining marinade over the calamari as you cook it. Turn several times, and cook for a total of 10 minutes, until opaque all the way through. Turn papaya quarters about every 3 minutes to sear each cut side, cooking them a total of 10 minutes. The idea is to have everything ready to come off the grill at the same time. Serve immediately on warmed plates.

Recommended companion dishes: **Steamed Bulgur (page 49), Asian Salad (page 74), and sesame bread sticks**

Each serving provides:

306	Calories	0.7 g	Omega-3
24 g	Protein	3 g	Fat
40 g	Carbohydrate		9% of calories from fat
191 mg	Sodium		1 g saturated fat
330 mg	Cholesterol		1 g polyunsaturated fat
			0.2 g monounsaturated fat

Mahimahi with Cilantro Red Pepper Sauce

ALMOST INSTANT

The flavor of this popular Hawaiian fish is delightful with pungent cilantro and sweet red bell pepper. This is a wonderful dish for a summer dinner party. If time permits, prepare the sauce ahead, as its flavor matures nicely.

Yield: 6 servings

Reduced-calorie mayonnaise	¼	cup
Plain nonfat yogurt	¼	cup
Red bell pepper, diced	¼	cup
Fresh cilantro, minced	3	tablespoons
Yellow onion, diced	2	tablespoons
Granulated garlic	¾	teaspoon
Mahimahi steaks or fillets	2	pounds

Preheat a coal or gas grill to medium-high (see page 340). Whisk together the mayonnaise and yogurt, then stir in the bell pepper, cilantro, onion, and ¼ teaspoon of the granulated garlic. Place in an attractive serving dish and set aside in the refrigerator.

Rinse the fish and pat it dry. Trim off any skin and remove any bones, using tweezers or pliers, if necessary. Rub both sides with the remaining ½ teaspoon granulated garlic. Place the fish on the grill and cook 6 minutes. Turn and continue to cook 6 to

8 minutes, depending on the thickness of the fish. Fish is done when mostly opaque, but still barely translucent at the very center. Serve immediately, passing the sauce.

***Recommended companion dishes:* Grilled Red Potatoes (page 54), steamed corn on the cob (see page 64), and Roasted Garlic Bread (page 58)**

Each serving provides:

152	Calories	0.2 g	Omega-3
24 g	Protein	4 g	Fat
2 g	Carbohydrate		26% of calories from fat
196 mg	Sodium		0.2 g saturated fat
97 mg	Cholesterol		0.2 g polyunsaturated fat
			0.2 g monounsaturated fat

Tomato Lime Barbecue Sauce for Sea Bass

Sea bass is our preference for this delicious barbecue sauce; however, it would also be wonderful with halibut or swordfish. It is likely to become one of your favorite summer meals.

Yield: 6 servings

Low-sodium tomato juice	1½	cups
Low-sodium tomato paste	2	tablespoons
Worcestershire sauce	2	tablespoons
Honey	1	tablespoon
Fresh-squeezed lime juice	2	tablespoons
Liquid smoke	4	drops
Yellow onion	¼	cup, minced
Garlic	2	cloves, minced
Sea bass fillets	2½	pounds
Lime wedges	1	per serving

Whisk together the tomato juice, tomato paste, Worcestershire sauce, honey, lime juice, and liquid smoke until smooth. Stir in the onion and garlic. Cover and refrigerate for at least an hour, or up to several days, to allow the flavors to combine.

Preheat a coal or gas grill to medium-high (see page 340). Rinse the fillets and pat them dry. Trim off any skin and remove any bones, using tweezers or pliers, if necessary. Place the fish in a large, shallow glass pan and cover with the barbecue sauce. Turn to coat. Allow to sit in the refrigerator for about 5 minutes before grilling. Grill the fish 20 minutes, turning every 5 minutes and saucing both sides each time. Serve immediately with lime wedges.

Recommended companion dishes: **Honey Mustard Salad (page 76), Grilled Red Potatoes (page 54), and steamed artichokes (see page 64)**

Each serving provides:

224	Calories	1.1 g	Omega-3
36 g	Protein	4 g	Fat
10 g	Carbohydrate		16% of calories from fat
189 mg	Sodium		1 g saturated fat
78 mg	Cholesterol		2 g polyunsaturated fat
			1 g monounsaturated fat

Golden Trout Grilled with Fresh Rosemary

Trout is widely available throughout the year, though golden trout from Idaho shows up in the autumn. This recipe works well with any variety of trout, so feel free to substitute whatever is available. Choose trout that weigh about ¾ of a pound each, so every person can be served a whole fish.

Yield: 4 servings

Fresh whole trout°	3	**pounds (4 medium)**
Fresh rosemary	4	**sprigs, 4 inches long**
Olive oil	1	**tablespoon**
Dry white wine	1	**cup**
Garlic	2	**cloves, minced**

Preheat a coal or gas grill to medium-high (see page 340). Rinse the fish under cold water, removing fins and cleaning the cavity. Place a sprig of rosemary in each cavity and secure with a toothpick.

In a bowl, whisk together the oil, wine, and garlic. Place the fish in a shallow glass dish, cover with the wine mixture, and marinate in the refrigerator for 1 hour, turning the fish halfway through. Remove the fish from the marinade and place on the preheated grill. Brush with a third of the marinade and cook 7 minutes. Baste with another third of the marinade, then turn the fish (the skin adhering to the grill is a sign that the fish has cooked properly). Cook an additional 4 to 7 minutes, until flesh is opaque all the way through. Baste again with the remaining

°Have your fishmonger remove the heads from the whole trout.

marinade and transfer to a warmed serving platter. Serve immediately.

You may need to instruct your guests in the art of deboning cooked trout. With the trout lying on its side on the plate, tail pointing toward you, grasp the tail with one hand. Insert a fork into the fish beneath the tail to secure the lower fillet on the plate, and lift the tail slowly to peel away the trout's bones from the lower fillet. Lay the unboned half flat on the plate, again insert a fork under the tail to hold the fillet in place, and slowly lift the tail to completely remove the bones and the tail in one piece. Discard.

***Recommended companion dishes:* Grilled Red Potatoes (page 54), grilled corn on the cob, and Honey Mustard Salad (page 76)**

Each serving provides:

357	Calories	1.6 g	Omega-3
50 g	Protein	12 g	Fat
1 g	Carbohydrate		30% of calories from fat
69 mg	Sodium		2 g saturated fat
136 mg	Cholesterol		3 g polyunsaturated fat
			5 g monounsaturated fat

Grilled Swordfish with Tarragon Dijon Sauce

ALMOST INSTANT

Swordfish is a great choice for grilling. It cooks fast and retains its wonderful firmness. This fish freezes well, so don't hesitate to buy it frozen when it is not available fresh.

Yield: 6 servings

Swordfish steaks	2	pounds
Canola oil	1	teaspoon
Granulated garlic	½	teaspoon
Unsalted butter	1	tablespoon
Garlic	2	cloves, minced
Green onions	3,	minced
Unbleached flour	1	tablespoon
Lowfat milk	½	cup
Dry white wine	2	tablespoons
Dijon mustard	1	tablespoon
Fresh tarragon leaves, minced	1	tablespoon

Preheat a coal or gas grill to medium-high (see page 340). If the steaks are large, cut into 6 equal-size portions. Rinse the fish and pat it dry. Place on a large platter and rub each side with canola oil and granulated garlic. Place in the refrigerator while you prepare the sauce.

Heat the butter in a medium skillet over medium-low heat. Add the garlic and onions and sauté for a minute or two, then stir in the flour. Allow the flour to cook for a moment, then gradually add the milk and wine. Whisk as the sauce cooks for about 4 minutes, until thickened. Cover and turn off the heat.

The Best 125 Lowfat Fish and Seafood Dishes

Place the fish on the preheated grill and cook 4 minutes, then turn and cook for 4 to 6 minutes, depending on the thickness of the steaks. Fish is done when mostly opaque but still barely translucent at the very center. Reheat the sauce briefly just before you take the fish off the grill and stir in the mustard and tarragon. Place the cooked fish on a warmed platter. Top with the sauce and serve immediately.

***Recommended companion dishes:* Steamed Couscous (page 51), steamed broccoli (see page 64), and Basil Balsamic Salad (page 67)**

Each serving provides:

231	Calories	1 g	Omega-3
31 g	Protein	9 g	Fat
3 g	Carbohydrate		37% of calories from fat°
180 mg	Sodium		3 g saturated fat
65 mg	Cholesterol		2 g polyunsaturated fat
			3 g monounsaturated fat

°Health experts recommend that we derive no more than 30 percent of our overall calories from fat. When served with our recommended companion dishes or on an otherwise lowfat day, this recipe fits the bill.

Grilled Salmon with Chardonnay Plum Sauce

This recipe was developed at Lake Tahoe after a day of sailing with friends. We had salmon, fresh plums, and Chardonnay on hand, and decided to see what we could cook up!

Yield: 4 servings

Santa Rosa plums	**4,**	**ripe**
Chardonnay	**1**	**cup plus 2 tablespoons**
Honey	**2**	**tablespoons**
Salmon steaks	**1⅓**	**pounds**

Blanche the plums (see page 34). Discard the peel and cut the fruit from the pits. Coarsely chop the fruit and combine in a small skillet with one cup of the wine. Gently heat over medium-low, mashing the plums as they cook. Increase heat to medium and cook, stirring frequently, until sauce reduces to a thick consistency, about 30 minutes. Stir in the honey and set aside in a warm place.

Preheat a coal or gas grill to medium-high (see page 340). Rinse the steaks and pat dry. Place the salmon on the preheated grill and cook 6 minutes. Turn and continue to cook 3 to 5 minutes, depending on the thickness of the steak. Fish is done when mostly opaque but still barely translucent at the very center.

Stir the remaining wine into the sauce and reheat briefly while the fish finishes cooking. Serve the salmon immediately, passing the sauce.

Recommended companion dishes: **Steamed Basmati Rice (page 45), steamed snow peas (see page 64), and Asian Salad (page 74)**

Each serving provides:

261	Calories	1 g	Omega-3
30 g	Protein	6 g	Fat
9 g	Carbohydrate		21% of calories from fat
78 mg	Sodium		1 g saturated fat
111 mg	Cholesterol		2 g polyunsaturated fat
			3 g monounsaturated fat

Blackened Red Snapper
with Lime Cilantro Aioli

ALMOST INSTANT

Blackened fish is usually cooked in a very hot pan that creates a lot of smoke. We prefer to cook ours on the outdoor grill. The aioli that accompanies this recipe tames the fire of the spices.

Yield: 6 servings

The aioli

Reduced-calorie mayonnaise	¼	cup
Plain nonfat yogurt	¼	cup
Garlic	2	cloves, minced
Fresh-squeezed lime juice	2	tablespoons
Dijon mustard	1	teaspoon
Fresh cilantro leaves, minced	2	tablespoons
Cajun Blackening Spice Mix (page 39)	½	cup
Red snapper fillets	1½	pounds

Whisk the aioli ingredients together in a small bowl until smooth; cover and refrigerate (it may be prepared ahead of time and refrigerated for several days). Preheat a coal or gas grill to medium-high (see page 340). Pour the blackening mix onto a plate and dredge the snapper in it to evenly coat both sides. Place on the hot grill and cook 4 minutes. Turn and cook an additional 3 to 5 minutes, depending on the thickness of the fish. Fish is done when it separates easily when a fork is inserted and twisted in the thickest part. Serve immediately, passing the aioli.

Recommended companion dishes: **Seasoned Black Beans (page 50), Steamed Basmati Rice (page 45), and Southwest Salad (page 70)**

Each serving provides:

211	Calories	0.4 g	Omega-3
26 g	Protein	6 g	Fat
13 g	Carbohydrate		26% of calories from fat
321 mg	Sodium		0.4 g saturated fat
45 mg	Cholesterol		1 g polyunsaturated fat
			0.6 g monounsaturated fat

Blackened Halibut and
Black Bean Burritos

*This is a delicious choice for a casual summer dinner party.
Margaritas or ice-cold beer would be the perfect beverage
accompaniment.*

Yield: 6 servings

Cooked black beans	3	**cups**
Halibut steaks	1	**pound**
Cajun Blackening Spice		
Mix (page 39)	3	**tablespoons**
Dry sherry	¼	**cup**
Garlic	4	**cloves, minced**
Ground cumin	½	**teaspoon**
Salt		**A pinch**
Flour tortillas	1	**dozen**
Green cabbage, finely		
shredded	2	**cups**
Salsa Fresca (page 40)	1	**cup**

Cook black beans according to directions on page 36, or rinse
canned beans and drain them well. Set aside.

Preheat a coal or gas grill to medium-high (page 340).
Rinse the fish and pat dry. Pour the blackening spice mix onto a
plate and dredge the fish in it to evenly coat both sides. Place the
fish on the preheated grill and cook 5 minutes, then turn and
cook 4 to 6 minutes longer, depending on the thickness of the
steak. Fish is done when mostly opaque but still barely translucent at the very center.

Meanwhile, in a medium saucepan over medium heat,
combine the cooked beans, sherry, garlic, cumin, salt, and ½ cup

bean cooking liquid or water. Bring to a boil, reduce heat to low, and simmer 10 minutes, until just heated through. The consistency should be thick and moist like a good chili, not runny. Mash some of the beans, if necessary, to thicken the mixture. Wrap the tortillas in foil and place in a 250-degree oven for 10 minutes to warm.

When fish is done, remove skin and bones and cut the fish into small chunks. Place the fish and cabbage on a platter. Serve the beans and salsa in bowls alongside. Place the hot tortillas in a covered basket and serve, allowing your guests to wrap their own burritos.

Recommended companion dishes: **Spanish Rice (page 47), tortilla chips with guacamole, and Southwest Salad (page 70)**

Each serving provides:

442	Calories	0.3 g	Omega-3
30 g	Protein	6 g	Fat
65 g	Carbohydrate		13% of calories from fat
335 mg	Sodium		1.5 g saturated fat
24 mg	Cholesterol		2 g polyunsaturated fat
			2.5 g monounsaturated fat

Honey Glazed Smoked Salmon

You will need a covered charcoal or gas grill for this recipe. Leftover smoked salmon is delicious with cream cheese and capers on crackers, or add it to a quiche.

Yield: 8 servings

Honey	½	cup plus 1 tablespoon
Salt	1½	tablespoons
Fresh ginger, grated	½	tablespoon
Whole cloves	6	
Bay leaves	3	
Ground allspice	1	teaspoon
Salmon roast°	2½	pounds
Apple or hickory wood chips	1	cup

Heat 2 cups of water in a saucepan and add ½ cup of the honey. Stir in the salt, ginger, cloves, bay leaves, and allspice. Bring to a boil and stir until the honey dissolves. Allow to cool to lukewarm.

Meanwhile, rinse the salmon, pat dry, and place in a single layer in a large shallow glass baking dish. Pour the barely warm brine over the salmon. Cover the dish and marinate in the refrigerator 4 to 8 hours. Soak the apple or hickory wood chips for 20 minutes in enough warm water to cover.

Meanwhile, preheat a coal or gas grill to medium (see page 340). Remove salmon from brine and rinse under cool water. Pat dry and place skin side down on a large piece of heavy-duty foil atop a large platter or cutting board. Discard the marinade. Rub

°Have your fishmonger fillet the salmon roast, leaving the skin intact, to produce fillets that are 1½ inches thick at the thickest point.

the remaining 1 tablespoon of honey over the exposed side of the salmon fillets. Place a quarter of the wood chips on the coals. Put the salmon, foil side down, on the grill. Cover and cook about 50 minutes without turning, adding the additional wood chips at three even intervals. During the cooking time the salmon will accumulate moisture on its surface; salmon is done when no moisture is present.

Use a wide spatula to remove the salmon from the foil. Serve it hot or at room temperature.

***Recommended companion dishes:* Mediterranean Pasta (page 52), Basil Balsamic Salad (page 67), and sourdough rye bread**

Each serving provides:

175	Calories	0.9 g	Omega-3
26 g	Protein	7 g	Fat
9 g	Carbohydrate		29% of calories from fat
323 mg	Sodium		1 g saturated fat
47 mg	Cholesterol		2 g polyunsaturated fat
			2 g monounsaturated fat

Index

Index

Carbohydrates, about, 25–26
Carrot(s)
  Braised sea bass and, with lentils and
    ginger, 278
  Braised shark with sauerkraut and, 274
  Halibut with, and ginger en papillote,
    282
  steaming time, 64
Cast-iron pans, tempering, 33
Catfish
  dumplings, in Creole, and rice, 190
  greens, and black-eyed peas with
    smoked cheddar and tomatoes, 310
  sweet potatoes and hot honey mustard
    en papillote, 292
Cauliflower, steaming time, 65
Caviar, lemon, cream, in Prawns and
  pasta with, 214
Ceviche, scallop and sea bass, 98
Champagne, in Salmon poached in, with
  capers and tarragon, 262
Charcoal, about, 338
Chardonnay plum sauce, in Grilled
  salmon with, 362
Cheddar cheese
  Risotto with spiced shrimp, beer, and,
    183
  smoked, in Catfish, greens, and black-
    eyed peas with, and tomatoes, 310
Cheese(s), about, 16. *See also names
  of specific cheeses.*
Cherry tomatoes. *See* Tomatoes, cherry
Chevre
  about, 16
  Crab spread with, dill seed, and dried
    tomato, 84
Chickpeas. *See* Garbanzo beans
Chili(es), green, canned
  Corn and, chowder with clams, 154
  in Huachanango with pickled
    jalapeños, 306
  in Red snapper and zucchini
    enchiladas with green sauce, 334
  in Salmon quesadillas with cilantro
    and salsa fresca, 106
  in Salsa Fresca, 40
Chili(es), green, fresh, in Tex-mex
  orange roughy, zucchini, and
  peppers en papillote, 284
Cholesterol, about, 24, 26
Chowder, clam, Manhattan style, 156
Chowders. *See Contents for list of
  recipe titles.*

about, 134–136
recipes for, 150–157
Chutney
  Curried salmon and artichoke
    chowder with, 152
  Mango, 42
  Pineapple jalapeño, 268
Cilantro, fresh
  Curried risotto with sea bass,
    garbanzos, lime, and, 168
  lime, aioli, in Blackened red snapper
    with, 364
  Orange, scallops over rice with snow
    peas, 186
  red pepper sauce, in Mahimahi
    with, 354
  Salmon quesadillas with, and salsa
    fresca, 106
  Stir-fry of scallops, shiitake, ginger,
    and, 246
Cinnamon, in Scallops, beans, and
  arugula with, and fresh basil,
  122
Cioppino with fresh fennel and brandy,
  162
Clam(s)
  about, 4
  chowder, in Manhattan style, 156
  cooking tips, 32
  Corn and green chili chowder with,
    154
  dip, in Australian, 81
  and leek frittata with potatoes, dried
    tomatoes, and oregano, 312
  littleneck, in Thyme and dill steamed,
    256
  Pasta with, white wine, and
    mushrooms, 200
  risotto with dried tomato and peas,
    174
  serving size, 6
Coconut, in Poached mahimahi with
  pear, and mint, 270
Coconut milk
  in Mahimahi and asparagus
    en papillote with Thai seasonings,
    288
  in Shrimp and rice noodle soup with
    lemongrass, 142
Cod
  baked with green bell pepper and
    tomatoes, 304
  in Oven-baked fish sticks, 330

Index
373

Eggplant(s)
　Skewered ginger prawns and,
　　with spicy teriyaki sauce, 350
　Szechwan, and orange roughy
　　risotto, 180
Enchiladas, in Red snapper and
　zucchini, with green sauce, 334
Enoki mushrooms
　about, 14
　in Halibut with carrots and ginger
　　en papillote, 282
En papillote. *See Contents for list of
　recipe titles.*
　about, 280–281
　recipes for, 282–301

Fats, about, 23–24
　monounsaturated, 23–24
　polyunsaturated, 23–24
　recommended intake, 23, 44
　saturated, 21, 23–24, 26
Fat-to-calories ratio, 22, 23, 44
Fennel
　braised halibut with calamata
　　olives, 276
　Cioppino with fresh, and brandy, 162
　Trout and, en papillote with lemon
　　caper cream, 298
Feta cheese
　about, 16
　in Mediterranean pasta, 52
　Risotto with red snapper, spinach,
　　and nutmeg, 176
　in Smoked salmon ravioli with
　　sherry cream sauce, 224
　in Swordfish and calamata olives
　　with rigatoni, 212
　Swordfish stir-fry with, and tomatoes,
　　250
　Tuna and leeks en papillote with
　　paprika, and fresh dill, 286
First Courses. *See Contents for list
　of recipe titles.*
　about, 78–80
　recipes for, 92–107
Fish and seafood. *See also names of
　specific species.*
　calories in, 22
　cooking tips, 31–32
　fat content of, 2
　odor, 8–9
　oils, 26
　rinsing, 9

selecting canned, 5–6
selecting fresh, 2–4
selecting frozen, 5
Fish market, choosing, 1
Fish sticks, oven-baked, 330
Florentine, Sole, with nutmeg and
　paprika, 314
Food guide pyramid, 14, 20–21
Freezing, 7–8
Frittata, Clam and leek, with potatoes,
　dried tomatoes, and oregano, 312
Frozen fish, 5, 7–8
Fruit, dried, reconstituting, 37
Fruit, fresh, about, 15
Fruit juices, about, 15

Garbanzo beans
　Curried risotto with sea bass, lime,
　　and cilantro, 168
　Mussels in spicy broth with
　　vegetables and, 137
Garlic
　about, 30
　Baked crab with red potatoes, pearl
　　onions, and, 332
　baking, 35–36
　mashed potatoes, 56
　Roasted, bread, 58
　Tofu, spread, 60
Ginger(ed), fresh
　Braised sea bass and carrots with
　　lentils and, 278
　dried tomato and, sauce, in
　　Poached red snapper with, 260
　Halibut with carrots and, en papillote,
　　282
　Lobster broccoli stir-fry with, and
　　fermented black beans, 236
　miso gravy, in Broiled orange roughy
　　with, 341
　peanut sauce, in Shrimp and snow
　　pea stir-fry in, 248
　prawns, in Skewered, and eggplant,
　　with spicy teriyaki sauce, 350
　Stir-fry of scallops, shiitake, and
　　cilantro, 246
Goat cheese, about, 16. *See also* Chevre
Gorgonzola cheese, lemon dressing,
　in Salmon, orzo, and cucumber
　salad with, 114
Gouda cheese, smoked, in Broiled
　swordfish and vegetables with
　smoked cheese and noodles, 222

Newburg, Crab, 188
Nut(s). *See also names of specific nuts.*
  about, 16–17
  butters, 17
  toasting, 34
Nutmeg
  Risotto with red snapper, spinach, feta and, 176
  Sole Florentine with, and paprika, 314
Nutrition Alert, 20–28

Oil(s)
  about, 16–17
  canola, about, 16–17
  olive, about, 16–17
  sesame, about, 17
Okra, in Scallop, snapper, and, gumbo, 160
Olive(s), in Lemon sole stuffed with, and Tarragon, 328. *See also* Calamata olives; Green olives; Pimiento stuffed olives
Olive oil, about, 16–17
Omega-3 fatty acids
  about, 20, 24
Orange(s). *See also* Mandarin orange(s)
  basil tomato sauce, in Mussels in, and linguine, 208
  cilantro scallops over rice with snow peas, 186
  hot tomato, marmalade, in Poached orange roughy with, 272
Orange roughy
  Baked, in grapefruit oregano sauce, 316
  Broiled, with ginger miso gravy, 341
  grilled, in Fettuccine with basil pesto and, 204
  Poached, with hot tomato orange marmalade, 272
  Stuffed, Sicilian style, 326
  Szechwan eggplant and, risotto, 180
  Tex-mex, zucchini, and peppers en papillote, 284
Oregano
  Clam and leek frittata with potatoes, dried tomatoes, and, 312
  grapefruit, sauce, in Baked orange roughy in, 316
  mustard dressing, in Smoked oyster, artichoke, and pasta salad with, 111

tomato coulis, in Linguine with scallops and, 210
wine, marinade, in Halibut baked in a, 322
Orzo, in Salmon, and cucumber salad with lemon gorgonzola dressing, 114
Ouzo, in Prawn scampi with anise liqueur, 242
Oyster(s). *See also* Oyster(s), smoked
  about, 4
  cooking tips, 32
  Sauté of, mushrooms, and sweet red pepper, 238
  stew, in Quick and light, 148
Oyster(s), smoked
  artichoke, and pasta salad with oregano mustard dressing, 111
  and fresh dill lovash, 88
  spread with fresh basil, 86

Paella, Seafood, with dried tomato and mango, 194
Papaya
  Crab, jicama, and kiwi with citrus poppy seed dressing, 132
  and tomato, grilled, in Skewered calamari steaks with, 352
Papillote. *See* En papillote
Paprika
  Sole Florentine with nutmeg and, 314
  Swordfish and potato salad with, capers, and horseradish, 118
  Tuna and leeks en papillote with, feta, and fresh dill, 286
Parchment paper, cooking in. *See* En papillote
Parmesan, about, 11
Parsley, fresh
  about, 18
  potatoes, 55
Pasta, main dishes. *See Contents for list of recipe titles.*
  about, 197–199
  "al dente," defined, 198
  recipes for, 200–230
Pasta, salads
  Dill marinated rock shrimp, 116
  Salmon, orzo, and cucumber, with lemon gorgonzola dressing, 114
  Smoked oyster, artichoke, with oregano mustard dressing, 111

Index   377

Photograph by Hope Harris.

Susann Geiskopf-Hadler and Mindy Toomay have been friends and feasting companions since 1971. They reside with their husbands in Sacramento, California, where an abundance of fresh vegetables, fruits, and seafood inspires their culinary efforts.

More **The Best 125** Cookbooks
by Mindy Toomay and Susann Geiskopf-Hadler

The Best 125 Meatless Pasta Dishes $12.95

Drawing on the cuisines of many nations, as well as the authors' seasoned imagi-
nations, this book expands your sense of pasta's possibilities. With its emphasis on
fresh ingredients and tantalizing flavors, this book proves we can eat less meat
without sacrificing enjoyment. Recipes include Dried-Tomato Pesto with Mint,
Savory Pumpkin and Pasta Soup, Spinach Lasagna with Port, and Tortellini Salad
with Roasted Walnuts.

The Best 125 Meatless Main Dishes $12.95

A follow-up book to their instantly successful first book, Toomay and Geiskopf-
Hadler once again team up to bring you another collection of tantalizing and
healthy meatless meals. Their inventive dishes include Filo Pastry with Asparagus,
Goat Cheese, and Fresh Dill; Risotto Laced with Fresh Basil, Peppers, and Pine
Nuts; Roasted Garlic and Wild Mushroom Calzone with Ricotta Cheese; and much
more!

Look for *The Best 125 Vegetable Dishes*—coming Fall of '93
to your nearest bookstore.

TO ORDER:

By *telephone:* Use Your M/C or VISA. Call Prima Publishing at (916) 786-0426,
9–4 PST.

By *mail*: Fill out the information below and send with your remittance to Prima
Publishing.

I am paying by (check one) ❑ Check ❑ Money Order ❑ VISA or ❑ M/C

Name _____

Address _____

City/State/Zip _____

VISA or M/C number (exp. date) _____

Signature _____

Quantity	Title	Unit Price	Total
_____	*The Best 125 Lowfat Fish and Seafood Dishes*	$14.95	_____
_____	*The Best 125 Meatless Pasta Dishes*	$12.95	_____
_____	*The Best 125 Meatless Main Dishes*	$12.95	_____
	Subtotal		_____
	7.25% Sales Tax (CA only)		_____
	Shipping and Handling		$3.95
	Total		_____